Contents

Preface

The title of this text conjures up an image of Karl Marx sitting at his PC, surfing the Web for the latest news on the apparent collapse of the Asian Tigers' economic model, the social explosion in Indonesia or the general strike in Denmark. I fancy he would be quite at home, and his analysis would be as acute as ever. Now, some years ago, it became commonplace to declare that the 'Century of Marxism' was over. The odd antiquarian might take an interest but his ideas would gather dust in sad secondhand bookshops. Yet now, Jacques Derrida, one-time scourge of marxist metaphysics, can declare boldly and confidently that 'There will be no future without Marx'. So this book explores what a Marx @ 2000 might be like. This will not be an exercise in Marxology, poring over the texts to discover their ultimate meaning. I may well be accused of constructing a 'Marx lite' in keeping with our superficial, consumerist times. I prefer to think of it as a 'Marx live' who is brought to bear on current controversies on how to make sense of our turbulent, even chaotic, globalized postmodern times.

My subtitle refers to 'late marxist' in a passing tribute to Ernest Mandel's *Late Capitalism* (Mandel, 1975), from which we learnt so much. But, as people asked Mandel, late for what? Really, capitalism was just getting into its stride when marxists were declaring it past its sell-by date. Marxism can certainly be seen as too late historically, given that the political systems claiming to build a new society on its principles have collapsed so ignominiously. Maybe, though, it was too early for marxism, because capitalism had not developed sufficiently for its transformative strategy to work. As marxism enters a deep crisis, so capitalism appears to become more 'marxist'. I felt that the term 'post-marxist' was too monochromatic, at once too confidently 'post', and too old-fashionedly marxist. So, for better or worse, I go for 'late marxist' as a floating signifier amenable to different, even contradictory, meanings. It opens up a polyvocal understanding of our fluid times and signals an openness to other oppositional discourses. It would be too late for marxism, I believe, if it persists in seeking to 'reconstruct' itself and to seek comfort in the current problems of capitalism while being blind to its own.

The subtitle also refers to 'perspectives', alluding to the perspectivism of post-structuralism. We all see the world from different subject positions and universalism can lead to oppression. But we can also read

Marx from different historical perspectives. Two hundred years ago the great French Revolution inaugurated an era of emancipation, equality and justice which now seems to have run its course. As Foucault used to say, Marx is nothing if not a nineteenth-century philosopher. Yet we could also adapt the gaze of the *Communist Manifesto*, which appeared 150 years ago, and note how relevant it is to the present era. Indeed, even establishment economists are doing just that now. Come back Marx, all is forgiven.... Or, we could cast a tired, jaundiced look back a decade to 1989 and the collapse of communism. Compensating for not having seen it coming, analysts from left, right and centre made apocalyptic judgements all round, including the 'end of history'. My point is not to adapt any one perspective but to refuse the suffocating 'end of century' blues and melodramatic predictions, in favour of accepting the confused and mixed temporalities in which we live.

Chapter 1 examines the proposition that Marx is a 'dead dog', as irrelevant for this era as Hegel was for his. For Ronald Aronson in a heartfelt coming to terms it is simply the case that: 'Marxism is over' (Aronson, 1995: 9). While a certain marxism is, indeed, suffering from *rigor mortis*, Marx can be seen as alive and kicking if approached in the right spirit. This probably cannot be said for his successors in German social democracy, who have produced today the likes of a Tony Blair. By the 1980s the history of social democracy as a reformist hybrid of marxism seems to have come to an end. The other Marxist–Leninist hybrid seemed more sturdy, but collapsed without a fight in 1989. Were these things inevitable? Were the European roots of marxism debilitating in terms of constructing a global alternative? And, finally, why was late marxism not able to construct a viable vehicle for the future, once the limitations of traditional forms of marxism were detected in the 1970s? This chapter addresses these problems and quandaries in what is, hopefully, an open manner and not in the style of 'I told you so' adopted by self-proclaimed marxists in sects more reminiscent of the religious right than anything else. This chapter is a scene-setter for subsequent engagements of Marx with key issues of his and our day.

The so-called greening of marxism, its acquiring of an ecological conscience, is a relatively recent phenomenon. Chapter 2 examines some of the background to this recent engagement from Marx's own ambiguous treatment of nature, through to the sorry lack of understanding of sustainability by the socialist states, through to current debates. One of the most interesting among these is the emergence of an ecofeminism. In spite of its essentialism, this current has provided an imaginative impetus to the idea of a sustainable good life. What has brought the notion of sustainable development to the fore in the last decade is, of course, the context of globalization. Ecological problems are, intrinsically, global in their manifestation and resolution today. Certainly there is no easy solution as advised by technocratic environmentalism. Nor are the interests of the industrialized North and the industrializing South easily reconciled. There are many ways in which the socialist red and the environmental green can combine to produce a new variant of sustainable socialist development. This chapter simply seeks to pose some of the challenges involved.

For Lenin, the Soviets plus electrification equalled socialism. Though crude, this equation neatly captures the economistic and productivist bias of much marxism, as described in Chapter 3. Marx's original theory of capitalist development has made an incalculable contribution to what has become known only relatively recently as development studies. Yet the big contradiction is that Marx foresaw socialism growing out of advanced capitalism but, in practice, the socialist revolutions of the twentieth century have occurred under conditions of relative, if not absolute, underdevelopment. Lenin seemed to sweep away the Eurocentrism of Marx's orthodox successors but Leninism, in turn, became more or less an ideology of developmentalism in the Third World. The theory of imperialism, and its Third World variants such as dependency theory, became crucial later marxist contributions to an understanding of development and underdevelopment. Today, with a big question mark over whether the globally dominant capitalism can deliver development, there is a turn towards 'post-development' discourses which seem to hark back to marxist and pre-marxist utopias and visions of the good society.

For Marx, the gravediggers of capitalism are the workers it produces and exploits. The working class assumes mythical, even heroic dimensions in the marxist discourse. Chapter 4 examines the role of workers in Marx's own conceptual edifice, stressing his confidence in workers' creativity and self-organizing capabilities. The Russian Revolution in practice substituted the Bolshevik party for the working class as historical agent for change. In conditions of underdevelopment and a largely rural society, it was unrealistic to expect the urban proletariat to act as an enlightened vanguard and carry the rest of society with them. This substitutionism was, however, to have a huge impact on the subsequent development of the socialist and communist traditions. In recent decades, debates have shifted towards the growing incorporation of the working class into bourgeois society, at least in the advanced capitalist countries. The new social movements have, in practice, created a more diverse anti-capitalist movement today. With the centrality of the working class gone, in practice and in theory, where does this leave the traditional marxist project of social transformation?

At various times the socialist and feminist political movements have come close together but any rapprochement has been temporary. In Chapter 5 there is an examination of the various attempts to 'marry' the two traditions, with their usually unhappy consequences. Marx's own writings on women were scattered and hardly satisfactory as a theoretical treatment, but his close colleague Engels did dedicate serious work to the 'woman question' as it became known in the socialist tradition. Our story goes from there, to the early Soviet debates and practices on gender matters and thus to current issues. For in the last 30 years, there has been a veritable explosion of feminist theory and practice for which the 'marxist question' is not the only one on the agenda. What does a 'socialist feminism' entail? What do we mean by 'postmodern feminism'? These are some of the questions considered critically in this chapter. Marxism is not the only androcentric theory in the world, but its predominantly male bias has inevitably constrained its prospects as a guide to the liberation of the whole of humanity.

The cultural domain was for long relegated by marxism to a 'superstructure' dominated and determined by an economic 'base'. Chapter 6 examines the implications of this reductionist schema and shows how the superstructures had their revenge in the new cultural studies. The story goes from Marx's conception of ideology, the early Soviet attempt to create a 'proletarian culture' (*Proletkult*), to Antonio Gramsci's break with determinism and recognition of the full role of the cultural domain in capitalist societies. Gramsci acts as a hinge for the emergence in the 1970s of a 'culturalist' turn in marxism, examined critically in this chapter. With postmodernism, culture appears to be everywhere, all is culture; or so it would seem. From the neglect of culture we seem to have passed to the premature proclamation of the death of society. What postmodernism, and more clearly postcolonialism, has done is put a question mark under the previously undisputed hegemony of European culture. So, not only has marxism's economism been largely overcome but its Eurocentrism has also been 'corrected' in these recent debates.

Nationalism, has long been considered one of marxism's weak points, but then the whole of the Enlightenment tradition has trouble with nationalism. Chapter 7 traces the early, troubled and contradictory engagements of Marx and Engels with what they called the 'national question'. From this ambiguous legacy Lenin went on to construct the far more influential, but no less contradictory, theory of the 'right of nations to self-determination'. The explosion of national rivalries in what was once the Soviet Union shows the limitations of that approach. There is in marxist engagements with the national one lasting contribution, apart from Gramsci's, namely that of the Austro-Marxist, Otto Bauer, whose partial breakthrough is considered here. Finally, the chapter turns to nation and nationalism in the era of globalized postmodernism. There are no easy answers but we do, for example, have to recognize that all national phenomena are gendered, a blind spot of monumental implications in marxist and liberal approaches to the national alike. We are at least now beginning to understand nationalism as a discursive formation in its own right and not just as an 'epiphenomenon' of economic processes.

After the deluge of 1989 when communism collapsed like a house of cards, what future can there be for marxism? Chapter 8 concludes this text with an examination of the varied responses from marxists to the fate of what was coyly known as 'actually existing socialism'. For some it led to a form of political amnesia in which marxism just evaporated. Others, like the Bourbons in France, simply learnt nothing and argued that their particular brand of marxist catechism had actually been vindicated. I think the previous chapters add up to a verdict that we are now post/past orthodox modernist-manicheist-marxism. But what about a 'postmodern marxism', if we can envisage such a hybrid? For orthodox marxists this would be inconceivable and conservative postmodernists would be horrified. Previous chapters had already begun the task of engaging the 'ghost of Marx', as Derrida puts it, with current postmodern themes in regards to development, gender and culture for example. This final chapter broadens out this theme and seeks to develop more explicitly a critical deconstructionist marxist (if you want) method to better understand the world about us. Coming full circle to Chapter 1 on socialist trajectories there is a broad discussion of what a postmodern socialism might look like.

This text is written in a time of danger but also, I believe, one of opportunity. There is much turbulence and confusion, even chaos, across the world and within our subjectivities. 'All that is solid melts into air.' It is a time of paradigmatic transition, where the old is dead but the new is not yet born. I might as well admit that this book is written from a postmodernist perspective but one understood as a critique and even subversion of accepted truths. To some extent, also, it comes from a postcolonial perspective. What I cannot help thinking about in May 1998, as the text is completed, are the famous *événements* of that other May, 30 years ago. In 1968 (1969, actually, in Latin America) there was a great speeding up of history, an irruption of culture into politics and the liberatory pulsations of the new social movements, especially the women's movement, began to be felt across the globe. In pursuing a theme such as Marx @ 2000 it would do no harm to bear in mind the slogan of May '68 ('Power to the Imagination!') and apply it imaginatively.

RONALDO MUNCK

1
Beyond the Labyrinth: Marxist Trajectories

The 'century of marxism' is over, most commentators agree. Yet, Jacques Derrida, a champion of the postmodern, post-marxist era, has recently declared that: 'There will be no future without this. Not without Marx no future without Marx, without the memory and the inheritance of Marx' (Derrida, 1994: 13). It is not a simple question of 'Marxism is dead, long live Marx!'. Yet there is now – a decade or so since the collapse of communism – a more sober reappraisal of the marxist heritage than was previously possible. This chapter traces some of the high (and low) points of the complex marxist trajectories from its origins in Marx, through the social democratic and communist traditions, to marxism's difficult engagement with postmodernism in recent times. I have inevitably simplified the complex labyrinth of the marxist discourse and the socialist communist movements. Sometimes, though, it would seem that the labyrinth – with its walls, dead-ends and Borgesian logic – is one that some marxists/socialists/communists have created for themselves or, more often, their followers.

Live Marx

At first glance we would read as counter-intuitive Etienne Balibar's confident prediction that: 'Marx will still be read in the twenty-first century, not only as a movement of the past, but as a contemporary author' (Balibar, 1995: 1). Just as we thought that Marx had become a 'dead dog' (as Hegel before him), he seems to spring to life. Now, the marxist project did not spring fully developed one summer day from the head of Karl Marx. The genealogy of marxism shows a complex, sometimes contradictory, development of the discourse we now know as marxism (to use capitals would signal a misplaced faith of the true believer). Nor can this be reduced to the 'young Marx' versus the 'mature Marx' or artificial distinctions between Marx as economist, philosopher or politician. It is even a simplification to argue, as Kautsky and Lenin both did, that marxism as world-view has three clear sources: German philosophy, French socialism and British political economy. This type of totalization, which is intrinsically and inevitably Europe-bound, will not do for a critical (thus 'live') Marx for today. Instead, we must delve into the real world of Marx and examine the shifts, retreats and advances he carried out in his bid to put revolutionary theory on a scientific standing against all the 'utopian socialists' of his day.

With the *Communist Manifesto*, written with Engels in 1847, Marx's political vision was made explicit. While often read for its dramatic images of a dynamic bourgeoisie, the *Manifesto* is also marked by a strong belief in an imminent and general crisis of capitalism. This would create the conditions for the proletariat to lead all the dominated classes towards a radical democracy, which, in turn, would create the conditions for a classless, communist society. This was the era of 'permanent revolution'. The proletariat is seen as the universal class of history. This, as Balibar notes, 'allows Marx to read off from the present the imminence of the communist revolution' (Balibar, 1995: 40). The themes of modernism and romanticism seem rolled into one. Marx's dialectic of modernity creates a politics of redemption, of universal fulfilment. The image of perpetual progress and the inevitable advance of history is a bold one. From a postmodern perspective we can also see the dark side of these images. Marshal Berman, admirer of Marx-the-Modernist, can write how in the *Manifesto* 'We can see, too, how communism, in order to hold itself together, might stifle the active, dynamic and developmental forces that have brought it into being, might betray many of the hopes that have made it worth fighting for, might reproduce the inequities and contradictions of bourgeois society under a new name' (Berman, 1983: 105).

As it turned out, history took a turn showing it would not always advance by the good side. The European revolution of 1848–9 could have been the implementation of the *Manifesto* but, instead, had relegated it by 1850. The collapse of capitalism and the proletariat as universal class had both been proven to be a mirage or wishful thinking. The notion of permanent revolution went out the window and Marx was forced to grapple with the power of nationalism and religious ideas. There was to be no smooth move towards a classless society. Marx turned, in *The Eighteenth Brumaire of Louis Bonaparte*, to seek strategies to confront the counter-revolution and to bridge the gap between what he began to call 'class in itself' and 'class for itself'. Capitalism would not magically unite the working class, this unity would have to be constructed politically. Marx also (re)turned to his ambitious research programme into capitalism, the critique of political economy, which would bear fruit with the publication of Volume 1 of *Capital* in 1867. Captalism's failure to oblige through a simple collapse and general crisis led Marx, thus, to uncover the hidden secrets of this mode of production, the sources of its dynamism and the nature of its contradictions.

The complex architecture of Marx's *Capital*, in its three volumes and the 'fourth' volumes of the *Theories of Surplus Value* is, of course, his most enduring and systematic legacy. Yet at this level only, read as an economist, Marx could be discussed as a 'minor post-Ricardian'. This perception changes if we move on to read *Capital* politically, as Harry Cleaver advised: 'it is a reading which eschews all detached interpretation and abstract theorizing in favour of grasping concepts only within that concrete totality of struggle whose determinations they designate' (1979: 11). With the rule of capitalism having been secured (almost) across the globe, it would seem opportune to return to *Capital*. Of course many of the problems which have exercised marxist economics over the years seem, and probably are, arcane today. However, a strategic reading of *Capital* can still be a useful aid towards developing a deeper conceptual understanding of capitalism today. With capitalism triumphant, Marx may still provide, as Żyg Bauman writes, 'a thoroughly critical utopia, exposing the historical relativity of capitalist values, laying bare their historical limitations, and thereby preventing them from freezing into an horizon-less commonsense' (Bauman, 1976: 99). In developing a new commensense for our new times, Marx still has something to say, if read critically.

The events of 1870–1 were, as those of 1848–9, also to have a mixed effect on the development of the marxian system. The Franco-Prussian war of 1870, followed by the great but tragic Paris Commune, set back even further the optimistic view of history. While Marx may have hailed the Commune as the first 'working-class government' in history, he was still shocked that the revolution had not broken out in the most developed capitalist country, namely England. Then, the merciless crushing of the Parisian working classes brought home the real, material military power of the ruling classes. There would be no simple, organic path to communism. Real politics came smashing into the developing Marxian paradigm. Again history was not developing on the 'good side', as testified by the dissolution of the First International in 1872. After 1871, as Balibar writes, Marx 'did not stop working, but from that moment on he was certain that he could no longer "finish" his work, that he could not come to a "conclusion". *There would be no conclusion*' (Balibar, 1995: 103). The marxian discourse became more open, less necessitarian and more 'political'. In Marx it led to the notion of 'transition', that phase before communism when the proletariat would have to dismantle the state apparatus. This 'rectification' would have serious effects in the later history of socialism.

After the shock of 1871, Marx again interrupted his research programme, this time to learn Russian among other things, and to rectify his theory of social evolution. The inexorable progress of capitalism towards communism with its evolutionary image had been shattered. It was a simple question, yet one inordinately difficult for Marx to answer, which prompted this epistemological rupture. The early Russian socialists, known as 'populists', sought Marx's opinion in 1888 on whether the rural commune could be the germ of a non-capitalist development prefiguring communism. In the 1867 Preface to the first edition of *Capital* Marx had argued famously that: 'The country that is more developed industrially only shows, to the less developed, the image of its own future' (Marx, 1976: 91). In 1881, Marx was able to articulate in his letter to Vera Zasulich that *Capital*'s law-like theory of capitalist accumulation did *not* apply regardless of historical circumstance. No longer is there a unilinear path of capitalist development, but a recognition of complexity, diversity and the distinct concrete paths to development in different parts of the world. For Teodor Shanin, who helped bring to light Marx's writings on Russia: 'His last decade was a conceptual leap, cut short by his death. Marx was a man of intellect as much as a man of passion for social justice, a revolutionary who preferred revolutionaries to doctrinaire followers' (Shanin [ed.], 1983: 33).

When Marx died in 1883, Engels became his literary executor, with huge effects for the development of what was to become marxism. Along with the notables of the German SPD (Social Democratic Party) Engels systematized or simplified and made mechanical Marx's fluid thought. His defining influence is felt in the volumes of *Capital* published after Marx's death, in his own doctrinal texts such as *Anti-Duhring* and his creation of 'historical materialism' as *Weltanschauung* (world-view). In his analysis of the critical reception of Marx after his death, Paul Thomas goes as far as to say that 'Engels's doctrines owed little or nothing to Marx, the man he called his mentor' (1991: 41). Perhaps this is going too far, but it is no coincidence that the Soviet translation of Marx's thought into state ideology began with the work of the Marx–Engels Institute. Against all the scientistic readings of Marx by Engels and others it should be recalled that Marx never referred to 'historical materialism' and certainly never that Soviet monster 'dialectical materialism' (or 'diamat' for short). It was, of course, Stalin's 1938 pamphlet *Dialectical and Historical Materialism* which cemented this 'Marxist' orthodoxy and helped convert it into state ideology and police method. None of this was inevitable and, as Thomas puts it, 'There is no good reason to suppose that Marx thought of himself as a kind of sybil, purveying timeless truths to an anxious posterity' (1991: 42).

We do not need rose-tinted spectacles to reject Kolakowski's concerted effort in his three-volume history of marxism to make the father responsible for the sins of his children. The religion of Marxism–Leninism can simply not be laid at Marx's door, if we place the latter in historical context and actually read what he wrote at the time, in the conjuncture in which he was living. This does not mean, of course, that Marx is immune from criticism, particularly as a modernist thinker. In this regard, we need to consider soberly Foucault's warning that: 'the claim to escape from the systems of contemporary reality so as to produce the overall programs of another society, of another way of thinking, another culture, another vision of the world, has led only to the return of the most dangerous traditions' (1984: 46). Marx was probably guilty of this type of arrogance, but *Capital* does not lead inexorably to the Gulag, as some of the more disingenuous 'nouveaux philosophes' tried to tell us (cf. Glucksmann, 1980). Even Foucault, as we shall see, who ran a mile from anything which smacked of 'dialectical materialism' can be seen to be in a constant engagement with the 'ghost of Marx', as Max Weber was before him.

Why would we imagine that the ideas of Marx might be relevant today? For Lukács, in a text he later disowned during the Stalinist heyday, 'Orthodox Marxism ... does not imply the uncritical acceptance of the results of Marx's investigations ... On the contrary, orthodoxy refers exclusively to *method*' (1971: 1). Though still a text of a 'true believer', to some extent the point is a sensible one. The method of Marx is that of the radical critique, with its inherent capacity of reflexivity and self-critique. If the 'diamat' is an integral part of Stalinist totalitarianism, Marx's critical method points instead towards all the radical trends in epistemology, from feminism to deconstruction. In Marx's own thought there was permanent innovation, adaptation and self-critical reflection. Marx's thought was/is as dynamic as the society it worked on, and its drive for social justice is as relevant today as then. There does seem to be considerable consensus that Marx was on surer ground as critic of capitalism, rather than as creator of a new society. In this regard we can but agree with Marshall Berman, for whom: 'The great gift [Marx]...can give us today, it seems to me, is not a way out of the contradictions of modern life but a surer and deeper way into these contradictions' (1983: 129).

If Marx sought a science, did he not also create a utopia with communism? Certainly in much of his writing we can detect a strong anti-utopian sentiment, but communism is still a utopia in the full sense of the word. There are many voices urging a reconsideration of this utopian element in Marx. For John Gray, no friend of marxism, to 'repress in the interests of criticism and objective knowledge the mythopoeic impulse which explains its appeal' is to reduce it to 'an eso-teric and barely intelligible cult' (1995: 232). Jacques Derrida, in his own settling of accounts with Marx, similarly, but more positively, notes that marxism *'carries with it, and must carry with it, necessarily*, despite so many modern or post-modern denials, a messianic eschatology' (Derrida, 1995: 59). It would indeed be a very reductive and 'cold' view of science which would divorce it from all positive human endeavour. The politics of utopia can be grounded and do not necessarily degenerate into totalitar-ian dreams. It is, perhaps, at this point that Marx speaks most clearly to the new social movements which many would see as the agents of change comparable to Marx's gravedigger of capitalism, the proletariat.

Unwinding socialism

The socialist clock (or bomb?) so passionately wound up by Marx was slowly but surely unwound by his followers, to become a pale reflection (even betrayal) of its former self. The Second or Socialist International was formed in 1889, some years before Engels died in 1895. Hopes were high that this new international body would take up and develop the heritage of the First International. Kolakowski has, with little exaggera-tion, called the 1889–1914 era the 'golden age of Marxism' (1981: 1). Yet as the First World War broke out in 1914, the socialist parties of the French and German proletariats lined up behind their national states and armies in the great conflagration. The great hopes of socialist inter-nationalism were dashed as its constituent parts succumbed to chau-vinism and jumped on, with varying degrees of reluctance, to their respective nation-state war machines. This watershed in the history of marxist ideas and practice was to give rise to a new, hardier offshoot, bolshevism or communism, to be examined in the next section. But first we have to consider in more detail the epistemological and political underpinnings of 'orthodox' marxism after the death of its reluctant founder, Karl Marx.

Karl Kautsky, the 'Pope' of marxism as he became known, carried out the organic systematization of the doctrine, for that is what it became. Even Lenin, for whom he was 'the great renegade', praised his role in developing Marx's theoretical legacy, notably in relation to the agrarian question. According to Kolakowski 'Next to Engels, Kautsky was certainly the chief exponent of the naturalist, evolutionist determinist Darwinist element of Marxism' (1981: 51). Yet Kautsky did develop a far more nuanced understanding of the relationship between the workers' movement and the complex society which capitalism was becoming in the early twentieth century. Kautsky was keenly aware of the importance of democracy in the development of socialism. His analysis of the new relationships emerging between society, the state and political parties prefigures the later developments of Gramsci. His opposition to the undemocratic nature of the Bolshevik revolution of 1917 repays attention even today. Finally, Kautsky was the guardian of 'orthodox' marxism against the 'revisionism' of Eduard Bernstein and others, who sought a wholesale revision and modernization of marxism to fit the new conditions of a stable, increasingly prosperous and democractic capitalism as they saw it.

Bernstein's views have been anathematized even more than Kautsky's in communist and revolutionary circles. His practically Fabian view of a smooth, non-violent evolution towards socialism was easily derided. His aphorism of the final goal (socialism) being nothing and the movement (social democracy) 'everything' has been willfully caricatured. Following the death of Engels, Bernstein developed a series of articles in *Problems of Socialism* (1993) criticizing the founders of marxism for their belief in a catastrophic collapse of capitalism. The crisis of capitalism did not seem much in evidence in the Germany of the mid-1890s. The advance of democracy in the more industrialized countries seemed to indicate the possibility that working-class parties could advance the cause of socialism through parliament. Perhaps legislation, institutional reform and piecemeal social engineering could create a smooth transition to socialism. Bernstein picked up, astutely enough, the contradictions between the late Engels's advocacy of strict legality in the pursuit of socialism on the one hand, and his lingering attachment to revolutionary rhetoric on the other hand. While Kautsky clung to 'orthodoxy' while developing marxism, Bernstein became a more open advocate of a reformist socialist ideology.

Both Kautsky and Bernstein are bridges between classical marxism (that of Marx primarily) and the modern tradition of social democracy. With these two thinkers, marxism emerges squarely into the modern era and shakes off most of its Romanticist heritage. As Beilharz writes, it is no 'accident that Kautsky and Bernstein have little patience for the Fourieresque idyll of *The Germany Ideology*' (1992: 118). An air of realism had crept into the socialist discourse and the utopian element faded away. The modern concept of identity was ill at ease with some of the idyllic, pastoral visions of labour utopias. This was the age of Max Weber now, and Hegel was very much in the past. Capitalist accumulation and social differentiation was producing a complex society irreducible to simple dialetical schemas. Beilharz has the interesting idea that 'Social Democracy takes this process of rupture the furthest, and consequently is the most modern or potentially "postmodern" of labour's utopias' (ibid.: 118). The illusions of a simplistic marxist teleology were dispelled and its belief in itself as a fixed and finished system was severely shaken. However, what was to become known as social democracy in this modern era was equally teleological and represented no answer to the failings of classical marxism.

The trauma of 1914 and subsequent events – such as social-democratic participation in 'bourgeois government' in Germany after 1918 – utterly transformed the social-democratic discourse. For one, the state became the undisputed matrix of all social democratic strategy. From this it followed that gaining more seats in parliament was the way to get access to state power and policy-making. Marcel Leibman goes on to argue that: 'As a result, reformism came to be redefined. Its gradualism and peaceful legalism were now so blatant that they did not need to be spelled out' (1986: 4). Just as the Russian Revolution was opening up a new heroic chapter in the marxist story, the Western European social democrats were extolling the virtues of the prosaic, and sinking into apathy over the viability of even mild reformist measures. Whereas in the past, even moderate social democrats were prepared to endorse mass action and even revolutionary rhetoric to gain advantage, now many leading social democrats began to fear the mobilized masses. Social democrats were becoming 'responsible' aspirants to hold state power and thus any attempts against this state were to be opposed, with force if necessary. Even the reformisms of a Kautsky and a Bernstein were beginning to seem dangerously radical.

By the time the Second World War had come and gone, social democracy had mutated into an ideology which could barely trace its history back to Marx. Keynes had replaced Kautsky as leading light, and a broad, classless appeal had replaced traditional reliance on labour and the trade unions. Even the commitment to nationalization of the means of production, through which the statist orientation had been implemented, was being drawn into question by the 1950s. This turn was symbolically ratified in the 1959 Bad Godesberg programme of the German social democrats. To the new Keynesian consensus was added the welfare state and political liberalism. This new hybrid liberal–social democracy was not a particularly stable ideological formation. As Padgett and Patterson note: 'Attempts to redefine social democracy met with only limited success and the parties entered a period of ideological disarray. The collapse of the social-democratic consensus led to an intensification of the ideological fission which is a primary characteristic of the [social-democratic] parties' (1991: 2). The compass of marxism, albeit reduced to a largely symbolic or theological function, had now been thrown overboard and a new mutant political discourse had been created.

By the 1980s, the 100-year-old history of social democracy as a discernible reformist interpretation or development of marxism had clearly come to an end. In essence social democracy had become assimilated with liberalism in the now globally dominant neoliberal discourse. With the decomposition and ultimate collapse of communism, social democracy could not even pose as a bulwark against radicalism or as socialism 'with a human face'. The 'Mitterand experiment' in France during the 1980s saw just how rapidly social democratic discourse would evaporate under the new liberal dispensation and the rigours of globalization. Reformism and socialization are now replaced by modernization and liberalization. What is most noticeable is that the label of radicalism was now more often seized by the right. Social democracy lost even that intellectual or political ascendancy it had in the postwar period due to its association with radicalism and reform. The democratic terrain no longer saw the uncontested hegemony of these descendants, however distant and however intermarried, of Karl Marx.

A blind spot of the social democratic tradition was always the colonial or 'Third' world. An implicit, even explicit, acceptance of European imperialism was matched by a particularly virulent Eurocentrism when it came to dealing with the colonial Other. As an example we find George Leichteim, in his 'classic' history of socialism, dedicating a short subsection to the Third World where he refers among other things to 'the infantile parody of Lenin's thought known as Maoism' and the 'childlike simplicity' of the Maoist model (1970: 282–3). Needless to say, no such derogatory language is deployed against European thinkers, even when the author disagrees with them. Of course, colonialism is a problem for the marxist tradition from the founders onwards. Marx may well have come to grips with the politics of development in Russia and nationalism in Ireland, but he still thought British colonialism had done a good job in India, and that the 'energetic' Yankees should obviously have the upper hand over the 'lazy' Mexicans (see Chapter 3). But in recent decades, social democracy as a political current largely shorn of its marxian heritage has taken an increasingly interventionist stance in some areas of the Third World. Perhaps it would take on a new lease of life there as its cycle in the advanced capitalist countries seemed to come to a close?

There was a certain boom for social democracy in Latin America during the late 1970s and early 1980s. It seemed that this European tradition might transplant successfully to the Americas. One inspiration was the success of Spain's Socialist Party in managing the transition from Franco to a parliamentary democracy. Another key factor was the decisive drive by German social democracy to support or even create Latin American social democrats to counter the hegemony of US imperialism in the region. Thus one determinant was to help make the region safe for Western European investment and to block any prospect for insurgency through preventative reform. Yet, the tradition of Willy Brandt in seeking a more conciliatory relationship between the North and the South in global economic and political relations is not a purely self-serving one. It is also the case that the social-democratic tradition has, or at least had, certain minimum articles of faith – such as the right of workers to organize, the inalienable need for free, democratic elections, and the responsibility of the state for the common good – which were truly transformatory in a Latin America coming out of the long night of military dictatorship.

Today, social democracy faces severe challenges in the developing world. To some extent its Eurocentrism has been overcome and it has developed strong hybrid offshoots in many countries. It is interesting in this regard to consider the challenges as seen by a social-democratic leader of a major developing country, Fernando Henrique Cardoso. For Cardoso the challenges for social democracy in Brazil and elsewhere in the Third World revolve around three main issues:

1. Social democracy's relation with the state, once seen as a saviour, but now subject to liberalism's privatization drive;
2. Social democracy's ambiguous relationship with nationalism now so clearly questioned by the advance of globalization;

3. Social democracy's relationship with democracy and the troubled relationships between the need of a strong executive to achieve modernization and the defence of a parliamentary system. (Cardoso, 1993b: 403–13)

Whether social democracy is able to deal with these tensions is an open question. Whether social democracy's economic and political reformism can provide solutions to the pressing social problems of developing countries is even more open to question. Certainly those still clinging to 'orthodox' marxism do not seem to have any viable answers.

Communist collapse

When the Russian communists took power in 1917 it seemed that the shame of German and French social democracy in 1914 had been expunged. Indeed, a new dynamic Marxist–Leninist hybrid spread throughout the world. Yet, in historical terms, a brief 70 years later this movement had definitively collapsed. This section traces the rise and decline of the communist idea and state. But first we must recall just what a landmark 1917 was in the world's political history. As Arrighi, Hopkins and Wallerstein write: '1917 became such a big symbol because it was the first dramatic victory of the proponents of state-power strategy … 1917 proved it could be done' (1989: 99). Whereas Marx and Engels had no clear conceptions of how proletarian political power would be achieved and Kautsky and Bernstein had developed a reformist, parliamentary road to socialism, Lenin and the Bolsheviks (albeit reluctantly for many of them) pioneered the revolutionary path to state power. Renewing the Jacobin tradition, the Bolsheviks were part of a broader wave of revolutions in China, Mexico and, in a different context, Germany. The undoubted founder of the Bolshevik discourse is Lenin, a historical figure who rightly become part of the Marxist–Leninist couplet.

Lenin sought to fill in the gap left by Marx in terms of political strategy. The whole nature of marxism, or historical materialism as it became known, was transformed by Lenin's particular vision of politics, organization and the state. Lenin's epistemological breakthrough dates from 1903 at the Second Congress of the All-Russian Social Democratic Labour Party. A seemingly trivial dispute over the definition of membership led to the unravelling of two distinct discourses. A whole style of Bolshevik practice and attitudes entered the political vocabulary. The 'professional revolutionary' made its debut as a political category.

Dogmatism in theory, or 'principle', was allied with a flexibility in tactics which bordered on duplicity. The Leninist machine – The Party – was launched or, as Felix Guattari put it, 'the fundamental signifiers, the cardinal positions, entered history at that moment' (1984: 190). To assess its significance we need to consider Lukács, for whom Lenin's 'admirable realism' was simply 'the consistent application of Marxism… to problems of socialism' (1971: 73) alongside the sombre verdict of those such as A. J. Polan, for whom Lenin forecloses politics and seeks to 'ontologize the apocalypse' (1984: 204) in an authoritarian discourse which has conspired against human freedom.

The notion of Lenin as the agent of *realpolitik* who simply sought to operationalize marxism is a problematic one. Lenin was fully part of the socialist tradition committed to rationality and with universal aspirations. Indeed it makes more sense to see Lenin as the epitome, and epitaph for, a doctrinaire socialism believing in the power of theory. Here is where we need to distinguish at least two Lenins. There is the Lenin of direct democracy, the architect of 'dual power' and the promoter of 'all power to the soviets'. This is also the Lenin of the last years when, already ailing, he agonized over the party-state bureaucracy, rapidly becoming a dictatorship over (rather than of) the proletariat. Yet, in practice, the Lenin who led to Leninism was the creator of the vanguard party, the admirer of Taylorist work methods and the firm believer in firm economic and political discipline. As everyone knows, there is an 'objective' basis for this particular resolution of Lenin's ambiguities, in the painful conditions of economic, social and political backwardness in the Russia of the early twentieth century. So, in many ways inevitably, Leninism became the marxism of backwardness, an under- (or mal-) developed socialism for an underdeveloped capitalist country.

The young Bolshevik revolution looked hopefully to Germany in 1918 for a revolution in the capitalist heartland that would give respite to their beleaguered enterprise. As marxists they were internationalists but also, more importantly, they clearly believed that socialism could only come about through capitalism. In this sense, they did not accept Marx's letters to Vera Zasulich, which opened up a less necessitarian development scenario. In the end, the headquarters of the world revolution would remain in Russia, as hopes for a European rising faded. Optimism remained and, as Lenin announced to the founding conference of the Comintern (Communist International) in 1919, 'the victory of the proletarian revolution all over the world is assured'. The colour of this new revolutionary wave was to be less than pristine

red however. Led by Lenin's conception of imperialism, national liberation in the colonies was to be the mainspring of the move against
international capitalism. At the 1921 Congress of the Peoples of the
West the leaders of the Bolshevik revolution were calling for a Jihad or
'holy war' against British and French imperialism. Communism turned
its eyes to the East (the 'South' of the early twentieth century) and
towards nationalism. This was a long way from classic marxist proletarian internationalism and belief that only the most advanced capitalist
countries could hope to achieve a transition to socialism.

After the First World War there was one beleaguered, if big, anti-
capitalist state on the world scene; after the Second World War, China,
Vietnam, North Korea and Cuba had joined the club. Albeit imposed
by Russian arms, most of Eastern Europe also fell under the sway of
pro-Soviet governance. Yet these were revolutions that were predominantly nationalist in character and the setting was mainly agricultural
(except for parts of Eastern Europe). By this stage few observers doubted
that the economic and political system which had emerged was far
removed from anything envisaged by Marx or even Lenin. Critical marxism was wracked by a debate on the 'nature of the USSR' which now
seems byzantine and theological. While the more or less critical supporters of the non-capitalist, but definitely not socialist, regimes
sought mitigating factors, the ideologues of capitalism waxed indig-
nant about the communist monster.

What is clear is that the Soviet Union after the death of Lenin embarked on a course of authoritarian modernization and totalitarian politics
under Stalin which has few parallels in modern history. Whereas Mao's
successors in China were able to retreat under control from such a course,
Stalin's successors found regime decompression a more difficult process
to manage. The Soviet monolith was, however, less solid than it looked,
even by the late 1950s. The increased centralization of the economic
model was not conducive to efficiency or technological innovation.
The virtual absence of political participation meant there was little
prospect for self-correcting mechanisms in the decision-making process.
At another, social or molecular level, the regime was simply losing consensus; this would ultimately lead to its decomposition. Within 40 years
the bright and shiny hopes of 1917 had been tarnished. The nationalist
element remained, heightened by Russia's experience in the Second
World War, as did, of course, inertia. A vicious cycle of instability
frustrated reform and decay led eventually to Gorbachev's *perestroika*,
a restructuring tune which became a funeral march. For Carl Boggs:
'Modernity in its diverse expressions (economic complexity, technology,

urbanism, increased levels of education) had finally destroyed the firmaments of the post-Stalinist order and now threatened to undermine Communist rule in any form' (1995: 89). Yet there was no ineluctable necessity to this process – as the modernization and convergence theories of the 1960s argued – which was mediated by a political struggle punctuated by popular revolts, labour organizing and human rights campaigns.

It was not long before resentment over the imposed 'state socialist' regimes in Eastern Europe boiled over. East Germany in 1953 and Hungary in 1956 saw impressive, if ultimately defeated, uprisings. The latter became a landmark for the international communist movement. Then Czechoslovakia in 1968 and Poland in 1979–81 saw even more impressive moves by the people against the ruling bureaucracy. The bureaucratic centralism of these regimes was more fragile than it appeared. Faced with these less than impressive models for an alternative society, Western communists began to develop a 'Eurocommunist' hybrid. Essentially the communist tradition began to occupy the ground ceded by social democracy in the mid- to late 1970s. There was not much distance now between the inheritors of the Gramsci–Togliatti tradition and that of Kautsky–Bernstein. Parliament became the privileged focus of political transformation and socialism was placed on a very distant backburner. However, these respectable reformist communists were not able to make a breakthrough and by 1990 'Eurocommunism no longer existed as a vehicle of social change in the Mediterranean or anywhere else, much less as the fruition of grandiose visions entertained by many Marxists in the 1970s' (Boggs, 1995: 129).

Contrary to the agonising, inward-looking debates on the 'crisis of Western Marxism', events in the wider socialist world would prove equally important. The Chinese revolution had been the second great act following Russia 1917. If the proletariat in the advanced capitalist countries would not rise, then perhaps the 'world of the country' (the agrarian or 'Third World' countries) would encircle and engulf the 'world of the city' (advanced capitalism). Following Hungary 1956, many radicals turned their eyes to what would become known as the Third World. Victorious revolutions in Algeria and Cuba cemented the legend of the people's war against imperialism. Jean-Paul Sartre used Franz Fanon to berate the impotence of metropolitan marxism. Emancipation had found another route in the Third World with many in the West acting as cheerleaders. Then Che Guevara died and Castro supported the Soviet invasion of Czechoslovakia in 1967. *Realpolitik* was taking over from utopia again. Even the long-awaited victory of the

Vietnamese revolution in 1975 was to turn sour. The internecine war in Indo-China and the 'boat people', finally buried Third Worldism as a progressive discourse. Now capitalism appeared once again, as in classical marxism, as the progressive agent of economic transformation.

In 1989, the Berlin Wall dividing East from West Germany came down, symbolizing the end of the communist era. In practical and discursive terms, the events of 1989 represent a watershed in global history. They are equivalent to the French Revolution and 1917 as events marking the death of an old regime. As Eric Hobsbawm put it soon after: 'We are seeing not the crisis of a type of movement, regime and economy, but its end. Those of us who believed that the October Revolution was the gate to the future of world history have been shown to be wrong' (1991: 117). There was no way to escape the conclusion that marxism had come to the end of the road in almost all its various manifestations. The idea of socialism as a totalizing discourse and privileged path to social transformation had evaporated. Yet Fred Halliday could read the events of 1989 as having 'restated, in a dramatic form, the most neglected facet of political life … namely the capacity of the mass of the population to take sudden, rapid and novel political action' (1991: 78). So, at the very moment when marxism as movement and marxism as government was coming to an end, the risen peoples of Eastern Europe were carrying out some very 'marxist'-like revolutionary actions.

In the capitalist ideological euphoria following the collapse of nearly all the communist states, Francis Fukuyama developed the 'end of history' thesis (1992). Certainly capitalism, in all its economic, political and social forms, seemed to be 'the only game in town'. The West had won. Neoliberal economies and parliamentary democracy had a clear field. Events since have confirmed Misha Glenny's verdict that: 'Far from coming to an end, history is being reborn' (1990: 183). Perhaps slightly carried away by the atmosphere, Glenny read the 1989 revolutions in 'Central Europe' (as it then became) as victories of the rational over the irrational, the democratic over the totalitarian. Where all this left marxism as a theory was not so clear. It is well to remember that in 1898 Thomas Masaryk had also diagnosed a 'crisis in Marxism'. From that crisis was born the revisionist marxism which led to social democracy. Will this end-of-century crisis (albeit pretty permanent looking) conceivably lead to a postmodern marxism? Will the end of redemption politics lead to a rebirth of radical democratic opposition to the resurgent capitalist world around us? These are the themes and this is the background to the final section of this introductory chapter.

Late marxism

In 1977, at a conference in Venice organized by the Italian communist breakaway movement *Il Manifesto*, Louis Althusser, then the recognized 'Pope' of marxist theory, officially declared the 'crisis of marxism'. For him, this seemed to be mainly due to the crisis of the official communist parties then beginning to go their own separate ways. It was left to Rossana Rossanda to declare more precisely that actually existing socialism had drawn into question 'the very idea of socialism, not as generic aspiration, but as a *theory of society*, a *different* mode of organisation of human existence' (Il Manifesto, 1979: 9). In fact, by 1977 it was only a belated recognition by the communist tradition of a process which had begun a decade earlier. For it is '1968' (1967–9) that symbolizes the death of the old left and the beginning of a new one which would become known as post-marxism, with its varying degrees of emphasis on the first and second term of the couplet. The events around 1968 led to the questioning of a whole series of premises of orthodox marxism/socialism: 'its discursive universality, its identification with single classes and parties, its premise of a simple representation of (economic) interests, its blindness to multiple forms of domination, its unbridled productivism in a world of ecological limits' (Boggs, 1995: 182).

We can take as part of the same historical moment the May Events of France in 1968, the 'Prague Spring' in Czechoslovakia and the 1969 '*Cordobozo*' in Argentina. The old bureaucratic, authoritarian statist way of being was under challenge. It was, indeed, a world revolution which transformed utterly both the world and the way we view it. Though a 'failure' in the military sense, it brought onto the political scene the new social movements which effectively buried the old Marxist–Leninist dogmas. An optimistic reading was that of Perry Anderson, for whom 'The re-emergence of revolutionary masses outside the control of a bureaucratised party rendered *potentially* conceivable the unification of Marxist theory and working class practice once again' (1976: 95). This conclusion was based on the assumption that there was, indeed, an uncorrupted marxist tradition waiting in the wings once stalinism was dead, but Trotsky's descendants were too late. As it was, the significance of 1968 was to prove far more important at the cultural level, that domain for so long dismissed by most marxists as a 'superstructure' at the mercy of the all-important economic base (see Chapter 6). It was the tradition of Gramsci which would provide the hinge between the old and the new marxisms.

In the marxist tradition it was mainly Antonio Gramsci who had developed the idea of socialism as cultural critique. Gramsci's concept of hegemony opened up a consistent critique of traditional or orthodox marxism. Seeking to capture the complex nature of authority under developed capitalist conditions it shows that consent is as important as coercion in maintaining the system. Gramsci's suggestive, if fragmentary, analysis refused the reductive temptation and sought to grasp the multiplicity of social reality. There was a flourishing of interest in Gramsci's writings during the 1970s which was far from restricted to Western Europe. One example is the individual and joint work of Ernesto Laclau and Chantal Mouffe which has developed a postmarxism in the footsteps of Gramsci but also keenly aware of poststructuralists such as Foucault and Derrida. One point they make insistently is that the traditional socialist yearning for totality needs to be abandoned, and in rejecting all essentialist a-priorism they argue that: 'The incomplete character of every totality necessarily leads us to abandon, as a terrain of analysis, the premise of "Society" as a sutured and self-defined totality. "Society" is not a valid object of discourse. There is no underlying principle fixing – and hence constituting – the whole field of differences' (1985: 111).

If a Gramsci-inspired 'open' marxism was one result of 1968, there was also a lot of disillusion and a turn towards irrationalism. The Revolution did not happen, the workers went home, the students became employees and the Communist Party carried on as before. From modernist millenarianism we pass to the conservative simplicities of the *nouveaux philosophes*. The latter, mainly ex-Maoist 'children of '68' became notorious for their intemperate denunciation of marxism as nothing more or less than the philosophy of the Russian Gulag or labour camps. A leading light of this school, Bernard-Henri Lévy in *La barbarie à visage humain* (Lévy, 1977) rejected the marxist theory of power in favour of a conception where power is 'everywhere and yet is nothing'. For Lévy the lesson was clear: liberation is impossible and the good society is but a dream. Political struggle is between ethereal theories such as domination, submission and the love of freedom. The boundaries between the oppressed and the oppressor are fuzzy at best. André Glucksmann, one-time Althusserian, was particularly virulent in his *The Master Thinkers* (1980) where Marx is seen as the epitome of the dominator philosopher who, with his 'cult of the total and final Revolution' and 'the State that terrorizes for the good of the collectivity', is behind all the oppression unleashed by socialist regimes.

The whole ambiguity of '1968' can be seen in the intellectual career of Jean-François Lyotard, who is more icon or demon than properly read. First of all it is worth recalling that for many years Lyotard was a member of the *Socialisme ou barbarie* political–intellectual grouping, which was committed to an 'internal' critique of marxism and which included such key thinkers of the left as Cornelius Castoriadis and Claude Lefort. Lyotard's disillusion with marxism derives from his experience in Algeria, where he witnessed Communist Party compromising, and the events of May 1968, in which he played an active part. Lyotard is far from being a simple apolitical metropolitan *penseur*. Lyotard's break with marxism is most clearly articulated in his 1974 text *Libidinal Economy* (1993) – which he himself later called an 'evil book' – in which he develops the idea of a libidinal economy to counter Marx's notion of a political economy. Marxism had failed to work for Lyotard and he adopted his 'incredulity towards metanarratives'. His 1979 text *The Postmodern Condition* (1984) went on to become the Bible of the postmodern cult, but the point is that it is squarely within the tradition of post*marxism*. Lyotard is not the only political thinker who still lives in Marx's shadow and who, while heavily criticizing and even disowning him, cannot refuse his history.

It is Michel Foucault who has probably most influenced the pro-gressive intellectual agenda in the last couple of decades and whose relationship with marxism is not really clear. On the one hand he has told us himself that 'what has happened since 1968, and arguably what made 1968 possible, is profoundly anti-Marxist' (1980: 57). Certainly Foucault's themes were developed counterposed to much of marxism, but to see '1968' (or Foucault) as anti- (as against post-) marxist is a different thing. We also know from Pierre Macherey that it is repudia-tion of his early adherence to marxism which explains why Foucault 'shunned like the plague everything which arose out of dialectical materialism' (cited in Balibar, 1992: 39). On the other hand, we have more recent interpretations such as that of Althusser's one-time collaborator, Etienne Balibar, for whom 'the whole of Foucault's work can be seen in terms of a genuine struggle with Marx, and that this can be viewed as one of the driving forces of his productiveness' (Balibar, 1992: 39). Following this line of enquiry we could think of Foucault as a lever to carry out a critique of Marx, as a privileged, if heretical, vantage point to assist in the development of a late-marxism more in keeping with the critical impetus of Marx himself.

Foucault once called himself a 'Nietzschean Communist' and seemed well pleased with this heretical concept. For Foucault, Marxism (with a capital M) is inextricably bound up with domination, in its pursuit of scientificity and its acceptance of power structures. As is well known, Foucault developed a 'capillary' theory of power, focused on the disciplinary mechanisms of 'micro' power. Though at odds with much statist marxist work, it fits readily into the work of creative marxists such as Nicos Poulantzas in his last work (1980). As Abdul Janmohamed notes: 'Foucault himself is aware of the problems involved in his conflation of Marx and Marxism and in the hasty skirting of Marx's notion of the function of power within the sphere of political economy' (1996: 34). I think it is possible to say that Marx was a positive reference point in Foucault's thinking. We can also agree that power needs to be analysed in all its diversity and not reduced to the orthodox marxist trinity of state, class and party. In studying the complexity of power relations in the current era of globalization, Foucault is probably an indispensable complement (and provocation) to any marxism wishing to break with dogmatism and the structures of domination.

Turning now to Jacques Derrida, we have a guru of the post-structuralist movement and scourge of marxism who has recently turned to acknowledge his (and our) debt to Marx. Derrida is quite explicit: 'To continue to take inspiration from a certain spirit of Marxism would be to keep faith with what has always made of Marxism in principle and first of all a *radical* critique, namely a procedure ready to undertake its self-critique' (Derrida, 1995: 88). Derrida focuses on the essential marxist character as critique as against the wooden Soviet doctrine of dialectical materialism. As is well known, Derrida has developed an approach known as deconstruction which, in a Nietzschean spirit, 'has produced a discourse of extreme sceptical rigour and rhetorical self-consciousness' (Norris, 1991: 75). What is less well known, perhaps, is Derrida's recent attempt to bring this approach more into line with marxism. For Derrida now: 'Deconstruction has never had any sense or interest, in my view at least, except as a radicalization, which is to say also *in the tradition* of a certain Marxism, in a certain *spirit of Marxism*. There has been, then, this attempted radicalization of Marxism called deconstruction' (1995: 92). Polemical this may be, but it at least signals the enduring pull of marxism for all intellectuals with radical aspirations.

This is not the place to discuss the relationship between marxism and deconstruction (see Chapter 8) but we should understand how important the distinction between Marx and marxism has been. As with Foucault, Derrida has always seen himself as someone who has implacably 'opposed, to be sure, *de facto* "Marxism" or "communism" (the Soviet Union, the International of Communist Parties, and everything that resulted from them, which is to say so very many things...)' (1995: 14). Now, with the 'dogma machine' dead, Derrida has no alibi to continue avoiding Marx. The heavy hand of orthodox Marxism–Leninism, Stalinism for short, had a deadening and alienating effect on a whole generation of political intellectuals who instead would have been revitalizing marxism. We are now reaching the end of an era which has been dominated by what Derrida calls 'the quasi-paternal figure of Marx' so that now we might be able to renew his *critical* heritage. It is perhaps not surprising, in retrospect, that this voyage took a detour via Nietzsche, who provided a much-needed demystifying critical edge. The labyrinths of marxism and deconstruction respectively may now achieve some clarification through Derrida's bold, if unfashionable, claim to Marx's spirit.

Though I shall return in Chapter 8 to discuss in more detail the complex relationship between marxism and postmodernism, I would like to advance some preliminary points. Marxism and modernity are inseparable; marxism and male dominance are inseparable (see Chapter 5); marxism and productivism (see Chapter 2) are inseparable. Of course these somewhat overstated propositions will need to be developed. Yet it seems that postmodernism, or strands of it, have located some of the weak points of marxism and socialism. Some postmodernists had revelled in these weaknesses and developed a nihilistic politics for the end of century. But others have sought to renew the critical impulse of early marxism, as a critique to take us beyond modernity. That new social movements such as feminism had related so positively (yet critically, of course) to postmodernism is, in this sense, no surprise. Peter Beilharz has argued that what postmodernism really signals 'is the moment in which modernity becomes self-reflective, more fully conscious and critical of itself, more critically aware of the discrepancy between its promise and its performance' (1994: 9). A 'postmodernist socialism' would be guided by a similar ethos. It seems a sensible and sober way to begin the (de)(re)construction of the marxist and socialist traditions and help us out of the labyrinth.

2
Red and Green: Marxism and Nature

The story of marxism's engagement with nature is an odd one. It abounds in sorry tales such as Engels and his 'dialectics of nature' and Lysenko's 'proletarian science' in biology. Yet for a living marxism in the twenty-first century, the coming together of red and green politics will, undoubtedly, be a critical issue. If we trace back Marx's own ambiguous legacy on the question of nature we find relevant lessons for today's debates. After summarizing this background, this chapter will move on to consider the subsequent attempts by various theorists to develop a rapprochement between socialism and the new politics of ecology. The underlying issue is the tension between an anthropocentric and an ecocentric approach to development. The third section explores some of the fascinating encounters between feminism and ecology, including the development of a radical, if debatable, conception of ecofeminism. Finally, in the last section, the current state of the debate around globalization and sustainable development is considered. The point of this chapter, as of most subsequent ones, is to consider 'classic' marxist debates but to also confront them with current concerns in a spirit of critical engagement.

Divided Marx

Marx himself is irrevocably associated with a hostile attitude towards the 'idiocy of rural life' and a belief in a *homo faber* who would dominate nature. While there is certainly a Promethean ethos running through much of Marx's scattered writings on nature, there is also considerable ambiguity. To seek to discover a 'green Marx', an ecologist *avant la lettre*, would not be particularly fruitful, but it would be wrong to flatten Marx's views on nature and refuse their ambiguities. At the same time, we should be aware of what Alfred Schmidt refers to as 'the technocratic and scientistic misinterpretation that Marx was solely concerned to secure a quantitative increase in the existing forms of mastery over nature' (1971: 12). While Marx did constantly refer to the 'domination of nature', he tended to conceive of this in terms of the need to achieve mastery of society by its members. The broader problematic within which Marx worked was the distinction between a 'realm of necessity' and a 'realm of freedom'. Nature is thus an issue for Marx as part of human practice. Marx put it bluntly in the 'Economic and Philosophic Manuscripts': 'nature taken abstractly, for itself, and fixed in its separation from man, is *nothing* for man' (1975: 398).

For Marx 'Nature builds no machines, no locomotives, railways, electric telegraphs, self-acting mules, etc. These are products of human industry; natural material transformed into organs of the human will over nature' (Marx, 1973: 706). This is the Marx taken up by the subsequent tradition of marxist developmentalism (see Chapter 3) with its self-confident, indeed arrogant, view of humankind's domination of nature. Yet Marx, when he wrote of the sharp division between town and country, so typical of the growing capitalist mode of production, could point out critically how this division had disturbed 'the metabolism between man and the earth; ie the return to the soil of its elements consumed by man in the form of food and clothing, and therefore violated the eternal natural condition for the lasting fertility of the soil' (ibid.: 505). Marx would probably thus fully understand the implications of the capitalist industrialization of agriculture in the contemporary era. There are, indeed, for Marx natural conditions for human existence. It is, further, possible in line with Marx's thought to distinguish between a transformative labour process and another, such as in agriculture, where human labour is applied in a way to facilitate natural processes of growth.

Marx could certainly pour scorn on the naturalists of his day: 'We can see this cult of nature is limited to the Sunday walks of an inhabitant of a small provincial town who childishly wonders at the cuckoo laying its eggs in another bird's nest, at tears being designed to keep the surface of the eyes moist, and so on' (cited in Grundmann, 1991: 110). Marx went on to explain to Herr Daumer, whose romantic cult wished to see 'the sacrifice of the human to the natural', that modern science had revolutionized the whole of nature. If nature is, for Marx, an object to be mastered, he did, however, recognize limits to this process. These natural limits are not purely 'natural' but result from humanity's interaction with its natural environment. Because, as Marx and Engels argued in the *German Ideology*, our relationship with nature is always dialectical, in harmony and in struggle with it at the same time: 'The celebrated "unity of man with nature" has always existed in industry and has existed in varying forms in every epoch according to the lesser or greater development of industry, just like the "struggle" of man with nature, right up to the development of his productive forces on a corresponding basis' (Parsons [ed.], 1977: 160).

There has been an interesting debate recently on Marx's conception of nature and the heritage it has left progressive forces today. Rainer Grundmann, on the one hand, has sought to defend Marx's record, arguing that 'the potential of Marxism...has not been exhausted' (1991: 52). Marx is seen as maintaining the modern conception of nature, going back to Hegel and Nietzsche and, ultimately Bacon. The idea of an ecocentric approach to nature is seen as inconsistent because it begs the question of who will define an ecological problem as such. Against an unproblematic ecological conception of pollution, Grundmann quotes Mary Douglas, for whom 'uncleanliness is matter out of place' (Douglas, 1966: 106). This means that pollution is a culturally specific phenomenon. Above all, Grundmann defends Marx's view that humanity must seek the domination of nature. For Grundmann this is no more problematic than him seeking to 'dominate' his violin. He has no empathy with Greens who criticize this Promethean attitude towards nature, rejecting their plea 'for a new harmonious relationship with nature' which he sees as part of some mystical move to seek 'a re-enchantment of the world' (Grundmann, 1991: 120).

In a polemic with Grundmann, and independently, Ted Benton has taken a far more critical stance with regard to Marx's views on nature. For Benton, 'the idea of a limitless mastery [of nature], the project of "controlling all natural and social processes", is literally unthinkable: it is incoherent' (1992: 67). Marx was simply immersed in a nineteenth-century conception of progress through scientific advance and industrial control over nature. To reject the project of 'domination' over nature is not to lapse into naïve nature worship and sentimentalism. Benton rightly draws attention to the political context in which Marx and Engels dealt with issues around the natural limits to human development. In particular their polemic with Malthus, who viewed population and resource-scarcity as limiting growth and hence social reform, meant that Marx and Engels 'were disposed by the *politics* of these debates to view with suspicion *all* natural-limit arguments'

(Benton, 1992: 56). Ultimately, Benton believes that Marx's views are deeply ambivalent and often contradictory on the way human life relates to its natural conditions. Marx the modernist, the ruthless 'dominator' can be matched by a more green, romantic, even bucolic Marx who had a utopian view of humanity's prospects.

It is probably not a question of seeking a balance or a reconciliation between Marx's diverse views on nature. It may be opportune to recall, in this regard, the distinction drawn by Ernst Bloch between a 'cold' and a 'warm' stream in marxism (1970). This is probably a more correct characterization than that of the 'two Marxes', one scientific, the other utopian. In Chapter 1, I have already argued that marxism as science is a project which is distinct from marxism as critique, a project which is much more defensible in the current era. In relation to nature, Marx and Engels could not but be bound by the scientific discourses of the 1860s: Darwin, Spencer and T. H. Huxley. The theory of evolution and the unitary conception of the universe provided a key to under-standing all phenomena. As Kolakowski notes: 'The day seemed close at hand when the unity of nature, hidden behind the chaotic wealth of its diversity, would be laid bare, to human view' (1978: 376). Marxism as critique can hardly take the same hostile attitude towards the green as Marx took against Malthus, guided by a scientific methodology, which was evolutionist and conservative to its core.

If Marx has left us ambiguity, Engels has left us a text dedicated to the *Dialectics of Nature* usually viewed with embarassment by critical marxists. For Engels, nature is the proof of dialectics: 'Dialectics, so-called *objective* dialectics, prevails throughout nature, and so-called subjective dialectics, dialectical thought, is only the reflection of the motion through opposites which asserts itself everywhere in nature' (Marx and Engels, 1987: 492). The laws of the dialectic derived by Engels from the current natural sciences are three: the transition from quantity to quality and vice versa; the interpenetration of opposites; and the negation of the negation. Engels was seeking, in a sense, the basis of universal causality. From his home-brew studies of biology, chemistry, physics, mechanics and mathematics Engels hoped to derive the ultimate scientific method. He was reworking Hegel's dialectics from what he conceived to be a materialist standpoint. It would be facile to poke fun at this rather strange book by Engels. Suffice it to say that this naturalistic evolutionism is at odds with the ideas of Marx. Specifically, Marx never advanced the notion that nature itself was 'dialectical' in any way; at most he could envisage a dialectical relation-ship between humanity and nature. Darwinism seems to have made its entry into marxism (Marx/Engels) through this route.

It is no simple matter to evaluate the views of Engels on nature in terms of their position in marxist thought. According to the editors of the Marx–Engels collected works, there was simply a division of labour between the two men: 'Since Marx was wholly absorbed in his main work, *Capital*, it was Engels who undertook the solution of the latest theoretical tasks raised by the whole course of development of the natural sciences' (Marx and Engels, 1987: xx). Others are far more reluctant to see *Dialectics of Nature* as a Marx–Engels product, and the most systematic reading of the marxist concept of nature by Alfred Schmidt concludes that it represents 'a naive-realist regression in comparison with the position both he and Marx had reached in their polemic against Feuerbach in the *German Ideology*' (1971: 195). It is from this work of Engels that Soviet diamat (dialectical materialism) developed its bizarre 'laws' of the dialectic. It also led, inexorably or not, to the Lysenko affair in Soviet genetics and agriculture, in which the absurd notion of a 'proletarian science' combating a 'bourgeois science' was promoted by the state. Lysenkoism and its grandiose plans for the transformation of nature promised a technical resolution of the problems of agriculture and served as 'scientific' ideological underpinning for Stalin's policies (see Lecourt, 1976).

Subsequent thinkers in the classic marxist tradition could not fail to engage with the question of society's relation to nature. Karl Kautsky, in his somewhat Darwinian development of marxism, argued that human history derived from natural history and that its laws of motion were reflections of biological laws. The history of humanity became an aspect of the laws of nature. Lukács, on the other hand, engaged in the binary opposite, arguing that: 'Nature is a societal category ... nature's form, its content, its range and its objectivity are all socially conditioned' (1971: 234). For Lukács's Hegelian-tinged marxism, nature is dissolved into a metaphysically conceived 'Spirit'. Of course, we cannot collapse nature into society, or society into nature. Karl Korsch was the classic marxist who understood rather better the complex dialectic of nature and human history, arguing that: 'It is not nature, or organic nature and the history of its development in general, nor is it the historical development even of human society in general, but rather modern "bourgeois society" which forms for Marx and Engels the real point of departure, from which all earlier historical forms of society are to be grasped materialistically' (cited in Schmidt, 1971: 47).

Whatever might be said about the gaps and inconsistencies of the marxist approaches to nature, they are certainly united in their anthropocentrism. That is to say, the debate on nature is always framed from the viewpoint of *human* emancipation. Conversely, an ecocentric approach may also espouse emancipatory projects for humans, but will do so within a broader conception which recognizes a moral standing for the non-human world. Thus, the concept of rights could be extended to animals and to various manifestations of nature. For Grundmann: 'It seems pretty clear that Marx would have scorned rights-based theories' (1991: 85). Whatever the case, marxists may still wish to embrace various ecological concerns, as we shall see in the next section. For now we can accept Robyn Eckersley's characterization of anthropocentrism, of which Marx was part, as a human-centred orientation towards nature in which 'the nonhuman world is reduced to a storehouse of resources and is considered to have instrumental value only, that is, it is valuable only insofar as it can serve as an instrument, or as a means, to human ends' (1992: 26). It seems on the face of it difficult, on this basis, for a socialist ecology to be established.

Socialists and ecology

Before considering the current engagements by socialists with ecology we need to allude to the Soviet experience in that regard. In the first flush of enthusiasm for the new Soviet revolution there were radical stances taken on all sorts of issues, including ecology. The energetic Soviet Commissar for Education, Anatolii Lunacharsky, threw his full weight behind the formation of an influential environmental movement, and he encouraged the development of ecology as a discipline. As Douglas Weiner shows in a pioneering study from the 1950s, 'In what will be a surprise to many, through the early 1930s the Soviet Union was on the cutting edge of conservation theory and practice' (1988: x). The Soviet Union was the first country to set aside protected territories for the study of ecological communities, and its early advances in community ecology and work on rehabilitating degraded landscapes is still worthy of study. Though this orientation towards conservation is probably not a Green one in the contemporary meaning, it did reflect an early Soviet awareness of the need for a certain balance between human needs and nature.

As is well known, however, the Soviet Union embarked on a course of accelerated industrialization which paid little heed to environmental effects. There was soon to be no conservation movement or any other which might act as a countervailing influence to the mighty development drive. The fate of the Aral Sea was but one example of this terrible process. Once the size of Ireland, the Aral Sea began to dry up in the 1970s as a result of diversion of its tributary rivers. As David Dyker notes: 'On present trends it will have dried up altogether by the early decades of the next century. Water apart, this is causing the release of noxious salts into the atmosphere in the Aral region which are creating grave public health problems akin to the effects of nuclear radiation' (1992: 127–8). This, of course, is but one example of the environmental damage caused by Soviet development strategies, at home, in Eastern Europe and in those Third World countries where it obtained influence. Socialism, for many, was to become a byword for dirty development, and it was no surprise that, when Soviet politics began to open up in the 1980s, there were many thriving environmental movements adding their weight to the democratization impetus.

If one event could symbolize the ecological disaster lurking in the Soviet development paradigm, it would be the 'accident' at the Chernobyl nuclear plant in 1985. The plume of radioactive gases which swept across parts of western Europe brought home the transnational nature of ecological issues. As Camilleri and Falk argue: 'The Chernobyl accident graphically illustrates how the physical environment is now integrated with human technology on a scale which is truly global' (1992: 178). This is an issue which I shall develop in a subsequent section of this chapter dealing with globalization and sustainable development. At this point we should take cognisance of Chernobyl as symbol and symptom of Sovet developmentalist lack of concern with ecology. The aftermath of the terrible collapse of the Chernobyl reactor was equally significant. At a turning point in Soviet politics, first attempts to contain the news were followed by a terrible helplessness. The sight of unprotected workers dealing with the radioactive aftermath and 'clean-up' was at once heroic and pathetic. The project to 'dominate' nature had come full circle and its terrible and terrifying consequences became plain to see with the naked eye.

Non-orthodox Soviet communist thinkers such as Ernest Mandel did adopt a grudging acceptance of ecology's main themes in the 1960s. However, this acceptance was still shaped by a fervent rejection of the 'natural limits' argument as the thin end of a Malthussian wedge. One author who received the Mandel *imprimatur* as a socialist-acceptable ecologist was Barry Commoner. According to Commoner: 'We can learn a basic lesson from nature: that nothing can survive on the planet unless it is a cooperative part of a larger, global whole' (1973: 299). Instead of a linear, self-destructive development course, Commoner called for 'closing the circle', through recycling and other measures designed to complete the great ecological cycle. What made this a socialist and not just an ecological vision was Commoner's bringing of poverty, racial discrimination, and war into the equation as blockages of the project to resolve the environmental crisis. The environmental debt had been presented to humanity and, in a modern version of Rosa Luxemburg's famous 'socialism or barbarism', Commoner argued that there was a stark alternative: 'either the rational, social organization of the use and distribution of the earth's resources or a new barbarism' (ibid.: 296).

Another early socialist engagement with ecology was that of Hans-Magnus Enzensberger. The editors of *New Left Review* said in their 1974 introduction to his *Critique of Political Ecology* that this was 'one of the first Marxist attempts to go beyond a simple reduction and dismissal of environmentalism' (Enzensberger, 1974: 1). Yet Enzensberger still argued that it was 'easy to understand that the working class cares little about general environmental problems' and that as an ideology 'ecology is a matter that concerns the middle class' (ibid.: 10). There seems a pale reprise here of Lysenko's fateful separation of a proletarian from a bourgeois science. Ecological problems were caused by capitalism, so this should be the focus of socialist energy rather than its unfortunate side-effects, which were focused on by middle-class liberals. For Enzensberger, 'the preoccupation with ecological crisis appears as a phenomenon belonging entirely to the superstructure – namely an expression of the decadence of bourgeois society' (ibid.: 17). It would seem that such a reductionist view shows socialists to be suffering from the 'blindness and naïveté' of which Enzensberger accuses the ecologists.

Without doubt, the two most developed and influential attempts to marry the red with the green have been those of Rudolf Bahro and André Gorz, which we shall consider in turn. Bahro first came to prominence with the East German dissident programme *The Alternative in Eastern Europe* (Bahro, 1978). Later, in exile in West Germany, Bahro joined the Green Party and developed in an ecological direction. He began with the assumption that 'Marx never asked whether the earth might have finite limits, because in his time there were no limits in sight' (Bahro, 1984: 143). Now the utopian socialist vision is simply no longer utopian: 'We have reached the limit. Nature will not accept any more and is striking back' (ibid.: 184). As Bahro became more and more Green he began to see ever fewer merits in the traditional socialist arguments. Bahro saw the trade unions as among the most conservative forces in society, especially in contrast to the peace and ecology movements. This was all part of the great cultural shift which had occured in 1968 and which Bahro was retrospectively embracing. While not denying a utopian socialist element in his thinking, Bahro was categorical: 'I am green and not red. The socialist concept, in theory and in practice, was tied to industrialism and statism' (ibid.: 235).

Bahro was eventually to leave the German Greens when the clash between 'fundamentalists' who cling to principles and 'realists' who wished to put them into practice, came to a head. Bahro could not accept the 'realist' turn towards parliamentary politics, seeing the Social Democratic Party and the unions as 'institutional prisons'. Instead, Bahro advocated staying outside the walls of the state, building parallel institutions such as a citizen's parliament. The whole industrial system is doomed for Bahro, so the task is to build a type of 'dual power' similar to that Lenin advocated in dealing with the corrupt capitalism of his day. Bahro, the postindustrial utopian, still tends to think in terms of traditional Marxist–Leninist categories. He also suffers from the traditional Eurocentrism of 'Western Marxism' and sees little role for the oppressed peoples of the Third World in transforming the global capitalist system. Bahro's limits in terms of developing a coherent ecosocialism are admitted openly: 'From scientific socialism I have returned to utopian socialism, and politically I have moved from a class-dimensional to a populist orientation' (ibid.: 220). Though a defensible political position, this does not take us further in investigating the compatibility between red and green politics.

André Gorz appears to be a far more eclectic thinker and political actor than Bahro, while pursuing a similar engagement with ecology from a marxist perspective. The starting point for Gorz is that: 'Growth-oriented capitalism is dead. Growth-oriented socialism, which closely resembles it, reflects the distorted image of our past, not of our future' (1980: 11). If this is the old, the new is ecology, a perspective Gorz sees as incompatible with the rationality of capitalism and authoritarian socialism alike. However, he argues that ecology is compatible with a libertarian or democratic socialism of the type he espouses. This ecosocialism which Gorz advances leans quite heavily on the work of Ivan Illich, in particular the notion of socially necessary labour which could be seen as ecologically benign. This postindustrial utopia is, somewhat contradictorily, associated with a benign view of automation and computerization and a view of the state as neutral technical administrator. Not surprisingly, radical ecologists have argued that: 'Gorz's technocratic postindustrial utopia is riddled with paradoxes in attempting to combine central planning with neighbourhood self-help initiatives and worker self-management' (Eckersley, 1992: 135).

Gorz cannot escape the dilemmas faced by the socialist movement since its origins – such as the issue of the state, planning and democracy. He has engaged with ecology in a bold way, just as he had earlier with the issue of new technology. Yet, ultimately, the eclecticism of his thinking seems to lead to inconsistency. Can we really have technology and 'small is beautiful', state planning and local control, high tech and Illich's 'convivial tools' all working together in harmony? Frankel has called his vision 'puzzling and paradoxical' (1987: 58). Eco-anarchist Murray Bookchin has summed up his ecological utopian as 'a childish "libertarian" Disneyland' (1980–1: 188). This is not to say that a more coherent ecosocialism cannot be imagined. This would be based on 'political pluralism, public accountability and widespread public participation in economic planning' (Eckersley, 1992: 136). The objectives of ecology and social justice are certainly compatible. Viable political forms are not that easy to develop, though, and 'ecosocialism' has no easy answers to the dilemmas that have bedevilled the democratic socialist project since its inception.

If our focus has been on the inconsistencies of socialism in approaching the issue of ecology it should not be assumed that the latter is unproblematic. To take a biocentric approach does not automatically take a discourse 'beyond left and right', an illusion of populists for a long time. Nor is eclecticism a prerogative of those trying to bring the red and green discourses together. As David Pepper shows in his careful dissection of British Green ideology, it is composed of inherently contradictory elements with a view of ideal society as 'both green and communal, with strong elements of liberalism (individual freedom) combined vigorously with dashes of anarcho-communism, eco-fascism, and a non-ecocentric belief in the supremes of "objective science"' (1993: 58). It is not surprising that, faced with this peculiar mix many socialist ecological activists have sought to develop a clearer perspective. Before turning to these more recent debates on sustainable development in the era of globalization, however, we need to consider the engagement of feminism with ecological concerns.

Feminism and ecology

If socialists have had a less than totally fruitful engagement with ecology, feminism, or at least some currents of this movement, has developed an influential symbiosis of the two discourses. Ecofeminism at its starkest produces a new unitary focus or discipline. Thus ecofeminist theorist and propagandist, Vandana Shiva writes that: 'women and nature are intimately related, and their domination and liberation similarly linked. The women's and ecology movements are therefore one, and are primarily counter-trends to a patriarchal maldevelopment' (1989: 47). Not only is there a confluence of interests between the women's and ecology movements but they are seen to be as one, because they face the same enemy. Ecofeminism, whatever nuances it may contain, starts from the premise of a nature/culture opposition as binary opposites. That nature might be culturally constructed is a notion quite alien to ecofeminism. Women are equated with nature and nature is seen as feminine. Thus the women/nature versus man/culture opposition is seen to replace any division between left and right politics seen as quaintly outmoded and irrelevant.

By far the most influential presentation of ecofeminism is that by Vandana Shiva in her book *Staying Alive* (Shiva, 1988). Shiva illustrates her work within a broad overview of the Enlightenment, and its associated view of progress and development which 'began to destroy life without any assessment of how fast and how much of the diversity of life on this planet is disappearing' (ibid.: xiv). It is science which is seen as responsible for the transformation of nature into a source of raw material for humankind. Women are seen by Shiva as privileged fighters 'for the protection of nature as a condition for human survival' (ibid.: xviii). There is a symmetry, and even equivalence, between the violence against nature resulting in the ecological crisis, and the violence against women resulting in their subjugation and exploitation by men. Women, for Shiva, are part of nature: 'At one level, nature is symbolised as the embodiment of the feminine principle, and at another, she is nurtured by the feminine principle to produce life and provide sustenance' (ibid.: 38). Women and nature share a different philosophy from that of men and science: one is based on nurture and co-operation, while the other can speak only the language of domination.

The political project of ecofeminism has a broad emancipatory sweep to it. Third World women, in particular, are seen to have privileged access to survival expertise. Thus, for Shiva: 'The ecological categories with which they think and act can become the categories of liberation for all, for men as well as for women, for the west as well as the non-west, and for the human as well as the non-human elements of the earth' (ibid.: 224). Ecofeminism thus advocates an ecocentric philosophy grounded in principles of harmony, sustainability and diversity.

The women of Chiipko, in India, were involved in a struggle to defend their forests in a way which Shiva has seen as paradigmatic. In gestures which created a powerful image, these women embraced the trees to prevent the loggers from cutting them down:

> Embrace our trees
> Save them from being felled
> The property of our hills
> Save it from being looted.

(quoted in Shiva, 1988: 73)

Ecofeminism is a holistic approach to nature, some may say it is spiritual. Its effect in the international environmental movement has been considerable.

The critique of ecofeminism has, however, been devastating. Ecofeminism starts off with a highly dubious separation and opposition between nature and culture. Following the nineteenth-century discourse of romanticism, this leads ecofeminism to extol the (sometimes imaginary) virtues of nature against the evil advance of modernity, industrialization or development. As Molyneux and Steinberg point out, ecofeminism is based on (mis)understanding of 'the dualistic and reductionist nature of scientific thinking and in the simultaneous romanticization of what science destroys' (1995: 89). This view is based on an overly reductionist view of science as though the benign view of science, as bearer and agent of all progress, has simply been turned on its head. Furthermore, this view of science seems to ignore the long-standing debates within feminism and in epistemology over the nature of science. The ecofeminist perspective of Shiva and other authors such as Maria Mies (cf. Mies and Shiva, 1993) works with an essentialist view of science as a monolithic enterprise. Science cannot be reduced quite so automatically and inherently to a male enterprise. There seems in ecofeminism to be more than a hint of reductionism at work.

The main weakness of ecofeminism is, probably, its equation between nature and woman. Nietzsche once said that 'Woman is more closely related to nature than man and in all her essentials she remains ever herself. Culture is with her always something external...(1964: 23). Feminism, in all its facets, has fought against this essentialist linking of women and nature. Yet some ecofeminists have followed in the footsteps of Mary Daly (1979) and Susan Griffin (1978) in asserting women's special relationship with nature. This essentialism, as Elizabeth Carlassare notes, 'refers to the assumption that a subject (for example, a "woman") is constituted by presocial innate, unchanging qualities' (1994: 52). The so-called nature-feminists have sought to celebrate the special link between women and nature, rejoice in their place in the world and transform their consciousness to be more in tune with nature. Women's 'innate' abilities in terms of co-operation and ecological sensibility are, in short, promoted against patriarchal polluting society. Whatever motivation might lie behind these attempts to link women with nature against men and culture, it is clear that this type of position from Nietzsche onwards has been used to oppress women. Its contribution to a politics of ecology is also open to question.

The critique of ecofeminism's essentialism is a powerful one, but this does not necessarily invalidate it as a political perspective. It would seem unlikely that feminist writers such as Daly and Griffin were articulating a position inherently designed to oppress women. Criticisms of their nature-feminism seems to be as much about style – often poetic and allusive – as about content. The critique of this current smacks of scientism and intolerance, especially in its reference to the 'irrationalism' of the nature-feminists and cultural ecofeminists. Nor is a discourse 'apolitical' simply because it does not conform to Western standards of what is an acceptable political practice. As Carlassare argues: 'Dismissing cultural ecofeminism on this basis, however, precludes the possibility of learning from this position and obscures the legitimacy of the variety of positions and discursive forms that are affiliated under ecofeminism's umbrella' (1994: 65). Certainly there is no doubting the energy and originality of the ecofeminists' arguments and policies. They seem a genuine contribution to a transformation politics in the era of global capitalism. Their attempt to bring together feminist and ecological concerns and movements must surely be a positive thing.

The critique of ecofeminism has been, on the whole, of its 'cultural' variant or current; the social or socialist ecofeminists are not necessarily prone to the same criticisms. Refusing all essentialist views of 'woman', this current argues instead for the social and material construction of gender in contemporary society. They argue that there is no such thing as an immutable essence of 'woman' which may make her closer to nature then men, or anything else. There is need to recognize the diversity of women's experience rather than seek to homogenize it under a common label. In particular this would lead us to distinguish the distinct interests of Third World women from those in the advanced capitalist countries. Nor could we stop at this, because the category of 'Third World women' is itself a form of essentialism which refuses to recognize diversity. On this basis it is possible to imagine an ecofeminism which does not suffer from essentialism, advocating a new universalism and being seen as a form of eco-messianism. In the rest of this section some hints at what this ecofeminism might entail are advanced.

It is well to recall, as Cecile Jackson summarizes, that 'technocratic environmentalism is largely gender-blind, either because it fails to recognize gender differentials at all, or, where women are recognized as a distinct category, because gender stereotypes prevail and the household continues to be treated as a unit' (1994: 123). If, as with marxism, we are dealing with a discourse which is largely (essentially?) gender blind (see Chapter 5), then ecofeminism has had a positive role to play. As a new social movement it has been seeking the democratic equivalent which might unite the struggles against gender oppression and environmental degradation respectively. It has shown an acute awareness of our relationship with the non-human world and its problematic nature. That ecofeminism has shown signs of a historical essentialism is more understandable when it is viewed as a political movement. To seek the common ground between feminism and environmentalism, and to call for more synergy between them, has been the overriding objective of a current of thought which has made some of the most original contributions to the radical environmental discourse.

A more social or material development of ecofeminism would probably focus on gender rather than women. As in the field of women and development there has been a shift in recent years to a focus on gender and development. The emphasis is thus on the gender relations of development (or environmental issues in this case) rather than on woman as problem or solution. A focus on women does not constitute a gender analysis, which would need to focus on gender-differentiated social roles and identities. This would lead us, in turn, to examine the household critically rather than assume it is unproblematic. The household is now understood to be a far from unitary phenomenon, and it is seen as subject to class and other social divisions – including, primarily, gender divisions. In terms of ecology, we need to understand, as Cecile Jackson puts it, 'that individuals within households will have different objectives and livelihood strategies' (1994: 122). This means that men and women will have different approaches to issues such as sustainable agriculture or forestry conservation. On this basis, we would be able to detect specific material or social causes explaining why women might have particular views and practices in relation to environmental issues.

Ecofeminism, as a politics, fits in with the new 'postmodern' orientation towards the local and the experiential dimension. It sees the body, especially those of women, as a site of struggle over power. The idea of 'ecocide of the body' is central to ecofeminism in its social variant, and highlights the effects of capitalist patriarchy. The new political economy, inspired by Foucault, points us towards a new liberation politics. This assumes a feminist, socialist and ecological orientation. What is being articulated is a new truth/power relationship, less repressive than the current one. Ecofeminism points towards a new regime where gender and environmental relations are more egalitarian. As Val Plumwood has argued, at this stage of human history, we now require 'an account of the human ideal for both sexes, which accepts the undesirability of the domination of nature associated with masculinity' (1988: 22). This entails a critique of all forms of dualism, be it that of masculine and feminine, mind and body, nature and culture, reason and emotion or public and private.

Globalization and sustainable development

Some time in the late 1970s, the ecological debate shifted from libertarian conceptions of the 'good life' to concerns with planetary survival. The earth's resources were seen to be finite, the 'limits to growth' were recognized, and the sober prospects for human survival were highlighted. The first phase of the debate focused on material shortages and on food shortfalls in relation to population growth. By the late 1980s, the focus on limits to growth had shifted to such issues as air pollution and water quality. The environmental agenda was largely set by people and agencies in the advanced industrial societies, with the South or 'Third World' dominated still by the development agenda. The huge gap between these two great masses of humanity can be highlighted by data from the 1991 World Conservation Strategy (Benton and Redclift, 1994:15) that showed that one-quarter of the world's population, living in the advanced industrial societies or North, consumed 80 per cent of the commercial energy produced worldwide, whereas three-quarters of the world's population, living in the South, consumed barely 20 per cent of the world's commercial energy. What was becoming clear in the course of the debates around the environment, from the 1980s onwards, was that ecology was increasingly a global issue.

The Chernobyl disaster of 1986 brought home how permeable national boundaries were to ecological phenomena. As Camilleri and Falk argue: 'The traditional description of a world broken into hermetically partitioned sovereign states was confronted by a biosphere emerging ever more deadly as a single integrated whole' (1992: 177). The danger of 'global warming' due to the emission of 'greenhouse gases' into the biosphere heightened this phenomenon. As with the thinning, or breaching, of the ozone layer around the earth's poles, here was a natural process where a fine balance was being disrupted by human economic activity. The Rio Earth Summit of 1992 saw some intergovernmental commitment to deal with these issues, but no real co-ordinated action. What there has been, is much anguished concern over the fate of 'spaceship Earth', the common vessel for the whole of humanity. Yet, as Enzensberger reminded us, the idea of spaceship Earth tends to ignore the difference between 'the bridge and the engine room' (1974: 15). For the peoples of the poor countries, much of the concern with environmental issues was perceived as a direct threat to their socioeconomic interests and, indeed, survival.

The Rio Summit brought out in the open the conflicting interests around the supposedly common global concerns of the environment. Failing to question in any way the sacrosant principles of the capitalist market, this gathering could not really address the underlying interlocking issues of environment and development. As Nicholas Hildyard explains, there was a move towards 'a convention on biodiversity but not on free trade; on forests but not on agri-business; on climate but not on automobiles' (1993: 22–3). Thus, while the rich countries achieved much of what they sought, the poor were hardly able to get on the agenda. The 'management' of the environment, as discussed at Rio, is not the same as radical concern with environmental degradation. Nor did it take long for the mystifying rhetoric of common concerns to dissipate as it became clear that the powerful and the rich would continue their 'management' of the environment in the same way that they managed the global economy. What we need to examine in some detail is whether the subsequent strategy of 'sustainable development' is more energizing and more viable in political terms.

The concept of 'sustainable development' has been called a 'development truism' (Redclift, 1987: 3) and a 'flag of convenience' (Adams, 1993: 218). We are dealing with a fluid, labile concept and a discourse which can take on different meanings according to the context. A fundamental document for the 'sustainable development' concept is *Our Common Future* (Brundtland, 1987) which followed in the footsteps of the influential Brandt Reports with their multilateralist North–South approach. Applying a type of globalized Keynesianism, this approach appeals to what it would see as the enlightened self-interest of Northern politicians to allow for some level of development in the South. *Our Common Future* (also known as the Brundtland Report, after the Norwegian prime minister who co-ordinated it) sought to place the issue of sustainable development back in the context of international development strategy. It recognized the links between the environment and poverty, which is seen 'as a major cause and effect of global environmental problems' (ibid.: 9). It sees sustainable development being based on meeting 'basic needs' and the idea of 'environmental limits' set by technology and social organization. *Our Common Future* calls for a new form of sustainable growth leading to integrated socioeconomic development which would be 'more equitable in its impact' (ibid.: 52).

The mainstream notion of sustainable development is based firmly on the modernization approach to development. Its vision is explicitly predicated on the need for 'more rapid economic growth in both industrial and developing countries…greater technology transfer… and significantly larger capital flows' (Brundtland, 1987: 89). There is little in this agenda to distinguish *Our Common Future* from the internationally dominant and dominating doctrines of neoliberalism. As for the element of 'sustainability', it appears to be merely a pious wish. The report argues, with little foundation or evidence, that it might be possible that 'the international economy must speed up world growth while respecting environmental constraints' (ibid.: 89). It would seem that 'sustainable development' has hitched up certain environmental concerns in the North, with the need of Third World dominant classes to foment development. The notion of 'sustainability' is simply not addressed in a rigorous fashion at all. How economic activity can be conducted in such a way that it is environmentally sustainable, cognisant of the issue of non-renewable resources and the environmental impact of this activity, has still not been addressed adequately.

The new ecological management approach has blurred the concept of sustainability and reinscribed it within the orthodoxies of modernization theory. Sustainable development, as Wolfgang Sachs puts it, 'emasculates the environmental challenge by absorbing it into the empty shell of "development"' (1993: 9). This is a totally anthropocentric strategy which, ultimately, ignores the current threat to ecological balance and perpetuates the utilitarian approach to nature. The world's poor enter this global stage as the principal culprits of environmental destruction. To 'save the planet' the poor are put in the frame. Global management of the environment is conducted in ways which, as always, marginalize the poor. Global control by capital entails removing all local, national and international constraints on its operation.

Indeed, the very notion of a global environmental problem is a dubious one. As Vandana Shiva points out, this notion has 'been so constructed as to conceal the fact that globalization of the local is responsible for destroying the environment which supports the subjugated local peoples' (1993: 151). While the North constructs its horizons on the global terrain of 'spaceship Earth', the peoples of the South live on the depressed, impoverished and environmentally degraded terrain of the local.

In developing his 'global sociology' approach, Leslie Sklair has argued that 'The hypothesis that there is a contradiction between capitalist development and global survival appears ... to have prima facie plausibility' (1994: 220). In this scenario, we can then intepret the 'sustainable development' movement as one designed to regenerate the development idea against cultural survivalist ideas. There would be many now who would think that the Earth cannot 'afford' industrialization of the Third World and the ex-state socialist countries. The 'greening' of sections of the transnational business class (for example, the International Chamber of Commerce's World Industry Council for the Environment) also responds to similar pressures and growing environmental awareness worldwide. Whether it is possible or not, transnational capitalists must act as if they can resolve the contradiction between development and survival. Given these imperatives, it is most likely that Third World countries will continue to act as 'pollution havens' as others might act as 'tourism havens', acting as a dumping ground for hazardous waste produced in the West. For global ecology this could presumably be classified as a kind of 'recycling'.

It is certainly the case that ecology has now become central to most debates on the future of capitalism. As Alain Lipietz puts it: 'Ecology, previously on the "periphery" of the economy, is today right at the heart of the problem' (1992: 55). Fordism was a form of capitalist development which held sway from the 1920s to the 1970s. We are now in a post-Fordist era in the sense that the old way of doing things is no longer viable. Fordism was based on productivism and on consumerism. It was the philosophy of quantity rather than quality. Perception of an ecological crisis, however we might care to define it, challenges the functionalist logic of production and consumption in their neat self-contained worlds. In the era of globalization, ecology is a clear example of the interconnectedness of all parts of the capitalist system. It is also part of the solution insofar as whatever development model replaces the now-defunct Fordist-productivist model, it will, of necessity, need to be a more social and ecological one.

Recently there have been some attempts to link ecology with post-modernism. Certainly many ecologists would have been open to the critique of marxism and other Enlightenment ideologies articulated by postmodernism. There is common ground in the critique of materialist productivism and a celebration of subjective knowledge. Arran Garé has, however, taken a slightly different approach in arguing that: 'Postmodernism is "eco-centric". It is associated with respect for non-Western societies and cultures, for the previously suppressed ideas of minorities ... and for non-human forms of life' (1995: 87). Some postmodernists have, further, endorsed Nietzsche's critique of Western thought on the basis of its anti-naturalism. Postmodernism would see the notion of a progressive humanization of nature as another form of metanarrative. The era of globalization is also the era of fragmentation of modern/ist culture. Postmodernism, at least potentially, opens up a terrain of debate where a new, more democratic world order could take shape. As with post-Fordism, this new world compromise would have to be, in all respects, an ecologically balanced dispensation.

Modern-day followers of Marx seek to keep postmodernism at bay in the arena of ecology as elsewhere. Thus David Pepper, in a useful review of ecological politics in Britain, examines the problems he sees arising because 'unlike most orthodox Marxism, at least, ecologism often flirts with postmodernism' (1993: 57). Postmodern ecologism is accused of cultural relativism, belittling notions of universal moral standards, and seeing the consumer as the locus of political action. As against this 'political eclecticism' which can only lead to 'nature mystification', postmodern ecologists should recognize 'as socialists do', that 'liberation should be a state in which we humans "dominate" the rest of nature, in the sense of having total control over our relationships with it' (ibid.: 57). All I can say is that marxism will not be able to develop a progressive ecological stance on this type of reductionist and domineering basis. This chapter has, however, shown that there are many progressive currents such as ecofeminism which have refused simply to reiterate the productivist Promethean themes of mainstream marxism.

3
Soviets Plus Electrification: Marxism and Development

Development is often seen as the over-arching need of the human condition. Marxism, like most other ideologies, has perforce had to face up to the issues of development. Indeed, development, in either its capitalist or socialist variants, is central to the marxist enterprise. This chapter surveys critically some of the main interactions between the discourses of marxism and development. Marx himself is shown to be ambiguous, with early fairly mechanical or unilinear views on progress matched by more nuanced writings on Russia, for example. Lenin begins a new trend in the marxist tradition which was to become, in many ways, an ideology of developmentalism in many Third World countries. A further section deals with the absolutely critical issue of socialism and underdevelopment, the fact that most socialist revolutions have not occurred in the states where the most advanced capitalism prevails. Finally, this chapter turns to more recent engagements of post-marxist currents, with the issue of development, now perceived much more critically, indeed rejected as an assumed human good.

Marx and development

For Marx, development and capitalism were almost synonymous. Marx's vision of development was also totally wrapped up with the era of modernity. Production was becoming increasingly internationalized and capital was being centralized. Capitalism advanced at an ever more frantic pace and development spread across the globe. This vision of what we might call 'Manifesto Marxism' is quite explicit: 'The bourgeoisie cannot exist without constantly revolutionizing the instruments of production, and thereby the relations of production, and with them the whole relations of society' (Marx, 1973: 71). For the Marx of the *Communist Manifesto*, 'everlasting uncertainty and agitation distinguish the bourgeois epoch from all earlier ones. All fixed, fast-frozen relations, with their train of ancient and venerable prejudices and opinions, are swept away, all new-formed ones become antiquated before they can ossify' (ibid.: 70). This exhilarating roller-coaster of modernization is the essence of Marx's conception of development. As the bourgeois era mounted the world stage it would sweep away all the old orders and transform all in its own image. The more developed country was a mirror in which the less developed could glimpse its own future.

The bourgeois era, for Manifesto Marxism, is one of unprecedented development of the productive forces: 'The bourgeoisie, during its rule of scarce one hundred years, has created more massive and more colossal productive forces than have all previous generations together' (Marx, 1973: 72). Nature is subjected to humankind, chemistry is applied to industry and agriculture, the railway and the telegraph revolutionized communications. The insatiable drive of bourgeois development tears up all obstacles in its path. Markets are constantly expanding, capitalist social relations corrode all others, productivity increases by leaps and bounds. Manifesto Marxism is a thoroughly modernist discourse, as Marshall Berman reminds us so eloquently:

> from its relentless and insatiable pressure for growth and progress; its expansion of human desires beyond local, national and moral bounds; its demands on people to exploit not only their fellow men but also themselves; the volatility and endless metamorphosis of all its values in the maelstrom of the world market, its pitiless destruction of everything and everyone it cannot use ... and its capacity to exploit crisis and chaos as a springboard for still more development, to feed itself on its own self-destruction. (Berman, 1983: 121)

Of course, Marx did not stop at his paean of praise for the bourgeoisie and its revolutionary development role for human society. This capitalist development process was also creating its own 'gravedigger', the proletariat or working class. In proportion as the bourgeoisie – that is to say capital – develops, so does that class of labourers who sell their labour, as a commodity, to this hungry new mode of production. The same process which revolutionizes society creates the revolutionary class which will overthrow the new order. Capitalism will be devoured by the product of its own incandescent energy in this vision.

The development of modern capital-less society produces 'dialectically' as it were the basis for its own surpassment. This organic process is conceived in fairly linear terms as dispersed workers combine first in trade unions and then in a workers' political party. As feudalism gave way to capitalism, so capitalism would cede to socialism. As Marx climaxed in the Manifesto: 'In place of the old bourgeois society, with its classes and class antagonisms, we shall have an association, in which the free development of each is the condition for the full development of all' (Marx, 1973: 87). This was a manifesto, but in practice capitalist development was just spreading its wings in Marx's era.

The ambiguity of Marx's views on development can be illustrated through his (admittedly journalistic) writings on India. In these famous passages Marx paid tribute to the progressive role of capitalist colonialism: 'England has to fulfil a double mission in India: one destructive, the other regenerating – the annihilation of old Asiatic society, and the laying of the material foundations of Western society in Asia' (Avineri [ed.], 1969: 132). Modern industry and the railway system would dissolve the old divisions of labour, break up the 'inertia' of the Indian villages and drag the country into the slipstream of global capitalist development. Of course, 'The Indians will not reap the fruits of the new elements of society scattered among them by the British bourgeoisie till in Great Britain itself the new ruling classes shall have been supplanted by the industrial proletariat, or till the Hindoos themselves shall have grown strong enough to throw off the English yoke altogether' (Avineri [ed.], 1969: 137). While those passages can be read as a support for the civilizing effect of Western capitalism over Eastern barbarism, in fact Marx's writings on India, admittedly one-sided, dated and not too well informed, are consistent with the message of the Manifesto. Capitalism is a revolutionary force but it begets the cause of its own eventual downfall.

Where Marx began to break with his previously mechanistic/modernist views on development was in relation to Russia. In 1881 Marx spent some considerable time and effort drafting a reply to Vera Zasulich on the nature of the Russian peasant commune. Marx had been studying Russia since 1861, the year of the 'emancipation of the serfs'. The question was whether the commune was a symptom of all that was archaic in Russian society or whether it was a harbinger of a progressive 'communist' future. Marx's intervention in this debate was quite clearcut. He foresaw two alternatives. The first would involve state capitalism penetrating and destroying the commune. The second option, however, was that the commune would become 'the fulcrum of social regeneration in Russia' (Shanin [ed.], 1983: 124). Following a 'Russian revolution', which both Marx and Engels thought was imminent, the commune would become a springboard for a new mode of social organization. The keepers of the Moscow archives after the revolution of 1917 discovered these letters of Marx and were shocked by their unorthodoxy. The 'populist deviation' which the orthodox 'marxists' discovered in these letters was put down to the master's senility (he was 63 at the time) or, according to another version, by his tactful wish not to discourage the Russian revolutionaries of the time too much.

The significance of Marx's delving into the affairs of pre-revolutionary Russia cannot be underestimated. What Marx was arguing against, on the basis of the Russian case, was the tendency to make his analysis of mature capitalism in *Capital* into a schema of historical inevitability. This has major implications for any theory of development and, seemingly, contradicts his earlier dictum that the backward country saw its future in the mirror of the advanced one. What Marx actually argued later, in a letter to another Russian follower, was that 'to metamorphose my historical sketch of the genesis of capitalism in Western Europe into a historico-philosophic theory of the general path every people is fated to tread, whatever the historical circumstances it finds itself, ... is honouring and shaming me too much' (cited in Shanin [ed.], 1983: 59). There is a refusal here of any deterministic, blanket application of 'laws' of historical development. Marx was engaging, in fact, with the combined and uneven nature of development in strikingly 'modern' terms. What Marx and Engels foresaw in the 1882 preface to the *Communist Manifesto* was the Russian revolution acting as a 'signal' for 'proletarian revolution' in the West so that the two would 'complement each other'.

Marx, as is well known, never developed a theory of imperialism as such. However, his theory of capitalism and its development does foresee the creation of a world capitalist economy. Already the *Manifesto* was eloquent on the mission of the capitalist class: 'it compels all nations, on pain of extinction, to adopt the bourgeois mode of production; it compels them to introduce what it calls civilization into their midst, i.e., to become bourgeois themselves. In one word, it creates a world after its own image' (Marx, 1973: 71). Marx understood that, following the process of dissolution of the old social structures, what would replace them would depend mainly on the character of the old mode of production itself. To this end he developed a sketchy theory of pre-capitalist modes of production including the classless primitive community, the slave-based society of the classical era, the feudal society characterized by serfdom, and, in some accounts, an 'asiatic' mode of production (cf. Bailey and Llobera [eds], 1981). However, it is clear that, for Marx, all modes of production prior to the bourgeois/capitalist society are simply part of this mode's prehistory. The structuralist cul-de-sac of the modes of production controversies is one of the more unproductive offshoots of teleological, not to say theological, marxism.

Marx did not, either, have a particularly developed idea of what we would today call the Third World. He was certainly aware of the role of colonial plunder in oiling the wheels of the industrial revolution. However, in analysing the internal and external factors in the 'primitive accumulation' which gave rise to capitalism, Marx undoubtedly prioritized the first dimension. Subsequent marxists, engaged in debates over imperialism and dependency would reverse the order and prioritize the external dimension as the explanation of why capitalism emerged in some regions of the world and not others. Anthony Brewer correctly points out that: 'A stress on external factors is consistent with a picture of capitalism in which a centre–periphery division on a world scale is a defining feature, but such a definition of capitalism is not to be found in Marx' (1980: 44). Certainly, for example in his writings on Ireland, Marx can be seen to be aware of the stunting effects of colonialism on development. However, the main thrust of his theoretical rather than journalistic writings is on the internal development of capitalism as a mode of production and its appetite to create a whole world in its own image.

What Marx does leave us with is an ambiguous legacy on the question of development. He would probably have agreed with the once heretical statement by Geoffrey Kay that: 'capital created underdevelopment not because it exploited the underdeveloped world, but because it did not exploit it enough' (Kay, 1975: x). This view is totally at odds with most subsequent marxist theories of development and underdevelopment. This is not, of course, a harmonious view of capitalist world development and does not exclude an emphasis on exploitation, as Marx understood from India or Ireland. Nor was Marx advising nationalist movements in these countries simply to wait until capitalist development made their countries 'ripe' for revolution. The key to Marx's arguments was that, whereas previous forms of capital (such as merchants) simply destroyed and pillaged, industrial capital also transformed while it destroyed the old modes of production. A simple glance at India today or Brazil would probably find support for the underlying approach Marx had to the question of development. The odd ethnocentric/Westernist/modernist flourish or emphasis should probably not detract from this fundamental confirmation of Marx's original research and predictions.

With Engels we have far less ambiguity on the question of development and a more firmly unilinear conception of modernization. Whereas Marx resisted attempts to make his theory of capitalism a theory of the *'marche générale'* of history, Engels was moving precisely in that direction. The evolutionary framework which Engels was developing is clear in his 1875 essay 'Social Relations in Russia', where he concludes that: 'only at a definite high level of development of society's productive forces does it become possible to raise production sufficiently for elimination of class distinctions to become really progressive, to survive without engendering stagnation or decline in the mode of social production' (cited in Bideleux, 1985: 23). By 1892 Engels was even more firmly committed to the necessity of capitalist industrialization, as shown in one of his letters to one of Marx's Russian followers: 'capitalism opens up new vistas and new hopes. Look at what it has done and is doing in the West... There is no great historical evil without a compensating historical progress' (cited ibid.: 27). In this way Engels led to the codification of a mechanistic 'marxist' development theory which was deeply fatalistic about the inexorable and mechanical advance of capitalism, and somewhat hard-nosed about its attendant social 'side-effects'.

Leninism and development

It is ironic, given the subsequent history of Marxism–Leninism, that when Lenin engaged with the issue of the Russian commune in the mid-1890s he was implicitly opposing Marx's views of the same phenomenon. Lenin's perceptions of the Russian peasantry were extremely negative, stressing their individualistic nature. Belief in the peasants' 'communist instincts' had naïvely infected many Russian socialists 'based on a purely mythical idea of the peasant economy as a special communal system' (cited in Bideleux, 1985: 71). Lenin developed the label of 'populism' to criticize those Russian socialists who sought in some way to bypass capitalism via the commune. For Lenin, following in the footsteps of Engels rather than Marx, only the industrial proletariat (however minuscule it might be) could lead a revolution: 'only the higher stage of capitalist development, large-scale machine industry, creates the material conditions and social forces necessary for... open political struggle towards *victorious communist revolution*' (cited ibid.: 73). We have here a conception of development which is quite unilinear and mechanical. The negative view of the peasant commune is certainly debatable and, politically, this explains the general lack of support among the peasantry for Lenin's Bohshevik Party.

Lenin developed his ideas further in his turn of the century book *The Development of Capitalism in Russia* (Lenin, 1967), considered by many as one of the best marxist studies of the emergence of capitalism from feudalism. Lenin's theme in this text is the apparently technical one of how the home market of Russian capitalism was formed. His task was to demonstrate how the commodity economy became established in all branches of economic life, and how the division of labour became dominated by capitalism. Against the underconsumptionist arguments of the 'populists', Lenin showed convincingly that capitalism had created for itself a home market in Russia. Lenin's conception of capitalist development is centred around the question of social differentiation, which he examined in detail in relation to the rural population. It should be pointed out that he clearly exaggerates the role of capitalism at this stage, treating as capitalist 'economic structures which Marx explicitly described as *pre-capitalist'* (Harding, 1977: 87). Lenin did admit that his earlier writings had led to an *'over-estimation'* of the degree of capitalist development in Russian agriculture but the point is clear that Lenin's early conception of development was absolutely focused on the internal development of capitalism in Russia.

What Lenin, or Leninism, is better known for is his theory of imperialism. In terms of Marx's view of the progressive function of capitalism on a world scale, and Lenin's own analysis in *The Development of Capitalism in Russia*, this theory, elaborated during the First World War, was a watershed. It is only somewhat exaggerated to state as Bill Warren did, that 'In effectively overturning Marx and Engels's view of the character of imperialist expansion, Lenin set in motion an ideological process that erased from Marxism any trace of the view that capitalism would be an instrument of social progress even in precapitalist societies' (1980: 48). From now on the marxist tradition would begin to view the world system as centre–periphery, and imperialism as a block or impediment to development. Certainly, it was easy to understand that a political movement which was setting out to gather support among the poor and downtrodden worldwide would find it difficult to maintain Marx's stance on India, for example. Though Marx never ignored the negative effect of capitalist expansion worldwide he, undoubtedly, stressed the positive effect it would have on the productive forces. In the period of crisis, expectation and uncertainty of the First World War lofty, detached observation seemed out of place.

Lenin's work on imperialism is not, and was not intended to be, a major or innovative investigation. It was based largely on the works of others, like the marxist Bukharin and the non-marxist Hobson. It outlined what it saw as certain key tendencies of the period, such as the concentration of capital, its export to 'underdeveloped' countries and the dominance of finance capital (a merger of industrial and banking capital). Lenin's political objective was to counter Kautsky's notion of 'ultraimperialism' which implied a fairly smooth and peaceful carve-up of the world by the major powers. Instead Lenin tried to show the inevitable trend towards world war implicit in increased worldwide competition. He was not really concerned with the impact of capitalist imperialism in the colonial world. He did recognize that: 'The export of capital affects and greatly accelerates the development of capitalism in these countries to which it is exported' (Lenin, 1970: 718). Yet Lenin also moved towards the underconsumptionist positions he had criticized in *The Development of Capitalism in Russia*. In particular, he became the forerunner of the neo-marxist underdevelopment school (Baran, Frank, and so on), with his argument that imperialism would become a fetter or a brake on development, referring to 'the tendency to stagnation and decay, which is characteristic of monopoly, continues to operate, and in certain branches of industry, in some countries, for certain periods of time, it gains the upper hand' (ibid.: 745).

Gradually the latter tendency, to view imperialism and monopoly capitalism as the highest or last stage of capitalism, prevailed. Not only that, but the view also prevailed that imperialism was becoming the major obstacle to development. All ambiguity had gone by the time of the 1928 Congress of the Communist International, where a key resolution argued that: 'The epoch of capitalism is the epoch of dying capitalism ... The capitalism system as a whole is approaching its final collapse' (quoted in Claudin, 1975: 600). This was the general diagnosis, but – specifically in regards to the colonial world – the communist movement now began to prioritize its alliance with nationalist movements. It is this political imperative which explains the resolutions explicitly and unambiguously portraying imperialism as retrogressive economically, and foreign capital investment not only as an affront to national dignity but also a simple drain on national resources. Development henceforth became synonymous with national development. Somehow capital acquired political colouring so that the same social relations of production could be seen as healthy if under national bourgeois control and exploitative if under international or imperialist control. The later school of 'development of underdevelopment' (Frank) has its intellectual/political origins here.

Within Russia itself, as the 1917 revolution succeeded and a new social order was established, an economic debate on alternative development strategies began in earnest. This debate was also part of the political struggle to see who, and what policy, would succeed Lenin after his death in 1924. The issues ranged from the technical aspects of planning, to the mid-range issue of the priority to be given to industry compared to agriculture, to the big political issue of whether 'socialism in one country' was in fact feasible at all. Many of the central issues in development economics over the last 50 years were first aired in the Soviet debates of the 1920s as the country recovered from the ravages of civil war. For Moshe Lewin these debates were essentially a battle for or against the instalment of a new development model: 'an entirely, or almost entirely, nationalized economy and a political system run by a unique state-party making the whole system into a *sui generis* party-state' (1975: xiv). In a sense this was marxism's first laboratory to try out its recipes for development, confront awkward realities, and adjust its theoretical dictums to the real world in which they now operated.

Nikolai Bukharin is a neglected figure, who developed a coherent gradualist socialist project during these debates (see Cohen, 1980). Bukharin held a more positive (or neutral) view of the peasantry then did Lenin, and conceived of the conciliatory New Economic Programme (NEP) of 1921 in a more long-term way. Bukharin saw the need for an organic development model and political stability. As summarized by Robert Bideleux, this entailed: 'balanced, mutually reinforcing, largely autarkic development of small-holder agriculture and light industries propelled by rising consumption levels...and by providing positive economic incentives for both town and country' (1985: 84). If this was the right position, the left side was argued most coherently by Evgeny Preobrazhensky (1979). In his version, the new Soviet state would need to prioritize forced state-funded industrial development. Preobrazhensky was going for the most advanced capital-intensive model of development – Fordism, in a word – with financing to come from various sources but including a squeeze on 'private capitalist profit' and the peasant sector. The gradualist model of accumulation versus forced industrialization was a debate which was to dominate, and to some extent still does, if in different forms, the development debate.

The best-known debate in the struggle between Stalin and Trotsky is, of course, that between 'socialism in one country' and 'permanent revolution'. In a sense, this big question masked some of the more detailed polemics between the two leaders following Lenin's death. Trotsky and a number of economists such as Kondratiev (of 'Kondratiev waves' fame) argued for a least-cost model of industrialization based on the increased international integration of the new Soviet state, strong industrial planning, and a balanced urban–rural exchange. This was a buoyant, modernist model of development. Stalin, on the contrary, was going for self-sufficiency when he launched a long tradition of supposedly socialist autarkic development models. He argued for large-scale import-substitution industrialization based on continued unfavourable terms of trade with the peasantry. A series of 'emergency measures' were inflicted on the peasantry, and then an outright terror which left some 5 million farmers either without land or in the labour camps. The Soviet model of development, under Stalin, was not only a travesty of anything Marx or Lenin ever advocated but also went far beyond the debates between the left and the right in the mid-1920s, terms which Stalin's authoritarianism certainly transcended.

As the Soviet Union became consolidated and Stalinism tightened its grip on society, so Leninism became transmuted into a veritable ideology of development for what was soon to become the 'Third World'. The ideology of proletarian revolution in the West became the ideology of peasant mobilization in the East, and then the ideology of modernizing elites in the South. David Lane puts it bluntly that 'Leninism is the developmental ethic of Marxism' (1974: 31). Of course, one could argue that this judgement is one-sided, but it does capture the trajectory of a certain state version of Leninism. The sanitized 'Marxism–Leninism' of the bureaucratic-authoritarian Soviet state served as legitimizing cover for what was a NIC (newly industrializing country) in its day. This Leninism is very close to the American modernization theory of the 1950s in many respects. Stalin, predictably, expressed the discourse clearly:

> Socialist industrialisation is the development of large-scale industry, and primarily heavy industry, to a level where it becomes the key to the reorganisation of the entire national economy on the basis of an advanced machine technology, it ensures the victory of socialism and strengthens the country's technical and economic independence and defence capacity in the face of the capitalist world. (Stalin, 1973: 351)

Whatever merits this statement may have in terms of development theory, it is certainly a long way from the *Communist Manifesto*.

Lenin, of course, himself inaugurated this productivist–economist–developmentalist version of marxism with his notorious definition of communism in 1920 as 'Soviet power plus the electrification of all the country'. This was an extreme but, undoubtedly, representative expression of Leninism as development ideology. It is not our concern here to decry its reduction of socialism to industrialization, but simply to highlight to what extent Leninism became a bridge between classical marxism and the more contemporary theories of development, from modernization theory to the radical dependency theory of the 1970s. For a whole historical period in the 1950s and 1960s in a range of countries in the Third World, not all of them even claiming to be socialist, the Soviet development model took a grip. Soviet marxism even fashioned a particular theory of 'non-capitalist mode of development' as a supposed third way between the Western model and a marxist model deemed utopian for the actual conditions of the Third World. In legitimizing many authoritarian or populist Third World industrializing regimes, this particular hybrid of 'Leninism' helped stabilize capitalist rule worldwide and allowed imperialism to overthrow many of the features of colonialism which were by now more of an impediment to capitalist development.

Socialism and underdevelopment

It is by now a well-known 'paradox' that, though Marx expected socialism to flourish in the most advanced capitalist countries, most socialist revolutions occurred in conditions of relative or absolute underdevelopment. Socialist practice seems to contradict socialist theory. At one level the case is unarguable and accounts for why socialism and development had become practically synonymous in many parts of the world. Yet at another level it is hardly surprising that, in conditions of underdevelopment, wide sections of the population might come to view socialism as potentially liberating. Furthermore, Lenin advanced within his account of imperialism the notion that the world capitalist system would break at its 'weakest link'. This points towards a realist interpretation of revolution, unencumbered by marxist or any other teleology, where a whole range of political, strategic or ideological factors, may create a situation 'ripe' for revolution. It is not a question of simply waiting for the development of the forces of production to reach the point where a country is 'ripe' for socialism.

Whether it is a paradox or a natural concomitant of uneven capitalist development, socialist regimes have almost always inherited the legacy of underdevelopment. The constraints on the fledgling socialist state are formidable. Not only must it seek a more even distribution of income, but it also needs to create a massive advance in terms of economic development. The 'gigantomania' of a Stalin is not just the product of his fevered imagination and lust for power. The country will, more than likely, be devastated by external or internal war. There will probably be a small industrial base and an underdeveloped internal market. Natural resources may exist but may well not be immediately available. Human resources will exist but will, on the whole, not be endowed with great training or education. These hardly add up to fertile conditions for the development of socialism. It is not surprising that Paul Baran once famously admitted that: 'Socialism in backward and underdeveloped countries has a powerful tendency to become a backward and under-developed socialism' (1968: viii).

Underdevelopment of the forces of production also means underdevelopment of the working class, agent of transformation in the classic marxist schema. It is possible to detect a working-class role in socialist revolutions usually deemed peasant-based, such as that in China. More often the 'workers' party' has substituted for the actual participation of workers *en masse* in the revolutionary struggles. The main point remains that it is hard to conceive of socialism developing in the context of what were often pre-capitalist social and economic conditions. Socialization of the means of production was often replaced by a socialization of misery. Even relatively optimistic accounts of the prospects of socialism in Africa, such as that of Kidane Mengisteab, admit that: 'Under these conditions, however, while the seizure of state power can be revolutionary, developing socialism can only be evolutionary' (Mengisteab, 1992: 86). It may be the case that the best that socialism in conditions of underdevelopment can achieve is (was) the development of capitalism under slightly more democratic conditions. Even this is unlikely, however, given the prevailing international political context in which the socialist revolutions occurred.

To the legacy of underdevelopment one must add the hostile international environment which socialist regimes faced from 1917 onwards. Being a 'weak link' in an imperialist chain may have facilitated a socialist revolution but, for sure, imperialist aggression would ensue. This was the case for Russia, Cuba, Vietnam or Angola. Revolutionary nationalist self-determination had its place in the imperialist system. Wars, boycotts, external aggression and blockades have been a fact of life for most successful revolutions. The transition to socialism has thus been 'over-determined' by the conditions prevailing in the international political system. This situation can only exacerbate the already difficult internal conditions for democratic, let alone socialist, development. The internal balance of forces between democratic transformation and restoration are, inevitably, tilted towards the latter. While in the short term external aggression may hasten the transformation of social relations after the revolution, in the longer term it needs only to be maintained to fatally weaken the transformation project or turn it in an authoritarian militarist direction, as happened in Nicaragua.

The twin constraints of economic underdevelopment and external aggression point many victorious revolutions towards self-reliance, if not outright autarky. The radical dependency theory of development, which built on Lenin's concept of imperialism, advocated some form of 'de-linking' from the world economy as the remedy for underdevelopment. National liberation, however defined, became a central goal of socialist movements and regimes (see Chapter 7). This is understandable, but it does not lead to socialism in the way Marx understood it. Nor do we need to look at the experience of Burma or Kampuchea to see the terrible cost of autarky as substitute for socialism. We can even question the end result of import-substitution industrialization as a means of promoting self-reliance and national independence. In a hard, but ultimately realistic, vein Bideleux comments that:

> In fact really all the communist states have become increasingly dependent on heavily subsidized Soviet fuels, raw materials, equipment, technical aid and credit; on preferential access to 'soft' Soviet markets for their relatively inferior and unmarketable manufactures; and on Western technology and finance. (1985: 152)

It is clear by now, that the socialist regimes of the twentieth century existed more in the 'realm of necessity' than in the promised 'realm of freedom'. In terms of the theme of this chapter this meant that socialism, as it actually materialized, had to confront above all, the problems of underdevelopment. As Ken Post and Phil Wright argue, the main characteristic of all socialist regimes is (was) that they are 'resource-constrained economies' the principal characteristic of which 'is the continuous reproduction of shortages or, alternatively, continuous underproduction, in contrast to the overproduction of capitalism' (1989: 72). In this scenario, it is inevitable that there will be distribution conflicts between industry and agriculture, investment and consumption, or military and civilian expenditure, for example. There is no plenty to be socialized, no irrationality to be ironed out to everyone's benefit, no benign or virtuous circle waiting to be activated. It is certainly easy to see how, from the very start, there would be a tendency towards full reintegration into the world market in a bid to escape the critical resource constraints which the new socialist economies faced.

The resource-constrained economy finds it very difficult to escape the capitalist 'law of value' and launch the system of planning deemed essential for a transition to socialism. The idea was that the state would control the means of production and distribution sufficiently to act as a countervailing power to the law of the market. Central planning was seen as a key element in gaining social control over the economy. E. V. K. Fitzgerald even argued, with Nicaragua in mind, that 'The advance toward the effective socialization of the enterprise sector of the economy through subordination to the plan may...be more rapid than in a larger, more developed economy' (1986: 44). The idea was that prices could be set through economic calculus by a central decision-making power without recourse to internal market forces. In practice, this model did not succeed and the international capitalist market proved totally corrosive of any national attempt at control over the levers of economic power. This central planning proved to be as much chimera as self-reliance. The fragmentation of the post-revolutionary state and the 'dollarization' of the economy was the seemingly inevitable result imposed by a hostile capitalist world.

Faced with the inevitable contradiction engendered by state socialist economic policies, economic reform was inherently unlikely to achieve its objectives. As Janos Kornai explains: 'Stalinist classical socialism is repressive and inefficient, but it constitutes a coherent system. When it starts reforming itself, that coherence slackens and its internal contradictions strengthen' (1992: xxv). According to this argument, which Kornai backs with vast experience and detailed historical material, reform is doomed to fail because the socialist system is unable to renew itself internally. This is where capitalism is undoubtedly 'superior' as a mode of production, given its almost infinite capacity to reform and transform itself, its knack of renewing itself even (particularly) through crisis. The debates about 'market socialism' which seemed so riveting 20 years ago, now seem just quaint. The revolutionary changes in Russia since 1989 are but one dramatic example of how piecemeal change and reformist tinkering could not make the socialist economy viable in the long run.

The balance-sheet of socialism and underdevelopment or underdeveloped socialism is, inevitably, a mixed one. Adrian Leftwitch argues that in the well-established socialist states such as China, Cuba and North Korea 'the grossest forms of pre-revolutionary oppression, inequality, disease and poverty have been eliminated; industrialisation has progressed *some way*; and average life expectancy and perinatal infant mortality ... compare well or begin to approach levels typical of industrialised societies' (1992: 38). More recently established socialist states such as Angola and Mozambique, the Yemen or Afghanistan, do not fare so well on any of the conventional social development indicators. One could go even further and question whether, for example, that showcase for Third World socialism, Cuba, has really done all that better than it would have done under dependent capitalist development. Cuba on the eve of the revolution was among the better off Latin American countries not just in terms of per capita income but also according to health indicators, for example. There are limits, of course, to the usefulness of this type of counter-factual exercise, but it is still the case that Cuba has failed to provide an alternative development model as originally hoped for by dependency theory.

Socialism was once seen as the best means to 'catch up' with advanced Western capitalist societies. In 1936, Jawaharlal Nehru spoke for many Third World nationalist leaders when he declared that: 'I see no way of ending the poverty, the vast unemployment, the degradation and the subjection of the Indian people, except through socialism'. Some years after that Nikita Kruschev could still, with some credibility, talk about 'catching up' with the West, as Sputnik reached for the stars and the combine harvesters reaped bumper crops. Yet 50 years after Nehru's desperate leap of faith, it was abundantly clear that 'socialist development' was just a pale imitation of its capitalist progenitor, with its own undesirable features and inefficiencies thrown in. There can be little justification for Gordon White's arguments, barely five years before the great anti-socialist popular revolts of 1989, that, for medium-sized Third World countries, with a reasonable resource base and 'a determined leadership and a relatively homogeneous population', 'the Soviet model cannot be discounted as a strategic option' (White, 1983: 13). North Korea is hardly a strong case on which to base this argument.

Post-marxism and development

If until now we have largely taken for granted the concept of development itself, we must now question its meaning. We cannot simply assume, from a supposedly critical perspective, that development is a common human good. Recent attempts to deconstruct the development discourse have helped highlight its less than benign role. Gustavo Esteva points to the apparent contradiction that while 'development occupies the centre of an incredibly powerful semantic constellation... At the same time, very few words are as feeble, as fragile and as incapable of giving substance and meaning to thought and behaviour as this one' (1992: 8). Development acts as a truism and its open-ended significance renders it almost meaningless. Yet its conceptual inflation has led it to dominate almost all treatments of the non-Western world. Development seems to act as a metaphor for the Western way; a word to represent a world to be built in its own image. Far from benign, a wholesome objective all political tendencies could agree to, development begins to appear as a disciplinary mechanism in the Foucaultian sense.

Foucault has provided some fundamental insights into the dynamics of power and knowledge in Western societies. It is from this persepctive that we can envisage development as the extension into the non-Western world of modernism's disciplinary and normalizing mechanisms. A discursive field has been set up under the umbrella of development which has determined which questions get asked and which do not. Development is the deployment of power/knowledge to deal with 'underdevelopment' in a similar way that psychiatry came into existence to deal with 'madness'. Arturo Escobar has argued forcefully in this regard that 'not only does the deployment of development contribute significantly to maintaining domination and economic exploitation but that the discourse itself has to be dismantled if the countries of the "Third World" want to pursue a different type of development' (Escobar, 1984/5: 378). From this point of view, it becomes pointless to qualify development, as it were, by talking of 'sustainable development', 'integrated development' or 'endogenous development'. While appearing to be progressive, these amendments to development are seen simply as a way of heading off challenges to Western dominance and co-opting resistance.

Marxism might seem to be above this type of critique. After all, marxism has hardly been on a par with Western imperialism as an agent of development. Yet marxism is an integral part of the modernist paradigm, in many ways its epitome. Development can, indeed, be seen as a central axis of the whole of Marx's work. The Hegelian concept of history as an unfolding of the Spirit, and Darwin's concept of evolution merge and intertwine in the classic marxist notion of development. As seen above, marxism exudes confidence in the onward march of history and the inexorable progress of development. The marxist stages of human history – the sequence of modes of production – are imbued with a modernist conception of development. Thus from a post-marxist perspective we need to establish some critical distance from this conception. Whatever contradictions marxism may contain within its various theoretical and political manifestations, it is clearly imbued with the spirit of the Enlightenment and its concept of development. One way of illustrating this argument would be through a discussion of the radical, marxist and otherwise, dependency theory.

This is not the place to carry out a genealogy of the concept of dependency (cf. Kay, 1989). The point is that the dependency approach emerged in the late 1960s as a supposedly radical critique of the orthodox, conservative theory of modernization. In all its tenets it simply reversed the arguments of the mainstream discourse. Where modernization theory saw the diffusion of progress across the globe, the dependency approach saw simply the 'development of underdevelopment'. Where one saw integration into the capitalist world economy as the only path to development, the other saw delinking from the world economy as the key to development. Where one saw capitalist development leading steadily towards democracy, the other saw only an inexorable slide into dictatorship or fascism. Thirty years later it would seem that modernization has won the battle of ideas hands down. Reform in development parlance has now become synonymous with neoliberal, free-market doctrines, where once it conjured up images of agrarian reform and income distribution. The dependency approach has even been disowned by its erstwhile authors, who see it as naïve, simplistic and, ultimately, misguided. Why did the radical promise of this development approach in the marxist tradition fail so miserably?

Basically we would have to argue that dependency shared the same discursive terrain as modernization theory. In this regard it is useful to refer to Derrida's notion of 'logocentrism', which refers to a Western tendency to impose hierarchy when dealing with oppositions such as man/woman, West/non-West modern/traditional, and so on. As Kate Manzo argues, this concept is important in relation to a critical understanding of development theory because 'it demonstrates how even the most radically critical discourse easily slips into the form, the logic and implicit postulations of precisely what it seeks to contest' (1991: 8). Thus dependency theory assumes most of the postulates of mainstream development theory, it just seeks different ways of meeting its objectives. To produce a mirror image of smaller theory is still to pay it homage. Dependency, in its marxist and non-marxist variants, rarely stepped outside the development horizon of meanings. Dependency's challenge to developmentalism can at best be seen as only partially countermodernist, and never postmodernist in a positive sense.

If the modernization and dependency theories are, at one level, simply mirror images of each other, what could break this impasse in development theory? From a post-marxist perspective, both feminism and ecology appeared to be attractive alternatives. The various attempts to carry out an 'engendering' of development theory – women in/and development, gender and development, and so on – have utterly transformed this area of study. In theoretical terms, however, some of the criticisms of development theory, such as its essentialism, can be applied equally to feminism, at least prior to the emergence of poststructuralist feminism. As to ecology, we now have a new radical/reformist orthodoxy of 'sustainable development', a blanket term covering various perspectives, but imbuing them all with the warm glow of 'motherhood and apple pie'. As noted in Chapter 2, there is also now a hybrid formation bringing both discourses together in the shape of 'ecofeminism'. While these new critical approaches have taken over at the margins of development practice, the mainstream carries on being dominated by the technocratic/Western-centred/evolutionist perspectives of modernization theory which has even brought under its sway many erstwhile dependency theorists.

Postmodernism would also see itself as breaking with the sterile counterposition of modernization and dependency theory, seeing both as part of a discredited modernist paradigm or 'grand narrative'. From this perspective, development theory operates a classic modernist procedure: 'a disposition to impose hierarchy between places and subjects a nostalgia for origins, and a philosophical predisposition to foundationalism which provides a standard or vantage point independent of intepretation' (Watts, 1995: 53). This critique allows us, for example, to situate dependency theory better, which always operated with an assumed binary opposite of 'non-dependency', some state of origin which was totally mythical. As to the privileged vantage point of the development theorists and practitioner, this is where we see best the arrogance of developmentalism, which assumes an Olympian perspective of humanity down in the mud. The radical dependency theorist also assumed an all-knowing perspective, presumed to speak for all sections of the population, and offered the most unlikely salvation, namely the state of Cuba, no paradise even before it became something like a socialist theme park extension of Disneyland in Miami.

Postcolonial theory has, more recently, sought to develop a novel approach to the question of development. It is much more 'Third-worldist' in its approach, foregrounding the colonial history of Third World countries. In this sense, though it is related theoretically to post-modernism, it would be critical of the latter's engagement with mod-ernism almost exclusively on the terrain of the West. Postcolonialism is critical of the Eurocentric universalism of development theory, its denial of ambivalence, alterity and heterogeneity, and its silencing of other voices. It criticizes the discursive homogenization of even appar-ently radical discourses such as those on 'Third World women'. In Chandra Mohanty's (1998) critique, this category serves as a narcissistic other for Western feminism, part of the paternalizing, colonial project dealing with the colonial native. Postcolonialism is more political than postmodernism, in spite of its origins in cultural studies, and operates in a reverse direction, taking Third World voices into the heartlands of capitalism rather than telling peoples that have not enjoyed/suffered modernism that a postmodern era is now upon us.

To attempt to develop a new post-marxist synthesis on the question of development would probably be futile. From feminism, ecology and other 'new' social movements we can take a critique of mainstream notions. From the emerging 'anti-development' school (see Sachs [ed.], 1993) we can take the sharp deconstruction of the developmentalism discourse and puncture its self-assuredness. Yet this school's anti-mod-ernism hardly takes us 'beyond' modernism or even a post-marxist terrain. There is also something arrogant about talk of 'another' devel-opment which preaches non-material values and evades the basic problems of material needs. The postmodern tack is a different one and at the very least has carried out an effective 'decentring' of the white European male who invented development to deal with the rest of the world when colonialism had had its day. A new era of scepticism towards metanarratives of progress is upon us, we stress self-reflexivity more, and we are much more open towards difference and local knowl-edge than in the heyday of development theory.

In conclusion, it might be salutary to remember that the problems of development and underdevelopment are still with us, whatever theoretical juggling we might carry out. This is one reason, of course, why a 'development industry' persists even while others proclaim that 'development is dead'. Arturo Escobar writes, in this regard, that 'development (as discourse) is a very real historical formation, albeit articulated around a fictitious construct ("underdevelopment") and upon a certain materiality (i.e. certain conditions of life bapitzed as "underdevelopment"), which we must seek to conceptualize in different ways' (1984: 389). Gunder Frank noted a long time ago that there was no such thing as *under*development, only *un*development. What we need to do now is to go beyond even this distinction and question whether development itself has any positive or progressive connotations. All attempts to repackage or relabel the destructive social effects of capitalist expansion across the globe must be questionable from a critical perspective in the 'spirit' of Marx.

4
Gravediggers Limited: Marxism and Workers

The working class is central to the marxist enterprise. There is a virtual marxist myth constructed around the concept of proletariat. Labour is seen as central to the development of modern society. Workers are seen as the 'gravediggers' of capitalist society. This chapter examines firstly how Marx himself conceived of workers and their role in the marxist conceptual edifice. This is followed by a consideration of the role of workers in the Russian Revolution. This was, after all, the first time when workers had a chance to build a new society along marxist lines. This is followed by a discussion of various subsequent debates on the role of the working class in politics, such as the 'new working class' debate. Finally, this chapter turns to certain postmarxist themes which reconsider the traditional marxist views of the working class. Current concerns with new technology and globalization are seen to link up with the more positive premonitions of Marx himself.

Marx's myth

The proletariat, for Marx, is the class under capitalism which has nothing to lose but its chains. This class of labourers 'live only so long as they find work, and ... find work only insofar as their labour increases capital' (1973: 73). This proletariat is created by the Industrial Revolution and was crowded into the teeming industrializing cities of this era. Their conditions of existence led them inexorably towards 'combinations', then strikes and insurrections. While they had nothing – no status, no property – they also were the bearers of a new universality as against the bourgeois or capitalist class they confronted, which exuded particular interest. The proletariat, in short, was to become for Marx

60

the new universal class in history. Their presence at the heart of the new capitalist society was its fatal flaw or contradiction. This new class, which traced its ancestry to the Roman slaves and beyond, carried within itself a new co-operative mode of production which prefigured the new classless society which Marx called communism.

In the *Communist Manifesto* the story of the proletariat is recounted lyrically: 'of all the classes that stand face to face with the bourgeoisie today, the proletariat alone is a revolutionary class. The other classes decay and finally disappear in the face of modern industry; the proletariat is its special and essential product' (Marx, 1973: 77). The organization of the proletariat into a class, and 'consequently' into a political party, is disrupted by competition among workers: 'But it ever rises up again stronger, firmer, mightier' (ibid.: 76). Thus the 'incoherent mass scattered over the whole country' (ibid.: 75) begins to organize and struggle against the dominant order. The expansion of capital requires wage labour and, at first, competition among these labourers prevents combination. Gradually this situation is overcome and big industry promotes associations among the wage labourers. The development of modern industry sows the seeds of its own destruction. In the famous passage of the *Manifesto*: 'What the bourgeoisie therefore produces, above all, are its own grave-diggers. Its fall and the victory of the proletariat are equally inevitable' (ibid.: 79).

The political agent of this transition is a political party, but one of a special type. For Marx: 'The Communists do not form a separate party opposed to other working-class parties. They have no interests separate and apart from those of the proletariat as a whole' (1973: 79). The Communists are not enlightened intellectuals bringing light where there was once only darkness. They 'merely express … actual relations springing from an existing class struggle, from a historical movement going on under our very eyes' (ibid.: 80). They seek the formation of the proletariat into a class and the overthrow of the bourgeois order. But it is a constant refrain of Marx that: 'The emancipation of the working class must be the act of the working class itself'. When bourgeois supremacy is overcome and the proletariat becomes the ruling class, the battle for democracy will be won. Class power will be used by the proletariat to sweep away the conditions for the existence of class antagonisms. In another famous passage: 'In place of the old bourgeois society, with its classes and class antagonisms, we shall have an association, in which the free development of each is the condition for the free development of all' (ibid.: 87).

Let us consider further who this proletariat is composed of for Marx. At one level, it is a straightforward question of those who work for a living. To the industrial working class of the factories Marx adds, in his writings on France, those such as the garment workers and construction workers who support the industrial proletariat in its struggles. However, Marx writes out of this definition of the new universal saviour class those whom he calls the 'lumpen-proletariat'. In the *Manifesto*, Marx refers to 'The "dangerous class", the social scum, that passively rotting mass thrown off by the lowest layers of the old society... [whose] conditions of life...prepare it...for the part of a bribed tool of reactionary intrigue' (Marx, 1973: 77). In his later writings, Marx goes on to distinguish between productive and unproductive labour, with the latter being seen as not part of the proletariat either. This distinction will be referred to again, but the point here is that Marx began a tradition of distinguishing so-called 'objective' criteria for class-belonging and as predictors of class activity.

The objectivist marxist definitions of class are currently sustained by G. A. Cohen, for example, for whom: 'A person's class is established by nothing but his [*sic*] objective place in the network of ownership relations, however difficult it may be to identify such places neatly' (Cohen, 1978: 73). Culture, politics and consciousness have nothing to do with definitions of class position in this orthodox tradition of marxism. It is a structural conception of class opposed totally to E. P. Thompson's action conception of a working class which is present at its own 'making' (Thompson, 1970). Against objectivist, and inherently economistic, definitions of the working class, Thompson argues that this was not Marx's meaning; rather 'class happens when some men [*sic*], as a result of common experiences..., feel and articulate the identity of their interests as between themselves, and as against these whose interests are different from ...theirs' (ibid.: 9). Both interpretations – a structural one and an action-based or experiential one – can be found in Marx's writings.

What is clear in the marxist tradition is how central the working class is to the marxist political project. Ellen Meiskins Wood engages in a forceful restatement of orthodoxy in an attempt to rebut all those involved in 'the retreat from class' in recent years. For her: 'The proposition that the working class is potentially *the* revolutionary class is not some metaphysical abstraction but an extension of...materialist principles, suggesting that, given the centrality of production and exploitation in human social life...certain other propositions follow' (1981: 14). These would include the notion that the working class suffers the most 'direct' form of oppression under capitalism, and that it has the most direct 'objective' interest and ability to overthrow capitalism. The proletariat, at the heart of the capitalist machine, is seen as the principal motor of its emancipatory transformation. The problems with this vision will be examined in a subsequent section of this chapter. At this stage we register only what the orthodox marxist position on the centrality of workers is.

In Marx himself, what we get is largely a philosophical account or justification of working-class centrality. In *The German Ideology* we have a picture of bourgeois society being superseded through a development of its own logic. The universal development of the productive forces seemingly demands a transition to a postcapitalist society. The universalizing of exchange, the generalization of commodity production and the emergence of the new universal class, or proletariat, go hand in hand. As Marx and Engels write:

> only the proletarians of the present day, who are completely shut off from all self-activity, are in a position to achieve a complete and no longer restricted self-activity, which consists in the appropriation of a totality of productive forces and in the development of a totality of capacities entailed by this. (1976a: 87)

With the emergence of the proletariat, as culmination of the division of labour, communism becomes immanent, as it were, within bourgeois society. As Balibar observes: 'The thesis of the proletariat as "universal class" ... allows Marx to read off from the present the imminence of the communist revolution' (1995: 40).

It may be useful at this stage to examine Marx's analysis of an actual labour movement, namely the Chartists in Britain. For Marx, the vibrant capitalism of Britain's Industrial Revolution was bound to produce a dynamic and radical workers' movement. The People's Charter of 1838 demanded universal male suffrage and other democratic reforms as well as a shorter working day. Engels even referred to this charter as the proposed 'law of the proletariat', which would replace the law of the middle classes. For Marx, as Alan Gilbert recounts, there was a condensation of the aspects of Chartism: 'unionization, formation of a radical party to fight for a shorter working week by legal enactment and the vote, and finally, socialist revolution – into a new strategy for the working-class movement' (1981: 53). This type of interpretation was pursued by other marxist interpretations, including that of E. P. Thompson in his *The Making of the English Working Class* (1970). In spite of his break with simple reductionism, Thompson still posited a direct link between 'social being' and 'social consciousness' in the making of Chartism.

More recent students of Chartism, such as Stedman Jones, have broken with this marxist tradition and helped us see the relationship between workers and politics in a new way. He is critical of Engels and others who examine reasons for discontent, such as unemployment and poverty on the one hand, and the evidence for class antagonism in the Chartist discourse on the other hand. What has been problematic, he argues, 'has been the way in which these two types of evidence have been connected' (Stedman Jones, 1983: 19). An intuitive connection between the discontent of workers and the political movement of Chartism cannot be based on simple terms such as 'experience' or 'consciousness'. In a novel, but persuasive, manner Stedman Jones counters the traditional argument arguing that 'it was not consciousness (or ideology) that produced politics, but politics that produced consciousness' (ibid.: 19). What this meant as a research programme, was a new emphasis on the language of Chartism in a non-referential way 'rather than setting particular propositions into direct relation to a putative experiential reality of which they were assumed to be the expression' (ibid.: 21).

To conclude then, Marx created a veritable myth of the proletariat as universal historical subject and harbinger of a new co-operative and, ultimately, classless social order. Marx was big on the 'vision thing' but weak on details. As is often the case with Marx's legacy, it is ambiguous in this area. While certainly prone to determinist, structuralist and economistic ways of thinking about workers, he also stressed workers' self-activity. There is no hint of substitutionism in Marx's conception of communist politics, which is also quite non-sectarian. His emphasis on the creativity and self-organizing capacity of the working class has inspired labour activists for over 150 years. Marx's more dogmatic followers have, however, accentuated the theological aspects of his work, and prevented recognition of new social and political realities. It was Marx's Soviet followers, though, who went furthest in creating a new agency, the Party, which would substitute for the self-activity of the masses and become the arbiter of truth and error among the marxist clergy.

Lenin, Soviets and workers

In the mid-1890s, the incipient Russian workers' movement came into contact with marxism. As has often been noted, industrial capitalism and marxism arrived in Russia almost simultaneously. In this particular situation, as Oskar Anweiler describes, 'The nascent Russian labour movement became totally dominated by the Marxist intelligentsia, which assigned to the proletariat the messianic role of redeemer in its revolutionary scheme of salvation' (1974: 27–8). So, contrary to expectations, it was Russia and not Germany where the first marxist-inspired workers movement played a key role in a revolutionary upheaval. From the 1905 Soviets to the democratic and socialist revolutions of 1917, this movement was to play a key role. A product of the particular uneven development of capitalism in Russia and the First World War, this revolution came to epitomize what became known as the 'workers' state'. But what, in brief was the fate of labour in this dramatic, since terminated, social experiment?

When the Tsar's government fell in February 1917, the workers in the factories moved into action. Unrealistic, even utopian, ideas about the end of all oppression prevailed. The discourses of anarcho-communism and anarcho-syndicalism competed favourably with the more staid marxism of the orthodox Mensheviks and even the Bolsheviks. Factory committees took over the running of many workplaces in an incipient, if semi-spontaneous, movement towards workers' control. Economic chaos and the collapse of planning added impetus and gave an edge to the growing radicalization of the working masses. While the orthodox marxists maintained their neat schema involving state control over production, workers in the factories were demanding direct control and self-governance. This was no doubt a confused, inchoate movement which probably did not address the economic realities of the new, semi-democratic nation-state. It did, however, force the Bolsheviks into reluctant support for the slogan of 'workers' control' for a couple of decisive years.

On a broader, if interrelated, front the Soviets were re-forming, involving workers and soldiers in particular in governance of the new order. The Petrograd Soviet was the leading player in this field, acting as a dynamic, semi-permanent, assembly of workers and soldiers. Memories of the Paris Commune of 1871 were no doubt stirred in the marxist participants in this chaotic assembly. Gradually order was established, delegations were regularized and committees began to do routine work. Within a couple of months, there was a small Bureau of the Executive Committee established with the power to take 'emergency' political decisions. As Anweiler notes, 'the Petrograd Soviet thus changed from a provisional revolutionary organ into a well-organized administrative machine' (ibid: 108). No doubt this was necessary, and should not be put down to some 'iron law' of bureaucratization, but it did lead to a distancing of this, and similar, bodies from the working masses.

The ferment of Soviet organizations and the movement for workers' control led to a fierce debate within the marxist movement in Russia. Lenin, the undisputed intellectual leader of this movement, had no real conception of workers' self-management in 1917. Although keen to foment grass-roots activity among workers, he conceived of self-management in fairly limited terms. Socialism, for Lenin, would come through workers' control of the state through the Bolshevik Party, rather than through workers' control over the means of production. By 1919 the inchoate movement for workers' control had been decisively replaced by a centralized administration of industry, an all-encompassing nationalization. Exemplifying the new mood was Lenin's call in his 1918 *Theses on the Immediate Tasks of the Soviet Government*: 'Obedience, and unquestioning obedience at that, during work to the one-man decisions of Soviet directors' (Lenin, 1970: 680). Piecework, Taylorism and payment by results was the new Soviet way, and any resistance to it was, for Lenin, simply the effect of the 'influence of petty-bourgeois anarchy'.

The trade unions would be the natural beneficiaries of this return from utopia to business as usual. By 1919, the Russian trade unions had broadened their scope practically to merge with the machinery of government to run industry. As Robert Daniels puts it, however, 'The reverse side of the unions' administrative prerogative was their responsibility for maintaining labour discipline and productivity and for preventing, rather than conducting strikes' (1969: 120). The language of workers' control was giving way to the language of 'efficiency' and the Taylorist labour process. The trade unions were becoming 'transmission belts' for 'the party of the working class' among the working masses. If this new labour discipline was not sufficient, Trotsky saw fit in 1920 to advocate the full militarization of labour:

> If we seriously speak of planned economy, which is to acquire its unity of purpose from the center, when labour forces are assigned in accordance with the economic plan … the working masses cannot be wandering all over Russia. They must be thrown here and there, appointed, commanded, just like soldiers. (cited in Daniels, 1969: 121)

The subject of this unprecedented attack, the working class which would supposedly be the leading class of the new order, was being decimated during all these debates. The First World War was followed by the war of imperialist intervention from 1918 to 1921, along with a catastrophic civil war between the Bolsheviks and their enemies. The number of industrial workers in the Soviet Union fell from 3 million in 1917, to 2.5 million in 1918, to 1.5 million in 1920 and, finally less than 1.25 million in 1921 (Furedi, 1986: 16). Whether this process of social decomposition of the working class forced the Bolsheviks to do things on their behalf is probably an open question. What is certain is that the social force behind the drive towards workers' democracy was in serious risk of disintegration. Mounting unemployment and exclusion from political life was taking its toll on a once vibrant labour movement throughout the 1920s. By the 1930s, the capacity of Soviet workers to act in any way as a class, coherently and collectively, had been crushed.

There are many stories of the 'degeneration' of the workers' state declared so precociously in 1917. What is important to note, from the perspective of this text, is the subsidiary role allocated to workers in this so-called workers' state by its leaders. The dominant marxist discourse shared by the Second and the new, Third, International to some extent, was inherently productivist. The seizure of political power and rational planning was sufficient in itself to usher in the promised land. As Carmen Sirianni notes: 'Lenin postponed the question of self-management to the distant future, when the entire population would be fully educated to the tasks of economic administration' (1982: 260). In the meantime, the development of the productive forces, in a crude evolutionist reading of Marx, would take precedence over the transformation of the relations of production. The workplace was conceived by Lenin as a place where objects were produced, not the site of conflicting social relations at the heart of Marx's original vision for transformation.

It is not a question of drawing up a crude counter-factual version of the Russian revolution whereby all the blood and conflict could have been avoided in a harmonious development of communism. For S. A. Smith, the Bolsheviks were facing a 'cruel dilemma' in 1918: 'They were intent on creating democratic socialism, but their priority had to be the re-construction of the productive forces, especially, the revival of labour discipline' (1983: 264). We might question the imperative nature of this dilemma, but the point is well taken. The problem goes deeper, however. One-party rule, the so-called 'dictatorship of the proletariat', and its substitution for working-class self-activity was more than just a difficult and reluctant choice. Even if adoption of a capitalist labour process, labour-discipline and labour-intensification was inevitable in the short term, the Bolshevik theorists, including Lenin, showed little awareness that this was incompatible with the construction of socialism in the long term. The question then arises as to whether other marxist currents had a better understanding of these issues.

There were various opposition currents in the young Soviet state, with varying degrees of consistency. The Left Communist leader V. V. Osinsky was, however, able to remind Lenin in the journal *Kommunist* of Marx's forgotten tenet that: 'The emancipation of the working class must be the act of the working class itself'. In a remarkable series of articles, Osinsky uttered some basic home truths which should have been familiar to all marxists, starting from the obvious one that nationalization was not the same thing as socialism; that without democratic, workers' control, the result would be simply bureaucratic centralization; and that 'Socialism and the socialist organization of work will either be built by the proletariat itself or it will not be built at all' (cited in Sirianni, 1982: 149). Osinksy understood that Taylorism, the epitome of the capitalist labour process, would destroy the solidarity of the working class. He understood that labour productivity needed to rise to secure the material foundations of the socialist state, but accused Lenin of confusing labour productivity with labour intensity. Lenin did not really respond to this detailed critique.

Within a broader context, we can point to an alternative marxist tradition during this period which had a far more positive attitude towards workers' self-activity. Rosa Luxemburg, Anton Pannekoek and Antonio Gramsci dubbed it the 'revolution against Capital' (Gramsci, 1977). By this he meant that, in practice, the Russian masses had carried out a revolution in defiance of the dominant evolutionary reading of Marx's *Capital*. In the period following the First World War there was an upsurge of factory committees in various European countries which led to a distinctive 'councilist' perspective. As Carmen Sirianni argues: 'Factory councils would be the material and organizational basis for the creation of a new consciousness, and would prepare workers technically and spiritually to run society without the bourgeoisie' (1982: 338). That this did not materialize does not lessen the significance of this submerged communist tradition, even today.

Where is the working class?

As the first workers' state went into decline and settled into a cold, non-capitalist – but hardly socialist – nature, the orthodox marxists worked hard to re-affirm fundamental tenets. The Third, or Communist,

International spread this proletarian messianism to many parts of the world, including those where a proletariat, in the marxist sense, hardly existed. In the Marxist–Leninist system, quasi-faith, the proletariat was still the key actor. The path to salvation still lay through the working class and the 'dictatorship of the proletariat'. As in any theological system, there were many convoluted and contrived attempts to keep theory in line, to some extent, with reality. New formulations on the nature of the 'revolutionary alliance' and the type of revolution and post-revolutionary state abounded. Fierce debates, ideological splits and actual fighting occurred over these theological niceties, until the collapse of 'actually existing socialism' in 1989.

One issue seen as important was the degree of working-class participation in revolutions. After all, a socialist revolution would not be up to much if its alleged agent, the proletariat, was nowhere to be found. Thus James Petras carried out a sociological survey of the major twentieth-century revolutions, seeking their working-class component and concluded that: 'In all cases, the revolution had a socialist character because working class struggles profoundly influenced the ideas and practices of the revolutionary organization' (1978: 40). From Russia, through China and Vietnam, through to Cuba, Petras thus detects the proletarian agent at work against all the evidence of historical studies of these revolutions. When the evidence is too incontrovertible, Petras falls back on the proletarian party 'representing' the interests of the actual proletarians. The problem of the working class in the socialist revolutions is 'complex and dialectical' (ibid.: 57) but the schema holds.

The orthodox marxist mechanism holds because it developed a somewhat mystical view of the working class and revolutions. Petras, for example, argued that 'The strategic importance of the working class in the development of the revolutions we have been considering derived above all, from its qualitatively greater capacity to pose socialist goals' (1978: 63). The source of this capacity is never examined, let alone confirmed however. When the self-activity of the working class could not be discerned by even the most sympathetic observer, then the Party was wheeled in to 'represent' the proletariat. And here the marxist tendency towards evolutionism is displayed to its fullest:

The *sequence* leading to the revolutionary transformation *begins* with the formative period involving the organization and ideology of the party. This is *followed* by class and political struggles in which forces are accumulated, roots are put down among the masses, a mass membership is won and, *finally*, power is seized. (Petras, 1978: 37, emphasis added)

Oh, that life were that simple ...

Another debate which preoccupied Western marxism for many years was who actually was part of the working class and deserved the marxist seal of approval. The composition of the working class was crucial if we were to know who, precisely, would be the agent of the coming socialist revolution. The epithet of 'petty bourgeois' to label any deviation from the true proletarian socialism gives an indication of the depth to which this struggle for proletarian purity went. Other non-proletarians would be accepted into the struggle for democracy but, when the socialist phase of the revolution began, they would become our enemy. The boundaries of the working class were not just some arcane sociological dispute but were perceived as crucial to the integrity of the revolutionary project. The unitary conception of capitalism held by orthodox marxists was matched by this very teleological view of class as the subject of the inexorable advance of history.

A seemingly bizzare, but quite critical, debate emerged over the correct marxist definitions of productive and unproductive labour, the latter being deemed beyond the proletarian pale. Nicos Poulantzas, before he discovered Foucault, built an elaborate framework to explain class and concluded that the working class consisted exclusively of productive, subordinated manual wage-earners (Poulantzas, 1975). While productive labour produces surplus value, unproductive labour for example, state employees, service workers or administrators – is paid from this source. While Marx himself had seen entertainers and school teachers as productive when they were employed by capital, Poulantzas was more 'marxist' than Marx. For him only those engaged in the production of physical commodities could be deemed productive. Leaving aside the strong moral connotations of this distinction, we must question the whole nature of a debate so reminiscent of that on how many angels could dance on the head of a pin. While this debate raged in the post-1968 period, the working class itself seemed to be disappearing.

A landmark event in this regard was the publication in 1980 of André Gorz's *Farewell to the Working Class* (1983). Since the early 1960s, industrial sociologists, especially in France, had been preoccupied by the 'dilution' of the traditional working class and the emergence of what was being called post-industrial society. Gorz took these theoretico-political elaborations to their logical conclusion. For Gorz, the 'crisis of socialism', increasingly apparent from 1968 onwards, is simply a reflection of the 'crisis of the proletariat' of marxist myth. He argued that: 'The disappearance of the polyvalent skilled worker – the possible subject of productive labour and hence of a revolutionary transformation of social relations – has also entailed the disappearance of the class able to take charge of the socialist project and translate it into reality' (1982: 67). Working strictly within marxist postulates, Gorz is driven into this impasse. He ends up advocating what can non-pejoratively be called a 'post-industrial utopia' (cf. Frankel, 1987) which is quite Eurocentric and quite unrealistic.

The post-industrial utopians are quite correct in their arguments that the marxist view of the working class mirrors that of capital. Workers are, indeed, distributed in the social division of labour according to the needs of capital. Workers' organizations, such as the trade unions, reflect the role of their members within capitalist society rather than challenge it. As Gorz puts it, 'In its struggle with capital, the proletariat takes on the identity capital itself has given it' (1982: 39). Demands for higher wages are a far cry from early socialist calls for the abolition of 'wage slavery'. Yet Gorz's new/old call for 'the abolition of work' seems simply an anarchist/utopian knee-jerk reaction to the degradation of work under capitalism. It does not, either, reflect the aspirations of millions worldwide seeking to enter the world of paid employment, to whom this call might appear bizarre in the extreme. What is probably beyond question is that the proletariat of marxist myth has now left the stage, if it ever did exist anyway.

With the traditional working class rapidly fading in revolutionary potential, many on the left turned elsewhere to find a revolutionary subject in the post-1968 period. The 'embourgeoisement' of the traditional industrial working class led some towards the technicians/engineers/computer specialists of late capitalism. Perhaps this was the new, anti-capitalist, vanguard being forged in the white heat of technology. Others, perhaps through participant observation, saw revolutionary virtue in the student activists of 1968 and its aftermath. Perhaps learning would clash with the constraints of capitalism. But the most far-reaching turn was towards the oppressed peoples of the Third World. If the Western working class had become soft and corrupt, the lean and hungry peasants of the Third World would encircle the cities and lead the way to the promised land. Some, however, saw even Third World workers as a 'labour aristocracy', bought off and reformist, and saw the untutored revolutionary zeal of the 'marginals' in the shanty towns as the possible saviours of the 'revolutionary' project.

The flourishing of post-working-class subjects prompted some on the left to call a halt to 'the retreat from class' (Wood, 1981). Alternative visions of the traditional marxist view of the working class are accused of 'strategic bankruptcy', and Gorz, in particular, is berated for his 'counsel of despair' (ibid.: 15). Faced with the 'randomization of history and politics' operated by the post-marxists, Wood hews her way back to fundamentals. To carry on arguing that 'the working class is potentially *the* revolutionary class' is not seen as a metaphysical statement in any way, and the fact that the working class has not produced a revolutionary movement is simply brushed aside. We are just told that the working class has the most direct 'objective interest' in establishing socialism, and that it is the one social force with the 'strategic social power' to achieve this transition (ibid.). The point of this narrative is to recall how common it is for thought systems to retreat into blind dogmatism when their consistency and adequacy are contested by events.

If we stand back from the particulars of these debates within marxism on the working class, we can see certain more general problems. It would seem that even some of the critics of traditional marxism, such as Gorz, operate on the same discursive terrain as those they criticize. The search for *the* revolutionary subject would seem to be the problem, rather than the suitability of the candidates for this role. Furthermore, all sides of the debate on the composition of the working class seem to suffer from the problems of seeking structures, instead of conceptualizing class, more productively, as processes. Against the language of social 'system' and class 'subjects' Gibson-Graham has called for 'the need to liberate class politics from these restrictive yet privileged scenarios ... [and] understand society as a complex disunity in which class may take multiple and diverse forms' (Gibson-Graham, 1996: 58). We are now more able to conceive of capitalism as decentred and fragmented, and the processes of class as diverse, and unevenly developed. This is not a simplistic 'beyond class' scenario.

Post-marxist workers

If the previous section has dissected some rather bizarre orthodox marxist concerns with the working class, we need now to examine some postmarxist themes. Against all essentialisms, the postmarxists theorists, such as Ernesto Laclau and Chantal Mouffe, stressed the plurality of contemporary social struggles and the contingent nature of politics. They argued in the mid-1980s that:

> What is now in crisis is a whole conception of socialism which rests upon the ontological centrality of the working class, upon the role of Revolution, with a capital 'r', as the founding moment in the transition from one type of society to another and upon the illusory prospect of a perfectly unitary and homogeneous collective will that will render pointless the moment of politics. (Laclau and Mouffe, 1985: 2)

The idea of a universal subject – the proletariat – marching towards its inexorable destiny did not withstand the critique of the poststructuralists or the events in the real world following the cataclysms of 1989.

The traditional marxist discourse on class and the working class has had a paradoxical effect. While its critics have proclaimed the 'death of class', the fundamentalists simply call for a halt to the 'retreat from class', while privately lamenting working-class demobilization. In fact, we could argue with Gibson-Graham that 'what has died or been demobilized is the fiction of the working class and its mission that was produced as part of a hegemonic conception of industrial capitalist development' (1996: 69). We are now much more aware of the diversity of capitalism and the plurality of social struggles. Race, gender, sexuality, religion, disability and region are all on this terrain, alongside and integrated with class. There is now no one locus or site of social transformation. Oppressions are seen to be multiple, and the sites of resistance are seen to be everywhere. The capacity for transformation is not held in the hands of a mythical proletariat – or any other single subject – but is dispersed throughout society.

These are themes which, of course, the 'new' social movements of the 1980s – the peace, ecology and women's movements above all – began to articulate. The transition from industrial to postindustrial society had apparently thrown up a new societal type. The old conflicts over distribution were being replaced by new concerns with identity and the qualitative transformation of society. An economic emphasis was replaced by a cultural emphasis, to put it one way. The 'new' social movements were seen as a response to new forms of antagonism which had emerged under late capitalism. As to the internal workings of these movements, David Slater has argued that 'the importance given to high levels of participation in internal decision-making, the search for cooperative relations, the respect of social differences, and the socio-cultural "signification" of inter-personal relations combine to form another key

constitutive element of the novelty of the new social movements'
(1984: 7). What we need to consider is to what extent these practices
have spread to the more traditional labour movements.

We can certainly detect in the last 10–15 years some signs of a 'social
movement unionism' more attuned to the themes and moods of the
'new' social movements. In semi-peripheral countries, such as Brazil
and South Africa, but also even in the United States, there has been a
flourishing of 'new unionism' practices and strategies. Concerns about
inner-union democratic procedures, gender equality and qualitative
rather than quantitative strategies are now much more common.
The old prevalent state-centric strategies are now much more com-
monly matched by an orientation towards civil society. Trade unionists
are more prone to accept that the working class has two sexes and that
race cannot be brushed aside with simplistic formulae. In a sense, the
practice of the working class has, however unevenly and sporadically,
outstripped the preconceptions of its self-appointed 'representatives'
within marxist orthodoxy.

If one factor can be said to have disrupted the traditional marxist
views of class, that would be gender. In an influential article, Heidi
Hartmann argued that:

> the categories of Marxist analysis, 'class', 'reserve army of labour',
> 'wage-labourer', do not explain why particular people fill particular
> places. They give us no clue as to why *women* are subordinate to *men*
> inside and outside the family and why it is not the other way round.
> *Marxist categories, like capital, are sex-blind.* (Hartmann, 1986: 8)

Once the floodgates of criticism were opened in this way, there were
few areas of marxist enquiry, like the social sciences and humanities
generally, which remained immune to feminist subversion. Our understanding of the formation of the working class, patriarchy at work, the
labour process and engendered citizenship were all transformed. It was
no longer possible to forget, as Ros Baxandall and co-authors forcefully
reminded Harry Braverman's classic *Labor and Monopoly Capital* (1974),
that: 'the working class has two sexes' (Baxandall *et al.*, 1976).

Yet even when marxism began to engage the feminist critique, it
often did this in a partial or distorted manner. One example of this
problem was the so-called domestic-labour debate on which marxists
expended considerable energies in the 1980s. This was an attempt to
situate women's domestic labour within the capitalist realm and to cat-
egorize it within marxist terminology. Its focus was not the oppression
of women, but the precise role of domestic labour under capitalism.

The type of question which prevailed was whether domestic labour was productive, unproductive or non-productive of surplus value. To have women's domestic labour recognized as work was undoubtedly a step forward, but to then wonder whether this was strictly productive or not was a step backwards. Marxism, even when it tried, tended to remain trapped within a productivist logic. Class was still reduced to production (albeit in 'the last instance') and forms of consciousness and action arising outside production relations were barely perceived.

In more recent years, it has been the theme of globalization which has most impacted the critical study of the working classes. Marx himself, in the *Grundrisse* notebooks, had some brilliant intuitions on this process:

> The tendency to create the *world* market is directly given in the concept of capital itself. Every limit appears as a barrier to be overcome ... In accord with this tendency, capital drives beyond national barriers and prejudices ... It is destructive towards all of this, and constantly revolutionizes it, tearing down all the barriers which hem in the forces of production, the expansion of needs, the all-sided development of production. (Marx, 1973: 408–10)

In recent decades economic relations, among others, have progressed from an international dimension to a truly global one. It is a process of integration which is having far-reaching effects on the world of work. Capital has, as Marx foresaw, brushed aside any national boundaries which stood in its way. Capitalism has penetrated (the word is used advisedly) into all spheres of economic, cultural and social life across the globe. In the new 'global factories' workers have become mere commodities once again. The nation-statist terrain of struggle gives diminishing returns in an era where the survival of the nation-state is considered to be in question.

Hand in hand with globalization, capital has been leaping into a new technological era dominated by information (see Castells, 1996) and knowledge. This has led to a historical redefinition of the relationship between labour and capital to the advantage of the latter. The gradual dispersal of the traditional working class was accentuated as capital gained in flexibility and the power of adaptability. Labour and its organizations were characterized, on the other hand, by rigidity and, on the whole by a failure to adapt to the new order. As Manuel Castells notes:

> Labour unions, the main obstacle to one-sided restructuring strategy, were weakened by their unadaptability to representing new kinds of

workers (women, youth, immigrants), to acting in new work places (private sector offices, high-technology industries), and to functioning in the new forms of organisation (the network enterprise on a global scale). (Castells, 1996: 278)

It would seem that the lessons of the 'new' social movements were learnt too late or that the dead hand of inertia and orthodoxy prevailed.

There have been various responses from marxists, and radicals generally, to these trends. One tendency is simply to bemoan the uneven playing field between the 'footloose and fancy free' transnational corporations and labour. Another line of thought preaches doom and gloom about a 'jobless future' (Aronowitz and Di Fazio, 1994), against the available evidence. Yet there is also a sign that a new poststructuralist understanding of work and workers is emerging. Catherine Casey, for example, has argued for a new conception of the 'decentred workplace' created through the ability of the new information technologies to disperse work across national boundaries (1996: 195). Furthermore, she argues that advanced information technology and the ensuing reorganization of work 'are decentering the workplace in even more complex ways', as where we work is becoming a more diffuse site compared to the office block or the manufacturing plant which prevailed until the 1980s (ibid.: 195). The new decentred workplace also has its internal effects within the enterprise as network begins to prevail over hierarchy.

If we now perceive of class as decentred, it does not necessarily spell the end of class as a *passé* modernist phenomenon. Denying privileged agency to the proletariat (however we are to define it) does not mean turning our backs on workers' struggles. We do need to recognize that the militant particularism of this or that struggle is not synonymous with socialism. We do need to understand that class is not only constructed in the workplace and has a crucial cultural component. We also need to address constantly the divisions between workers of the industrialized North and the poor South, between women and men, and the running sore of racism in all its guises. The decentring of the world of work is a fact of contemporary capitalism. This cannot be counteracted by any bid to put the clock back and (re)centre a mythical proletariat. Instead, a postmarxist critical theory is being built which starts from the decentred nature of society, understands, even welcomes diversity, and looks to the future and not the past.

5
Unhappy Marriage: Marxism and Women

It is probably not coincidental that when the 'crisis of marxism' was noted in the 1970s, feminism was increasing in theoretical stature and political influence. While marxism tried to incorporate, even domesticate, women under the 'woman question' label, feminism was setting its own agenda. This chapter examines the attempted 'marriage' between socialism and feminism after a brief retrospective of the 'classic' engagement with women. Socialist feminism proved not to be a sturdy hybrid, as both partners came under scrutiny by postmodernism in the 1980s. There is a case for a new postmodern feminism as a radical vehicle for women (and men too, perhaps). Marxism is not the only androcentric mode of thought but its male-centredness in so many aspects, as we shall examine, would probably be enough to disqualify it as adequate guide and programme for the construction of a new society. One aspect of this chapter which distinguishes it from the others is that for once Karl Marx is the silent partner and it is Frederick Engels who comes to the fore in an early 'marxist' engagement with gender. The extent to which this was successful is still debated by Marxologists.

Engels and the family

There have been attempts to find in Marx's mature works an adequate basis for a materialist understanding of the position of women under capitalism (see Vogel, 1983), but on the whole it is recognized that Marx delegated 'gender' (along with religion, science, war and other 'non-central' topics) to his colleague Engels. As Michèle Barrett notes in a volume commemorating the centenary of Marx's death in 1983, 'his treatment of the issue [gender] is now widely regarded as scattered, scanty and unsatisfactory' (1983: 199). Nor can Marx, in all honesty, be 'excused' by the political culture of the era, which was hardly that 'pre-feminist'. It would even be doing Marx a disservice to see him as a simple product of his time, when his analytical vigour was so evident in other areas where he stripped away the naturalistic illusions of bourgeois commonsense. At a much later stage the categories developed by Marx in his analysis of capitalist society would be deployed by the socialist feminist current in seeking to articulate a coherent marxist understanding of gender relations under capitalism. For the time being, we need to examine what Engels – factory owner, slightly unconventional, personally more 'liberal' than Marx – had to say on gender in his famous *Origin of the Family, Private Property and the State* (Engels, 1990). Women are approached via the family in this foundational text.

Written in 1884, 'The Origin' became a more or less instant classic and was accorded, in the socialist tradition, the status of definitive treatment of the family and, hence, the 'woman question'. Essentially, what Engels was seeking to theorize was the relationship between the division of society into classes (and the emergence of the state) and the subordination of women to men. His main empirical anthropological source was Lewis Morgan's *Ancient Society*, published in 1877. One of the formulations used by Engels was later to spawn a whole area of marxist debate: 'According to the materialist conception, the determining factor of history is, in the final instance, the production and re-production of immediate life' (Engels, 1990: 131). Hailed as an insight by many contemporary socialists and feminists, it directed attention to the social and material aspects of reproduction of society, usually neglected by productivist narratives. However, it still takes as a given that the domain of reproduction is a female one, counterposed to a male realm of production. Not only does this perpetuate androcentric categories and ways of thinking, but it also inaugurates a long tradition of dualist thinking in this regard. Moira Maconachie is understated in arguing that: 'This conceptual dualism which separates the family from social production and which confines women to the sphere of domesticity is not especially useful to feminism' (1987: 107). History and social change is seen to spring from the 'male' sphere of production.

It flows logically from this conception that Engels would see the liberation of women coming from their increased entry into the sphere of production. For Engels:

> to emancipate woman and make her the equal of the man is and remains an impossibility so long as the woman is shut out from

social productive labour and restricted to private domestic labour. The emancipation of woman will only be possible when woman can take part in production on a large, social scale, and domestic work no longer claims anything but an insignificant amount of her time. (Engels, 1990: 262)

Not only does this statement suffer from a crude productivist logic – why should factory work liberate anyone from anything? – but it continues with the gendered assumption that women 'naturally' take responsibility for domestic labour. Nor is there any location of this process in terms of the division of society into social classes. In the state socialist societies which emerged after the Russian Revolution of 1917 this confident assertion by Engels was repeated *ad nauseam* to justify their productivist logic and their failure to address the emancipation of women in a meaningful way. The ultimate expression of this wilful blind spot was articulated by a Yugoslav official in the 1970s, for whom: 'Marxists have ascertained that the causes of the unequal position of women do not lie in their oppression by men … Hence the only way to achieve the emancipation of women … is by pursuing … the road to revolutionary struggle' (quoted in Molyneux, 1981: 177).

In terms of his anthropological account, derived largely from Morgan, Engels sees the shift to the patrilineal clan system as a turning point in gender relations. It was to create the conditions for the emergence of private property and the development of class society. As to gender relations, for Engels, 'the overthrow of mother right was the *world historic defeat of the female sex*. The man took command in the home also; the woman was degraded and reduced to servitude; she became the slave of his lust and a mere instrument for the production of children' (1990: 165). Descent by the female line and the supremacy of women in the communal household is the *status quo ante* according to Engels, but this is by no mean uncontroversial. The myth of 'man the hunter' has been largely discredited. Basically, Engels held a naturalistic view of gender relations and assumed women's responsibilities regarding home and family. The above account further subordinates an account of women's role to the broader story of how families were seen to have evolved by contemporary anthropology. It also tied gender inequality to the development of antagonistic class societies seen as the sole 'material' basis for women's subordination. For Engels; 'The supremacy of the man in marriage is the simple consequence of his economic supremacy, and with the abolition of the latter will disappear in itself' (ibid.: 181).

If we accept that Engels at least paid serious attention to gender, unlike Marx, there are still serious limitations to *The Origin,* even as a preliminary sketch of an area of enquiry. We have already mentioned the productivist bias in Engel's account of the development of capitalist society. It suffers, furthermore, from the economic determinism which is undoubtedly partly, but not the sole, legacy of Marx (see Chapter 1). There is also a strong naturalistic strain in the account Engels gives of the sexual division of labour. While this undoubtedly has a technical ('material') side which Engels examines, he seems oblivious to the hierarchical gender relations constructed socially around the sexual division of labour. As Maconachie puts it: 'Naturalizing women's domestic relationship to men blinds us to the strategic possibilities of any interchangeability of tasks between men and women, so making current domestic practices appear particularly immutable' (1987: 11–12). For precapitalist societies Engels ignores, more or less, the role of women outside the domestic sphere. Nor does he explain how the emergence of a specific sphere of social activity related to the reproduction of labour power (child rearing, socialization, feeding, clothing, and so on) is related to the emergence of capitalist society.

Taking a broader look at Engels and Marx's treatment of gender issues, we can usefully focus on two issues, namely the family and wage labour. In *The German Ideology* Marx and Engels developed a conception of the family as rooted in the social division of labour. This division of labour, for the founding fathers of marxism, 'was originally nothing but the division of labour in the sexual act' (Marx and Engels, 1976a: 44). From this arises the supposedly 'natural' division of labour in society as simply an extension of this 'natural' division of labour within the family. However, increased needs create new social relations and the family was becoming subordinate to the emerging capitalist system. In *The German Ideology*, Marx and Engels also go on to make the general theoretical claim that 'the production of life, both of one's own in labour and of fresh life in procreation, now appears as a twofold relation: on the one hand as a natural, on the other as a social relation' (ibid.: 43). What is significant in the present context is that this strong dualism posited between the natural and the social was explicitly overcome in Marx's own mature works such as *Capital,* but Engels chose to reproduce it nearly verbatim when dealing with gender relations in *The Origin.*

Where *The German Ideology* retained its utopian, even feminist, edge was in relation to the future of the family. In an admittedly fleeting passage, nevertheless, Marx and Engels declare that in communist society 'the supersession of individual economy is inseparable from the super-session of the family' (Marx and Engels, 1976a: 76). However, in *The Origin* Engels tends to extoll the virtues of the proletarian family to an unwarranted extent. While for the bourgeoisie marriage is a matter of convenience, and Engels is eloquent on the various double standards, for the proletariat 'all the foundations of typical monogamy are cleared away. Here there is no property, for the preservation and inheritance of which monogamy and male supremacy were established; hence there is no incentive to make this male supremacy effective' (Engels, 1990: 179). Among the working class, for Engels, 'personal and social conditions' decide and 'individual sex love' is paramount. This ideal-ized view of the working-class family is not even excusable for a man in Engels's position, as he would have been well aware of contempo-rary denunciations of domestic violence, for example. On this issue he somewhat tamely referred to it as 'a leftover piece of the brutality towards women that has become deep-rooted since the introduction of monogomy' (ibid.: 181). State socialist societies would later excuse the subordination of women as an unfortunate 'leftover' of capitalism.

On the question of wage labour, to put it bluntly, Marx simply assumed that the wage labourer was a male. Scattered throughout Marx's *Capital* are many references to women workers and their condi-tions. Marx focused particularly on the impact of the introduction of machinery, which allowed the capitalist to shift towards the employ-ment of 'cheap labour' such as women, children and the unskilled. Some of the most eloquent pages of *Capital* deal with the social degra-dation of women workers, for whom Marx continually called for better 'protection'. However, the focus was always the 'modal' male worker, with Marx typically denouncing how: 'By the excessive [*sic*] addition of women and children to the ranks of the workers, machinery at last breaks down the resistance which the male operatives in the manufac-turing period continued to oppose to the despotism of capital' (Marx, 1970: 402). So, not only is the male worker centred in Marx's account, but he sounds quite unjustifiably (given contemporary knowledge of the subject) shocked by the numbers of female workers being employed in industry. Again, Marx succumbs to 'commonsense' notions and percep-tions where, in relation to other topics, he would have sought to deconstruct received wisdom. This is also typical of later marxist use of gender-blind categories which tacitly accept the precepts of a sexist society.

Central to Marx and Engels's attitude towards gender relations at work is the notion of the 'family wage', whereby male workers are seen to receive a wage sufficient to sustain a family. In the context of discussing how the introduction of machinery brought 'under the direct sway of capital, every member of the workman's family, without distinction of age or sex' (Marx, 1976: 517), Marx went on to describe how this 'spreads the value of the man's labour-power over his whole family. It thus depreciates his labour-power' (ibid.: 518)[Marx had simply assumed that the male breadwinner had earned enough to sustain a family until women and children fell under the sway of capital.]He also simply assumed that this would depreciate male wages, a conception which lay behind many subsequent struggles over 'dilution'. The issue of the 'family wage' – more discourse than reality in practice – is a symptom of one of the deepest divisions in the labour movement. Socialist historians and trade unionists have, on the whole, portrayed the world of work in a way which simply assumed it to be a male domain.[Women workers were, and were conceived rightly to be, part of the 'reserve army of labour' to be called into service and dismissed back to the home when their services were no longer required.]

I believe, finally, that the most serious political critique of Marx and Engels in relation to gender is that they took at face value the tenets of liberal feminism. Here was a form of bourgeois liberal ideology which simply went unchallenged by the founders of marxism. Why was this, when they had offered such a sharp critique, for example, of Duhring's 'ethical socialism' based on vague notions of truth and justice? As Barrett puts it: 'Neither Marx nor Engels saw fit to attempt to rebut the classic statements in favour of women's rights. Wollstonecraft and Mill remain unanswered where similarly egalitarian and liberal arguments on other topics are dispatched with vigour' (1983: 201).[So it is not that Marx and Engels were 'prefeminist', but that they failed to see how the cause of socialism and the cause of women's rights might come together or point in the same direction towards a better society.] To this day Engels's *The Origin* stands as both a solid contribution to a materialist understanding of gender – witness its influence on the active school of marxist anthropology – and a symbol of its limitations. This text continues to be important, paradoxically, as Ros Coward says, in revealing 'the political theory by which the woman question became such a problematic area in Marxism while at the same time being absolutely central to it' (1983:141).

Socialists and feminism

After the ambiguous engagement by Engels and Marx with questions of gender, the international socialist movement sought to establish a more organic relationship with the 'woman question'. A crucial landmark was the 1878 text *Woman and Socialism* by a contemporary of Engels, the German Social Democratic leader, August Bebel. Its core was an analysis of the oppression of women under capitalism, which Bebel related to the penetration of the cash nexus into all areas of social life. While advocating equal rights for the sexes, Bebel believed they were fundamentally different, with women needing protection, especially from work which would threaten their femininity. As with other social-ist thinkers, Bebel believed that under capitalism only palliatives were possible and that only after the socialist revolution would women's lib-eration be possible. Although dubious in its marxist pedigree (Engels did not seem to have been too impressed) *Woman and Socialism* had an incredible impact on the European socialist movement, becoming a bestseller in Germany and being a major influence on subsequent socialist feminist pioneers such as Clara Zetkin and Alexandra Kollontai. It probably showed again how important the 'woman question' was to socialism even when it had immense problems in accepting feminism in any meaningful sense.

Clara Zetkin was to become the undisputed leader of the socialist women's movement in Germany at the turn of the century and a major influence on the European and Russian scenes. Her personal his-tory made her as much a feminist as a socialist. She followed Engels in advocating economic independence for women as a precondition for emancipation, but began to recognize that this was not a sufficient condition on its own. Influenced by current feminist writings, Zetkin developed a dialectical view of women's condition where class and gender both played a full role. While continuously stressing that her role in organizing working-class women was not in competition with the male socialist leaders, in practice she knew chauvinism was alive and well in those quarters. Thus, while attacking 'bourgeois feminism' and refusing common platforms on suffrage issues, for example, Zetkin began to move towards the concept of an autonomous women's move-ment in practice. The German Social Democratic Party's women's movement had 175,000 members when the First World War broke out in 1914, they had unionized some 215,000 women workers and Zetkin's magazine *Die Gleichheit* (*Equality*) had a circulation of around 125,000 subscribers.

In Zetkin's view, autonomy for socialist women within the party was essential to stimulate initiative and maximize the potential of the women involved. Taking advantage of laws that forbade mixed-sex political gatherings for a time, Zetkin developed a feminist agenda within the socialist movement. When a change in the law in 1908 allowed women to organize politically with men, the party leaders moved rapidly to dissolve separate women's organizations within their ranks. In return one seat on the party executive was to go to a woman – but that was not to be Clara Zetkin. She still retained a loyalty to the party that blinded her to the conscious move to nip radicalism and separatism in the bud. As Karen Honeycut puts it, there was a deliberate strategy by the party leadership 'who as males, as Marxists and as bureaucrats committed to revisionist tactics and organizational uniformity, opposed autonomy for socialist women' (1981: 41). Clara Zetkin goes down in history as the woman who not only created and led the Socialist Women's International but also took the initiative in establishing International Women's Day in 1907, a symbolic confluence of the socialist and feminist movements which is still having an impact today.

After the First World War, the centre of gravity of the international socialist movement shifted to Russia, where the revolution was brewing. In 1900, Nadezhda Krupskaya published *The Woman Worker*, drawing largely on Bebel and Zetkin but enormously influential as, for a long time, the only Russian text on the 'woman question'. Krupskaya did give much more attention to peasant women than the two German writers had, and helped focus the attention of the Russian social democrats on the question. Lenin, himself, wrote more than most male Bolsheviks on the 'woman question' but he tended to just follow a basic line. For Lenin:

> The female half of the human race is doubly oppressed under capitalism. The working woman and the peasant woman are oppressed by capital, but over and above that, even in the most democratic of the bourgeois republics, they remain, firstly, deprived of some rights because the law does not give them equality with men; and secondly – and this is the main thing – they remain in 'household bondage', they continue to be 'household slaves', for they are overburdened with the drudgery of the most squalid and backbreaking and stultifying toil in the kitchen and the individual family household. (Lenin, 1966: 83–4)

Lenin is perhaps best known for his frank personal conservatism in sexual matters expressed in conversations with Clara Zetkin.

Alexandra Kollontai was, undoubtedly, the leading Bolshevik who engaged with the 'woman question'. Yet she did not call herself a feminist and much of her early political work was in vociferous

opposition to the feminists. During the First World War, feminism in Russia had grown significantly, with women's movements springing up everywhere. The Bolshevik women's group was, in contrast, defunct at this stage. So, when the (first) Russian Revolution began on 23 February, International Women's Day, it was not the Bolsheviks who were to the fore. The feminist movement lost no time in pursuing the question of universal suffrage with the provisional government. Kollontai was scathing about these 'upper-class ladies' who sought suffrage rights from bourgeois governments. She would attend feminist meetings to rail against 'bourgeois feminism' and to urge the women attending to focus on the war and on class exploitation. Shortly after the October Revolution the First Conference of Working Women of the Petrograd Region was held. At this, Kollontai urged women to vote for the Bolshevik list for the Constituent Assembly and not for the candidates of the feminist League for Women's Equality. A feminist delegate showed the distance between feminist and Bolshevism in declaring that: 'Everywhere women are subjected; everywhere they struggle for their rights…*Men cannot defend our interests*; they do not understand us' (quoted in Stites, 1978: 306/7).

In the new government, Kollontai went on to become Commissar for Social Welfare, her priority being the achievement of full independence and equality within marriage. Under Kollontai, equal pay for women was instituted, abortion was legalized and illegitimacy disappeared as a legal category. Many of these gains were, of course, to be reversed under Stalin's regime. But in the 1920s, the cause of women was advanced vigorously by Zhenotdel (Women's Section or Department), led first by Inessa Armand and, after 1920, by Kollontai. She told Emma Goldman that the work of Zhenotdel, in relation to raising the consciousness of women and addressing gender-specific issues such as maternity care, was not 'feminism' (Stites, 1978: 332). In reality her work with women, especially in the East – where hundreds of women were killed because the patriarchal society would not accept their new status as equals – is nothing if not feminist. Certainly, Kollontai did not stop at political emancipation (if that can be taken as 'feminism') and it was her leading role in the radical Workers' Opposition which soon saw her removed from the head of Zhenotdel and sent, eventually, to diplomatic exile in Norway. Her removal was a bitter blow to the women's and socialist movements in Russia.

Where Kollontai really drew her distance from the male marxists of her day and can be seen as a bridge to the 1960s is in relation to sexual politics. The normally restrained E. H. Carr declared that Kollontai 'preached the uninhibited satisfaction of the sexual impulse, supported by the assumption that it was the business of the state to take care of the consequences' (1970: 41). Indeed, her theories and personal example were seen as the main causes of the 'sexual excesses' or 'new morality' of the 1920s. The truth is more prosaic. Kollontai believed in the sacred function of motherhood, saw marriage as a free union which was impossible under capitalism, and saw that under communism 'Eros will occupy a worthy place and be a source of emotional experience and of ever increasing happiness' (cited in Stites, 1978: 353). This is hardly a libertine manifesto. However, it was sufficient for Aron Zalkind, founder of the Society of Marxist Psychoneurologists, to develop a counter-theory of 'socialist sexuality' which boiled down to sex and love being akin to fixed capital which should be involved in 'class' activities and not squandered frivolously. As in the cultural domain (see Chapter 6) the rolling back of the Russian revolution involved considerable psycho-sexual repression, sublimation and domination. Kollontai, for her part, signalled a new area of marxist enquiry, to be taken up by Wilhelm Reich and others some time later.

If we now take a broader look at the policies of state socialist societies in regard to the oppression of women, that record must be an ambiguous one. The context was not usually favourable, as virtually all these societies were characterized by material scarcity and external aggression or internal conflict. Yet there is no doubt that at least formal gender equality was high on the agenda of most socialist states and, due to the productivist bias of marxism *and* the needs of development, women were brought into the workforce in large numbers. Lenin was not totally deluded when he declared that the Russian Revolution led the world in according equal rights to women and in doing away with traditional patriarchal barriers to their advancement. Yet the sexual division of labour continued to prevail. Economic independence has not secured, cannot secure women's emancipation. For this to be achieved, as Maxine Molyneux puts it 'the complex combination of mechanisms, non-economic as well as economic, through which women's subordination is mediated, must form the object of a *specific* struggle' (1981: 179). Only a reductionist form of economism could see oppression being derived solely from economic, or even only class, factors. Thus the legacy of a mechanical marxism thwarted the cause of women's liberation.

Another legacy of state socialism was the Leninist model of party organization, endowed with quasi-mystical revolutionary virtues. The hard professional revolutionaries who stressed leadership, sacrifice and a knowing vision were, invariably, male. More to the point, this can be seen as an inherently male form of organization. The Leninist language of power politics is hardly reflective, it certainly does not favour any consideration of the personal. For all the talk about proletarian democracy's superiority over mere bourgeois democracy, the Leninist party is no school for democracy. This party model also operates with a rigid (if variable) hierarchy of activities from the political (state power), to the economic (the workplace), to the social (the workplace), to the community (housing, for example), to the cultural and other assorted low-priority issues. What feminism did (does) was bring prefigurative politics back to the fore; the form of organizing for socialism is as important as the objective. As Sheila Rowbotham puts it: 'The recognition which was present within preLeninist radical movements of the importance of making values and culture which could sustain the spirit and help move our feelings towards the future, has been reasserted by the women's movement' (1979: 128).

In conclusion, the socialist engagement with feminism after Marx and Engels was not a particularly fruitful one. Most socialists cling to the notion that engagement with paid work was the path to women's liberation, a goal that was, anyway, subordinated to the socialist revolution as they saw it. Socialists and feminists were often competing for the same political constituency and this accounts for much of the antagonism between these currents. Socialists would certainly seek to co-opt the politics of feminism and, sometimes (but not always) became enthusiastic supporters of universal suffrage. Socialist women often had to mask their feminism and make continuous declarations of faith to the party male-stream. When all the context is allowed for, most socialist organizations remained deeply patriarchal movements. As Richard Stites writes in relation to the aftermath of the Russian Revolution:

> Male workers continued to resent the competition of females, and would do so long after the Revolution. Male leaders of the various Marxist factions had little interest in organizing women. Some opposed it as a waste of time, energy, and funds; others as smacking too much of mere feminism – a movement that was held in contempt by every self-respecting socialist, man or woman. (1978: 257)

It would be 50 years later before a rapprochement between the socialist and feminist discourses would occur.

Socialist feminism

When the great 'second wave' of feminism surged forward in the 1960s, alongside the liberal and radical feminism was socialist (sometimes marxist) feminism. It seemed at first rather bereft of counter-arguments to radical feminism's claim that marxism was, at least, gender blind. Dusty texts by Engels, Bebel and Lenin, and the forgotten lives of Zetkin and Kollontai, could hardly compete with the drive and originality of the Germaine Greers and Shulamith Firestones. Yet a socialist feminist political theory and practice was gradually constructed. It was in this context that the 'marriage' between marxism and feminism (referred to in the title of this chapter) emerged as a strategy. Marxism was usually the lead partner, as in Juliet Mitchell's drive in *Women's Estate* to 'ask the feminist questions but try to come up with some Marxist answers' (1971: 99). How successful these marxist answers were is now open to question. Furthermore, the whole proposal that feminism should melt into socialism also seems misconceived. However, from the late 1960s to the late 1980s these socialist feminist debates advanced our knowledge of gender oppression considerably.

What Engels bequeathed the modern socialist feminists was, above all, a view of capitalism and patriarchy, or class and gender, as autonomous systems. This is the 'dual systems' approach which runs through much of the socialist feminist discourse. There is an underlying assumption that capitalism creates the slots in the hierarchy of classes and workers, but it is gender (and race) which establishes who will fill these slots. The concept of patriarchy enters as a transhistorical and geographically universal construct to explain the domination of women by men. In some variants of this theory, capitalism is deemed dominant in the 'material' world, while patriarchy is seen as dominant ideologically. This would be the case for Juliet Mitchell's *Psychoanalysis and Feminism* (1974), where marxism appears as the explanation for class and psychoanalysis becomes the theory for the analysis of patriarchy. Another variant is Christine Delphy's view that there are two modes of production in contemporary society: 'The first mode of production gives rise to capitalist exploitation. The second gives rise to familiar, or more precisely, patriarchal exploitation' (1984: 69). All forms of dual systems theory are, to my mind, examples of Derrida's binary oppositions, they reproduce hierarchies, and they fail to contest the capitalo-centric logic of marxism, its productivist bias and its essential economism.

By the mid-1980s the critique of the dual systems approach had gained ground to such an extent that it was largely abandoned. As

Barbara Marshall says: 'There appears to be general agreement that analytically separating the ideological and the material is fruitless, and that capitalism and patriarchy are so interwoven as to be one and the same system' (1994: 84). One of the writers who developed the conception of a unified 'capitalist patriarchy' was Zillah Eisenstein, for whom capitalism and patriarchy are so interwoven as to make their analytical separation impracticable. Engels, we recall, brought patriarchy ('the world historic defeat of women') into the marxian system to account for gender oppression. Now it was being integrated with capitalist logic because, for Eisenstein, 'Capitalism uses patriarchy and patriarchy is defined by the needs of capital' (1979: 28). It now seems that patriarchy is totally subsumed under the logic of capitalism, dancing to its functional needs in a seamless logic. The concept of patriarchy itself had become deeply problematic by this stage. There was little agreement on its origins, its meaning and its effect. Nor was it clear whether it was independent from capitalism, interdependent in some ill-defined, perhaps symbiotic way, or simply a dependent functional variable of the 'needs' of capital.

The legacy of Marx himself on the question of gender was equally ambiguous because his actual writings on it were sparse, but he did leave the concept of 'reproduction', which was to play a key role in the development of the socialist feminist approach. The problematic of social reproduction to some extent overcame the economism of productivist marxism. There was now a dynamic, processual aspect to the marxist story of capitalist development. Gender could be integrated into this story and social reproduction could embrace sexual as much as class aspects. Gendered relations of domination and subordination could now be seen as integral to the reproduction of capitalist society. Yet there was a conceptual confusion at the heart of this new problematic because, as Edelholm, Harris and Young (1977) showed, it could mean social reproduction proper (that is, of the relations of production); reproduction of the labour force (the domestic economy and socialization coming in here); and the biological aspects of human reproduction. Women were involved in all three aspects of reproduction but there was a strange conflation of women's biological and social roles. Nor do we get any convincing explanation as to why women play the key roles that they do in reproduction, with the biological aspect always hovering around unmentioned.

In the reproduction of capitalist society, ideology is seen to have a crucial role. Socialist feminists correctly drew their distance from the economistic recipe of Engels that women's liberation depended on their entering the paid labour market.) The oppression of women was deeper-rooted than this and was seen to have strong ideological roots. So, as marxists gradually began to recognize that ideology was relatively inde-pendent (see Chapter 6) feminists saw that it was possible 'to accom-modate the oppression of women as a relatively autonomous element of the social formation' (Barrett, 1980: 31). A whole new area of critical feminist research opened up, focusing on the gendered construction of identities, the nature of familial ideologies and the submerged issues of feminine and masculine subjectivities. From this cultural turn came a much deeper understanding of the discursive construction of gender and, indeed, of feminism as a discursive movement. For this work to advance it was also, however, necessary to abandon marxism as an overarching framework because of its debilitating restriction by the base/superstructure division and its granting of, at best, 'relative auton-omy' to the ideological and cultural domains. This was another way in which socialist feminism created the conditions for the surpassment of orthodox marxism.

As the understanding of capitalism's gendered reproduction advanced, attention naturally turned and focused on the domestic economy, of which the 'domestic labour debate' was one result. If capitalism needed to reproduce its labour force, women could 'fit in' here, structurally as it were, because they bore, fed, clothed, educated, nursed and nurtured the workers the system needed. Domestic labour, which had previously been unseen, was now foregrounded. From being valorized politically or culturally, it was a short step to discuss the value of housework in terms of marxist economic categories. A long and convoluted digres-sion followed, on whether domestic labour could be considered pro-ductive in the marxist sense of producing surplus-value, or whether it was 'merely' unproductive labour. In retrospect, there was a quite unnecessary struggle to establish an orthodox marxist economic pedi-gree for women's oppression and value to capitalism. Even Lise Vogel, who remains committed to a marxist–feminist synthesis, admits that 'many in the women's movement regarded the debate (on domestic labour) as an obscure exercise in Marxist pedantry' (1983: 21). It was hard to see how the domestic labour debate could advance either an understanding of women's oppression (beyond making their domestic labour visible) or contribute to a strategy for overcoming it.

One strategy advanced in this regard was, of course, the famous 'Wages for Housework' campaign. From this perspective, as Valerie Bryson puts it, 'women should not enter the paid workforce as earlier Marxist analysis had suggested but they should demand that housework itself be paid for' (1992: 238). It would be easy to take up this analysis for its impracticality but this would not invalidate it as a 'transitional' political programme. It could also be said that it simply perpetuates the domestic drudgery of women, seeking only to normalize it through a wage. However, like ecofeminism, it could also be seen as an imaginative way of putting the capitalist state on the spot. It makes plainly visible to all the undervalued contribution of women to the continuance of human society. It also challenges the assumption that women have perhaps some innate affinity for domestic labour (like the 'nimble fingers' supposedly characteristic of female electronics operatives) by demanding a crude cash nexus. In realistic terms, the notion of 'Wages for Housework' also exposes the limitations of the type of female employment opportunities actually available to women today. That marxist categories are subverted in this rhetorical strategy would probably not be a problem for Marx himself.

In all these convoluted debates on the relationship between gender and class oppressions, there was the underlying issue of marxism's relationship with feminism. Socialist women obviously wanted to see some kind of rapprochement or, at least, friendly interaction. Marxism would help us understand the historical development of capitalism, and feminism would provide the critical insight into the relationship between men and women. Some marxists tried to show the usefulness of their categories to understanding the oppression of women. Some feminists tried to make marxism more useful to the half of humanity it tended to neglect. Yet if there ever was a 'marriage' of marxism and feminism it was, as Heidi Hartmann put it in a landmark article, 'like the marriage of husband and wife depicted in English common law: marxism and feminism are one, and that one is marxism' (1986: 2). Yet she did not do the obvious thing and sue for divorce but, rather, sought a more progressive union. Marxism's categories might be gender-blind but feminism, left to itself, tended to be ahistorical. However, what Hartmann called for – essentially a dual systems theory where capitalism and patriarchy were seen as independent but complementary forms of domination – seemed inadequate even for the time at which it was written.

The relationship between marxism and feminism became much worse than an unhappy marriage eventually. There was a growing realization, expressed for example by Sandra Harding, that marxist categories 'are fundamentally *sexist as well as sex-blind*' (1986: 137). If this was the case then, as Audre Lorde put it poetically, it followed that 'The master's house cannot be rebuilt with the master's tools' (Lorde, 1994). Too much of the masculinist marxist apparatus lay intact, too much of the marxist engagement with gender issues smacked of co-option. Perhaps the marxist construction of a 'woman question' could now be replaced and understood by the 'man question'. Men simply *did* have more to lose than their chains from the advance of feminism. The crisis of the patriarchal order across the West and the new feminist-influenced (at least) commonsense showed how far-reaching the issues were. Socialist feminist androgyny was being replaced by an unapologetic gynocentrism even by thinkers who saw its 'theoretical' flaws. For this new feminist politics: 'We are at the moment in history when women must seize the lead in creating a theory and practice which are truly scientific in that they are more comprehensively historical and materialist. Women are now the revolutionary group in history' (Harding, 1986).

The socialist feminist project was an ambitious one. For Michèle Barrett, in a landmark text, the object of 'Marxist feminism' (as she called it) was no less than 'to identify the operation of gender relations as and where they may be distinct from, or connected with, the processes of production and reproduction understood by historical materialism' (1980: 9). It sought to clarify and analyse the relationship between capitalism and the oppression of women. It changed the hitherto dominant socialist understanding of gender, sexuality and the household. It did not, however, succeed in its own terms of producing a new unified discourse of socialist (or marxist) feminism. Michèle Barrett herself, in a new edition of her text in 1988, admits that the marxist feminist analysis had largely failed and distanced herself from the original political project which it represented insofar as 'the arguments of postmodernism already represent, I think, a key position around which feminist theoretical work in the future is likely to revolve' (Barrett, 1988: xxiv). Feminism had not been co-opted by marxism, but had, rather, along with post-structuralism, destabilized some of its key tenets. As marxism's unity was shattered, so was that of socialist feminism. It is this new heterogeneous landscape of the postmodern/postmarxist feminisms which we now must turn to explore.

Postmodernism and feminisms

If marxism was thoroughly imbued with the spirit of modernism, as we have seen (Chapter 1), so, arguably, was feminism. The bid for sexual equality is 'modern' in its decisive break with 'traditional' notions of gender roles and inequalities. Modernity and the development of capitalism led to the breakup of a whole series of social relations once assumed to be frozen and immutable. The classical 'first wave' feminist texts were inserted into this process, which they both reflected and influenced. Modernity also promises that the arbitrary authority of the old order will no longer hold sway. This would mean, or could be made to mean, equality and not absolutist authority based on 'tradition' or religious prescriptions. Feminism is based equally on the notion of 'universal reason' central to the Enlightenment and modern politics. Feminism is also, and most eminently, a movement committed to the Enlightenment notions of 'autonomy' and 'emancipation'. It would seem natural in this context that feminism would line up with those political currents who believe in the 'incomplete project of modernity' (Habermas) and not with those radical 'postmodernists' who question, root and branch, the logic and the politics of modernism and Enlightenment. However, certain parallels and convergences between postmodernism and the now multiple feminisms can be located clearly.

Postmodernism has effectively challenged many fundamental and long-standing dichotomies essential to the Enlightenment way of thinking about the world. The separation between the subject and object of knowledge strengthens the feminist critique of male knowledge and recognizes that all knowledge is interpretative and positional. The Enlightenment duality of reason versus the irrational is also undermined by postmodernism in a way which parallels and strengthens the feminist critique of the 'Man of Reason'. Postmodernism has also undermined the modernist opposition of nature and culture, often associated with woman and man in the Enlightenment discourse and popular culture. This critique of the rationalist philosophy of science, at the heart of modernism, also feeds into the feminist critique of masculinist treatments of nature and science. A postmodern feminism would thus be in a good position to deconstruct the rationalist epistemology on which all dualist forms of thinking and knowing the world are based. As Susan Hekman argues: 'A postmodern feminism would reject the masculinist bias of rationalism but would not attempt to replace it with a feminist bias. Rather it would take the position that there is not one (masculine) truth but, rather, many truths, none of which is privileged along gender lines' (1992: 9). But would this not undermine the feminist movement?

Not only does postmodernism unsettle claims to truth or falsehood but would also undermine a unified subject such as 'woman' which is central to feminism as a political movement. The very notion of 'woman' from a postmodern (or poststructuralist) perspective would be 'essentialist' in that it posits a human 'essence'. For Chris Weedon, 'Humanist discourses presuppose an essence at the heart of the individual which is unique, fixed and coherent and which makes her what she is' (1987: 32). Thus radical feminism appeals to an 'essence of womanhood', liberal feminism believes in a unified, rational political consciousness from which women are excluded, and socialist feminism is based on a notion of a 'true human nature' which has been alienated by capitalism. Against these universal human subjects postmodernism conceives of the self as fluid and contingent, always the site of conflicting identities and subjectivities. The stress is on fragmentation and heterogeneity against the unifying homogenizing vision of modernism. The diversity covered by the word 'woman' has now largely been recognized and difference has been legitimized. The abstract universals of the Enlightenment were having a diminishing purchase in a feminist movement which was breaking up in the 1980s in spite of, or because of, its considerable successes.

Finally, if postmodernism is a critique or a suspicion of metanarratives, where does it leave socialist feminism as a political project? For Di Stefano 'the postmodernist project, if seriously adopted by feminists, would make any semblance of a feminist politics impossible' (Di Stefano, 1990: 76). This is a reference to the supposed relativism and political nihilism of postmodernism (see Chapter 8). It does seem odd that white Western males who supposedly have a unified confident subjectivity should now deny to women the possibility of a subject-centred politics. However, it is also possible to discern the potentially enabling aspects of postmodernism for a radical/socialist feminist practice. Grand narratives of emancipation can be seen as potentially oppressive and their false universalism can be extremely ethnocentric. With its reliance on gender as the main, if not sole, variable in its social theory, classical feminism can suffer from the binary opposition it was seeking to undo. Postmodernism frees feminism from the futile search for an essential female nature: 'It would replace unitary notions of woman and feminine gender identity with plural and complexly constructed conceptions of social identity, treating gender as one relevant strand among others, attending also to class, race, ethnicity, age, and sexual orientation' (Fraser and Nicholson, 1990: 34–5).

If we are to locate a political point in which the coherence of feminism was shattered and postmodern feminism emerged, it would be the eruption of black and Third World feminism. If marxism was gender-blind, much of the 1970s feminism appeared to be race-blind. The 'woman' it refered to seemed Western, white and middle class.

bell hooks argued eloquently (1991) that the origins of the feminist movement inevitably shaped its agenda. Black women 'could be heard only if our statements echoed the sentiment of the dominant discourse' (ibid.: 11–12). If gender differences are seen as primordial and always paramount then, inevitably, racial differences and oppressions are seen as secondary. The liberal feminist rhetoric of equality was itself seen as problematic: was this white woman also to be equal with white men, or were black women also to be equal with white women? Black critiques of white feminism (see hooks, 1994 and Collins, 1991, for example) not only question its false universalizing tendencies but also draw attention to the arena of representation and ideology, where the ideal-type feminine image is invariably white. It would be a mistake to take from this literature only the accusation of racism, which can then foreground once again the white theorist 'working through' their racism. It should help to decentre white Western feminism from its hegemonic pedestal, though.

By the 1990s, gender was a legitimate area of enquiry in the academy. As Chandra Mohanty argues 'the crucial questions of the 1990s concern the construction, examination and, most significantly, the institutionalization of difference *within* feminist discourses' (1992: 74). The challenges from black and Third World feminisms posed questions for feminism's assumed unity and universality, but also pointed towards a more differentiated politics of transformation. It was no longer possible to believe, as Robin Morgan and others had, in 'global sisterhood' (Morgan, 1984) with women granted a cross-cultural coherence and unity they patently did not have. Third World feminisms had for long advanced by paths quite different from Western feminism. Issues of ethnicity, rurality and nationalism loomed larger than the 'personal politics' that dominated some strands of Western feminism. Then black feminism and working-class feminism showed that even feminism in the West was a mansion with many houses. The stories of these feminisms cannot be simply subsumed under the generic labels deployed in the standard Western texts, such as 'liberal', 'radical' and 'socialist'. Here was a difference which could not be so easily accommodated. They were not just a distant, alien 'Other' to serve as a useful comparison.

White Western feminism did try at first to marginalize colonial and post-colonial women by constructing the monolithic category of 'Third World women', which homogenized and, ultimately, obliterated difference. Chandra Mohanty has shown in considerable detail how 'Western feminist writing on women in the third world subscribes to a variety of methodologies to demonstrate the universal cross-cultural operation of male dominance and female exploitation' (1993: 208–9). Women in Third World countries are often perceived as helpless victims of male violence, as dependent in gender, race and class relationships, and as subordinates in familial and religious ideologies. Third World women are subsumed under these various oppressions, they are seen as devoid of voice, incapable of agency and virtually without history, always already colonized. This blatant ethnocentrism has recently been challenged in the literature on the interface of gender, development and postmodernism. Paternalism towards the 'non-Western' peoples has a long history in the Enlightenment tradition. It is not surprising that it has permeated much of Western feminism. Now, however, women in the Third World are beginning to set their own agendas, which can only strengthen feminism as a whole (because there can be unity in diversity).

The rise of black and Third World feminism was part of a broader process of debate and fission within the feminist movement. Where modernist feminism stressed 'equality', for example, the new postmodern feminist discourse stressed 'difference'. The belief in a transcendental Reason was giving way to a more culturally situated understanding of people's positions and possibilities. Large-scale intellectual and political projects for political transformation lacked credibility or even attractiveness. This was all part of a broad shift in paradigms in feminist theory in the 1980s. Yet, with just some hindsight, it is easy to see how new false polarities can be created, binary oppositions which can only divide. Joan Scott argues eloquently that the equality/difference opposition should be refused in the name of an equality based precisely on differences: 'the antithesis itself hides the interdependence of the two terms, for equality is not the elimination of difference, and difference does not preclude equality' (1990: 138).

It has been argued that the great feminist slogan of the 1960s and early 1970s 'the personal is political' has actually backfired insofar as the new 'politics of identity' has 'meant women found they had less, not more in common and a bitterness developed in the will to discover who had the most "authentic" voice in the women's movement' (Whelan, 1995: 129–30). The new notion of 'speaking from one's position' could actually become an excuse for not confronting hierarchy, racism, homophobia and other forms of oppression. The new tone is captured by a statement from a women's collective in the US which argued that: 'This focusing on our own oppression is embodied in the conception of identity politics. We believe that the most profound and potentially the most radical politics come out of our own identity, as opposed to working to end somebody else's oppression' (Comabhee River Collective, 1981, cited in Adams, 1994: 345). Not only is there a considerable accommodation to the rampant individualism of the New Right which set the tone for much of the 1980s, but a return to the old essentialism, as if 'experience' were something unambiguous and transparent from which the 'right' politics would spontaneously and naturally flow.

It is now possible, and necessary, to move beyond 'equality' and 'difference' and other such oppositions. From a postmodern perspective the notion of 'equality' is problematic insofar as it assumes that it is equals that are being dealt with, which from a feminist perspective can mean simple assimilation to the male norm. That 'equality' is not 'innocent' does not mean that a postmodern feminism turns its back on justice. Even those feminist currents which stress difference against the Anglo-American emphasis on equality do strive for 'a different conception of justice conceived as an equal liberty to shape oneself in accordance with whatever differences one finds significant' (Buck and James, 1992: 7). Sexual difference cannot, from this perspective, be subsumed under a bland conception of gender equality or, to put it differently, gender neutrality cannot lead to justice. In practice, neither an appeal to an undifferentiated equality nor an undifferentiated difference can suffice. Equality certainly needs deconstructing from the perspective of the various feminisms (including Third World feminisms) but, following Moira Gatens, 'to understand "difference feminism" as the obverse of "equality feminism" would be to miss entirely the point' (1992: 135). To recognize a multiplicity of differences is to open the door for a more pluralist politics of transformation.

6

Superstructure's Revenge: Marxism and Culture

Culture has made a remarkable move in the story of marxism from dependent, determined and subordinate part of the 'superstructure' of society (the economy being the 'base') to centre-stage in the new marxist cultural studies and, even more, in forms of marxism influenced by postmodernism. This chapter begins with Karl Marx's own engagement with culture and ideology, emphasizing the ambiguous legacy it left. It then turns to the post-Russian Revolution attempt by marxist cultural theorists to create a socialist culture, including the Soviet Proletkult movement. Any ambiguity in the marxist discourse is dissipated as culture is recruited to fight the class struggle. Then Antonio Gramsci, from his jail cell in Mussolini's Italy, began to break away from marxist determinism in regard to culture. The culturalist turn in marxism had begun, and its effects are still being felt today. Finally, this chapter turns to postmodernism and poststructuralism, which finally broke culture away from the orthodox marxist grip. The 'superstructure' had its revenge, but where does this leave a critical study of culture in society today?

Marx and ideology

Marx was no philistine and had a highly developed appreciation of the culture of his day, especially literature:

> In his private life Marx constantly demonstrates the way in which literature may embellish, enliven and heighten existence ... He reads tales and poems with his children ... He declaims aloud poems and dramas in several languages ... He characterizes his acquaintances by means of literary nicknames ... As a public figure too, as author and

as orator Marx constantly draws on the writers of the past and present whose work he admires. (Prawer, 1978: 415)

Indeed, S. S. Prawer spends 444 pages describing Karl Marx's intense relationship with world literature. Marx the writer certainly understood the creative process and would not dream of reducing it to impersonal class or economic determinations. Marx's taste in literature was quite traditional and he probably would not have liked the Latin American 'magical realism' texts, but there was nothing crude, instrumental or reductionist in his approach to literature. The problem lies in that literature, and culture more generally, fit within the broader understanding Marx developed of bourgeois society.

Where culture fitted into the marxist system was in the box called 'ideology'. Marx argued famously in the 1859 Preface to *A Contribution to the Critique of Political Economy* that: 'a distinction should always be made between the material transformation of the economic conditions of production, which can be determined with the precision of a natural science, and the legal, political, religious, aesthetic or philosophic – in short, ideological forms in which men become conscious and fight it out' (Marx, 1968: 182). This is a broad conception of ideology and one which, in its last manifesto-like sentence prefigures the concerns of the new cultural politics. Ideology is not seen here as simple misperception, illusion or clever bourgeois ruse. Yet there is no agreed or consistent version of Marx's theory of ideology which, elsewhere, did appear as a defective perception of reality (see Larrain, 1983). What does seem clear is that Marx counterposes, as in the above passage, science or knowledge more broadly with ideology. The truth claims of the marxist conception of science and knowledge are as evident – witness marxism as the science of historical materialism – as they are contested.

Foucault cut across much of the convoluted marxist debates on science and ideology in a few lines:

The notion of ideology appears to me to be difficult to make use of for three reasons. The first is that, like it or not, it always stands in virtual opposition to something which is supposed to count as truth. Now I believe that the problem does not consist in drawing the line between that in a discourse which falls under the category of scientificity or truth, and that which comes under some other category, but in seeing *historically* how effects of truth are produced within discourses which in themselves are neither true nor false. (Foucault, 1980: 118)

Even in its own terms the science/ideology couplet is dubious when we consider the close imbrication of the natural sciences, say biotechnology, with the political and ideological realms. Of course Foucault's objection is a more sweeping one which cuts the ground from under all assumed privileged vantage points, be they white, male or marxist. The banishing of epistemology may not be as simple as Foucault's practically throwaway comment in an interview implied. However, it is a telling critique of one of the fundamental tenets of marxism, and Marxism–Leninism in particular, namely its claim to scientificity.

It is interesting to recall that Louis Althusser had begun 'to wonder whether art should or should not be ranked as such among ideologies, to be precise, whether art and ideology are one and the same thing' (1984: 173). Thankfully, he concludes that '*I do not rank real art among the ideologies*, although art does have a quite particular and specific relation with ideology' (ibid.). This 'authentic' art, not to be confused with the 'average or mediocre', does not seek to replace 'scientific knowledge' but does help us 'see' or 'feel'. What we see, feel or perceive is the ideology from which this non-popular art is born, according to Althusser. He also praises Lenin's critical analysis of Tolstoy (dubbed 'brilliant' by Terry Eagleton), in particular that the literary 'greats' are able partially to detach themselves or step outside the ideology which bathes them in a particular political light. In his conception of ideology as 'lived relation' between people and ideology, Althusser moved beyond mechanical marxism. In his willingness to let art out of the science/ideology binary opposition he was also helpful. Yet, Althusser remained trapped, to a large extent, in the orthodox marxist architectural analogy of society as base and superstructure.

Raymond Williams, in his *Marxism and Literature*, has written that 'Any modern approach to a Marxist theory of culture must begin by considering the proposition of a determining base and a determined super-structure' (1977: 75). For Marx, there are relations of production which constitute 'the economic structure of society, the real foundation, on which rises a legal and political superstructure' (Marx, 1968: 182). In a typical logocentric manoeuvre we have the economic/real/material/primary/determinant on the one hand and the non-economic/non-material/determined on the other hand. Whether Marx would have wished it or not, the base/superstructure became central in the marxist apparatus and, in particular, where cultural analysis is concerned. Thus Terry Eagleton, who is by no stretch of the imagination a mechanical marxist, can write that: 'Art, then, is for Marxism part of the "superstructure" of society. It is (with qualifications we shall make later) part of society's ideology' (1976: 5). The trouble with these qualifications – such as the notion that the economic base is (only) determinant 'in the last instance' is that that lonely hour never seems to come.

It was Althusser, of course, who pushed the base/superstructure analogy furthest and disputed the notion expressed by Engels (not Marx) that the economy was determinant 'in the last instance'. For Althusser, there was clearly a 'relative autonomy' for the areas usually described by marxism as superstructure. Althusser developed instead the notions of 'structure in dominance', 'articulation', and, above all, 'overdetermination', which implied that all social phenomena have complex causation mechanisms and cannot be reduced to unidirectional causation by any 'base'. Since then, one-time followers of Althusser such as Paul Hirst (1979) have abandoned the whole notion of causality and autonomy (autonomy from what ?). The fact remains that Althusser's critique of the totality-based theorizing of traditional marxism had an enabling effect on critical cultural studies in general and on literary and film studies in particular. The problem was, as Michèle Barrett puts it, 'Althusser's recasting of Marx pushed Marxism further than it can logically go' (1991: 45). What Althusser's intervention in marxism achieved, notwithstanding his 'scientific' intentions, was to liberate marxism from its Second International shackles as regards the idea that culture, for example, could be seen as a simple 'reflection' of the economic relations of production in society.

It is hard to overestimate the damage done by the base/superstructure topographical analogy to the possibility of a marxist theory of culture. It is not only the question of economic reductionism, which is debilitating in itself to any critical cultural work, but the implicit reproduction of the idealist separation of culture from supposedly material social life. Thus, as Raymond Williams says 'the full possibilities of the concept of culture as a constitutive social process, creating specific and different "ways of life" ... were for a long time missed, and were often in practice superseded by an abstract unilinear universalism' (1977: 19). Rather than move into 'cultural materialism' as Raymond Williams did, most marxist cultural theorizing was hampered and restricted by the notion that arts, customs, religion and so on were simply 'ideas'. We could say that the enterprise undertaken by Williams in this regard was more in keeping with the critical spirit of Marx than the mechanical elaboration of subsequent marxist theories of culture and even the marxist literary critics, notwithstanding their considerable impact in the field of literary studies itself.

Having deconstructed Marx's concepts of ideology and the super-structure, where does it leave a marx(ist) theory of culture? Marx did not develop such a theory and some of his isolated formulations have created some quite horrible offspring. Christopher Caudwell, the British marxist critic of the 1930s, was one 'who heroically attempted to construct a total Marxist aesthetics in notably unpropitious conditions', according to contemporary marxist literary critic Terry Eagleton (1976: 79). In his *Studies on a Dying Culture* Caudwell saw all branches of 'bourgeois culture', from art and philosophy to biology and physics, undergoing a fundamental crisis. His main work, *Illusion and Reality* (Caudwell, 1973), is seen, even by his admirers, as a somewhat crude and slipshod attempt at creating a total theory of art as an economic activity arising from the labour process. It is not the individual Shakespeare or Wordsworth who writes poetry, for Caudwell, but the man-class, or genotype. In his *Romance and Realism* (Caudwell, 1970), he moves on to the terrain of 'socialist realism' (see the next section of this chapter) and proclaims that revolutionary truth is foreclosed to 'fellow travellers' and even accuses the likes of Stephen Spender of 'an anxious solicitude about the freedom of the writer' in the USSR, not realizing that 'whatever methods are necessary for a social transformation must be necessary in art' (ibid.: 132). That Caudwell died fighting fascism in Spain symbolizes both the high and the low points of Stalinism.

Another 'powerful and original study which analyses the relations between Marx's aesthetic views and his general theory' is, according to Eagleton (1976: 86), Mikhail Lifschitz, also writing in the 1930s. Lifschitz, a Russian critic, seeks to draw a parallel between Marx's analysis of the contradiction between the development of the forces of production and the relations of production and a 'contradiction between the development of the productive forces of society and its artistic achievement, between technology and art, between science and poetry, between tremendous cultural possibilities and meagre spiritual life' (Lifschitz, 1973: 106). For him, the objective of marxism is not only the abolition of the contradiction between mental and manual labour, and that between oppressor and oppressed, but also the creation of an unalienated universal culture. For Lifschitz, the marxist view of the development of art and culture is clear: 'Decadence of artistic creation is inseparable from bourgeois civilization' (ibid.: 99) but Marx and Engels 'knew full well that a new cycle of artistic progress can begin only with the victory of the proletariat…only then can all the forces now exhausted by capitalist oppression be liberated' (ibid.: 114–15). Basically, the interpretation of Marx by Lifschitz argues that through creating a new society, the proletariat will resolve the contradictions of the cultural development of humanity.

It is Terry Eagleton himself who, undoubtedly, has sought to create the most coherent modern marxist theory of literature (the 'cultural materialism' of Raymond Williams being a much more explicit departure from Marx). For Eagleton:

> To understand *King Lear*, *The Dunciad* or *Ulysses* is ... to do more than interpret their symbolism, study their literary history and add footnotes about sociological facts which enter into them. It is first of all to understand the complex, indirect relations between those works and the ideological worlds they inhabit. (1976: 6)

Marxist cultural critics need to examine the historical conditions which give rise to cultural products. This is not the same as a view of literature or culture as nothing but ideology, a form of 'vulgar Marxist' criticism Eagleton is keen to dismiss. Eagleton follows Lukács in arguing that 'the true bearers of ideology in art are the very forms, rather than abstractable content, of the work itself' (ibid.: 24). Thus developments in literary form, for example the novel, can be traced to shifts in ideology which lead to new ways of perceiving social reality and the new relations between culture and society. At the end of the day, in the last instance, and in the last sentences of Terry Eagleton's punchy review of marxism and literary criticism: 'Marxist criticism is not just an alternative technique for interpreting *Paradise Lost* or *Middlemarch*. It is part of our liberation from oppression, and that is why it is worth discussing' (ibid.: 76).

Proletkult

For Lenin: 'Every artist, who considers himself an artist, has a right to create freely according to his ideals, regardless of anything. But then, we communists cannot stand idly by and give chaos free rein to develop' (Solomon [ed.], 1979: 166). Where Marx's own cultural outlook would have been liberal, Lenin's was sternly functional: why, for example, should the Soviet state provide an expensive subsidy to the Bolshoi Theatre 'when we haven't enough money to maintain the most ordinary schools in the villages'? (ibid.: 166). In this atmosphere it was not surprising that in post-revolutionary Russia a cultural movement called Proletkult emerged, committed to the creation of a purely proletarian culture purged of all bourgeois components. At its height in 1920, Proletkult had some 84,000 members, published an influential review, *Proletarian Culture*, organized some 300 writing workshops across the country, and controlled thousands of amateur companies and theatres in small towns and villages. How successful was this move to 'Bolshevize' culture? Was Lifschitz accurate in stating that 'the communist revolution of the working class lays the necessary basis for a new renaissance of the arts on a much broader and higher basis' (1973: 101)? If not, why not?

The Russian Revolution of 1917 led to a great ferment in the cultural domain. Osip Briz, one of the main theorists of the Futurists, wrote of how the new art would break completely with bourgeois art, it would create new and unprecedented things, Futurism and the proletariat would march hand in hand (Struve, 1972: 20). The great poet Mayakovsky threw his lot in with the proletarian revolution and sang its praises. While Lenin liked some of his satirical anti-Western work and even his anti-bureaucratic tirades, on the whole he preferred the old school of Pushkin and company. Alongside the Futurists, Proletkult was set up to foster a specifically proletarian literature. Its guiding spirit was Bogdanov, with whom Lenin had a famous philosophical controversy (*Materialism and Empirio-Criticism*) in pre-revolutionary times. For Bogdanov cultural action was a crucial component for building socialism. The first Soviet Commissar of Education (or 'Enlightenment'), Anatolii Lunacharsky, while sympathetic towards Futurism and the Proletkult movement, was warning the cultural far left in 1919 that it should not have a fully negative and alternative attitude towards the culture of the past, and that it should not seek to speak for the government while it was only an artistic current (ibid.: 29).

It was this last point – implicitly contesting Bolshevik hegemony – which brought down the wrath of Lenin and other Bolshevik leaders. In 1920 the Central Committee of the Communist Party issued a declaration on Proletkult which, among other things, said that 'Under the guise of "proletarian culture" the workers were offered bourgeois views in philosophy (Machism) and in the cultural field absurd, perverted tastes (Futurism) began to find favour' (Vaughan James, 1973: 114). Well, the techniques and methods of the new 'proletarian poets' were derivative of Symbolism, with a strong dash of romantic heroism, but this was hardly the problem for a state under seige. The problem was, as the Central Committee made explicit, that the 'decadents', 'idealists' and 'drop outs' of Futurism seemed to be directing Proletkult, which 'continued to be "independent", but now this was "independence" of the Soviet regime' (ibid.). Trotsky, for his part, was against total Party control of the arts and also opposed the notion of a specifically 'proletarian' culture. However, Trotsky's own conception of marxism and culture was quite mechanistic, seeing art as simply a passive reflection of the social order, and postponing the cultural advancement of the people until some unspecified date in the future when they had 'caught up' and classes had been abolished.

The Proletkult initiative was followed in 1925 by the formation of the Russian Association of Proletarian Writers (RAPP) committed to 'proletarianizing' Russian literature, while, against Proletkult, stressing the need to 'learn from the classics'. As the Russian peasantry was being forcibly collectivized, so would RAPP assert the hegemony of the proletariat in the cultural domain. For RAPP's leading light, Leopold Averbakh, only the proletariat could create an art that was in harmony with the new way of life, and hence class warfare was required in culture as much as in the countryside. By 1929 Stalin was encouraging RAPP to take on the 'fellow travellers' – non-communist but sympathetic cultural workers – and thus purge the cultural domain of 'non-proletarian' elements. Literature must be placed at the service of the Five Year Plan. Writers were to become 'shock workers'. These 'excesses' were condemned belatedly by the Party in 1932 and the dissolution of RAPP was ordered. While it seemed that more moderate 'popular front'-type policies in culture would now apply, the grip of the Party actually tightened. Some of the sorriest episodes in so-called marxist dealings with culture would now take place.

While in exile in 1905 Lenin had written about the party press and the need for a party line by its writers. The formulations are categorical: 'Literature must become *part* of the common sense of the proletariat, "a cog and screw" of one single great Social-Democratic mechanism … Down with non-partisan writers! Down with literary supermen!' (cited in Vaughan James, 1973: 104). Against all concessions to 'bourgeois individualism', the socialist proletariat demanded 'party literature'. Yet this was not a crass call for censorship of all the arts: 'Calm yourselves [said Lenin] … ! First of all, we are discussing party literature and its subordination to party control. Everyone is free to write and say whatever he likes, without any restrictions' (cited ibid.: 16). Whether Lenin would have approved or not is impossible to tell, but around 1928–9 the Bolshevik Party used these early statements to legitimize a naked subordination of cultural workers to the party diktat. By 1932 all existing workers' organizations were 'liquidated' by party decree and a single state-run body, the infamous Union of Soviet Writers, was set up, which would henceforth regulate professionally, ideologically and morally all Russian writers.

As the party of 'Marxism–Leninism' moved to take over the cultural domain, it obviously needed to discipline the 'fellow travellers'. In 1929 a volume entitled *Literature of Fact*, edited by N. Chuzhak, declared that fiction was but 'opium of the people' to be countered by factual literature, which would lead to the 'concretizing', 'activizing' and 'rationalizing' of literature (Struve, 1972: 216). Art had nothing to do with inspiration, it was simply a skill to be learned. At the 1939 First Congress of Soviet Writers (of which more later) Karl Radek could declare without a hint of irony: 'I don't write novels, but if I did I think I would learn how to write them from Tolstoy and Balzac, not from Joyce' (cited ibid., 1972: 275). The watchword of this period was 'social command', which meant that art would be obliged to 'mirror' social reality and 'encourage' socialist transformation. Gorky, a writer of some repute, sponsored a massive *Histories of Factories and Plants* during this period, one of the volumes of which 'celebrated' the building of the Stalin Canal linking the Baltic to the White Sea, built on the basis of forced labour by common-law criminal and political prisoners. The effects on creativity and cultural freedom of this type of venture would be dramatic, of course.

As literature became handmaiden of the state, so the confidence of the new cultural commissars increased. In his inaugural address to the First Congress of Soviet Writers held in 1934 Zhdanov, the new culture supremo, declared proudly that 'Our Soviet literature is not afraid of being accused of tendentiousness. Yes, Soviet literature *is* tendentious, for in the age of class struggle a nonclass, nontendentious, would-be apolitical literature does not and cannot exist' (cited in Struve, 1972: 261). Led by the great 'Comrade Stalin', socialism had triumphed and Soviet literature was the greatest and most progressive in the world. Soviet culture was 'optimistic' because it was linked to the rising class of the proletariat. Cultural workers, for Zhdanov, should be 'engineers of human minds', provide uplighting and heroic tales, and not divert people towards impossible utopias. This was to be a new cultural philosophy, Socialist Realism, portraying reality 'objectively' and assisting the great masses to understand history and their role in it. The 1934 Congress paid special attention to the need to produce 'national defence literature' to boost the fighting spirit of the glorious Red Army. Literature would serve the people/party/army from now on.

What is not always so obvious, even to leftist critics of Soviet cultural terrorism, is the deep psycho-sexual implications of these moves towards control. Maynard Solomon is one critic who understands that 'it was inevitable that Zhdanov's and Radek's 1934 call for Socialist

Realism coincided precisely with cancellation of the liberal abortion and divorce laws, with passage of strict laws against homosexuality and with the arrest of a large number of homosexuals among the intelligentsia, accused of conspiracy with the Roehm Nazis' (Solomon, 1979: 239). Zhdanovism became a fanatical bulwark against all forms of 'irrationality', by which was meant any deviation from 'normal human emotions'. Not only were 'paranoics', 'schizophrenics' and 'gangsters' to be targeted, but also 'pimps', 'adulterers', 'chorus girls' and, quaintly, 'rogues'. Thus, it is not surprising that Karl Radek launched a vicious attack on James Joyce at the 1934 Congress for his 'madhouse phantasmagorias' and 'delirious ravings', as a writer with a small view of life– 'no great events, no great people, no great ideas' – and whose writing was simply 'a heap of dung, teeming with worms' (cited in Struve, 1973: 173). Thus so-called Socialist Realism made its intellectual mark on world culture.

As the grip of Stalinism tightened over Soviet society, so did its control over culture in all its manifestations. Successive party decrees between 1946 and 1948 meant that:

> the Soviet creative intelligentsia lived in a constant state of fear, and the political demands made on writers were so excessive as to destroy even the propaganda value of literature. Socialist realists were now required to ignore the grim realities of Soviet postwar life and present instead fanciful pictures of material abundance and social harmony. (Hayward, 1983: 65)

Socialist Realism had become a straightforward means of bureaucratic and administrative control of culture by the state. Even allowing for the hostility of the cold war critics of the Soviet state's dealings with writers, the picture is a grim one indeed and a travesty of anything Marx ever said on culture. It is said that Stalin himself coined the phrase 'Socialist Realism' while attending an artistic soirée at Gorky's flat, where he intervened to end a discussion between proponents of 'proletarian realism', 'tendentious realism' and 'monumental realism':

'If the artist is going to depict our life correctly, he cannot fail to observe and point out what is leading it towards socialism. So this will be socialist art. It will be socialist realism' (Vaughan James, 1973: 86).

As Soviet culture went on to decline, and many of its more radical exponents were executed, accused of being 'Trotskyite'/'Zionist'/whatever agents, there were few voices left to denounce this cultural terror. Many 'fellow travellers' abroad felt it best to go along with things, for whatever reason. Lukács did in the 1950s apply a subtle critique to this regime, which reversed Marx's view of uneven development to claim that Soviet cultural evolution unfortunately lagged behind its dynamic economic development. However, as Henri Arvon recounts, 'immediately thereafter Lukács is obliged to retract his statement, and in a most humiliating way moreover, for he is forced to attribute what he now describes as his errors of judgement to his lack of familiarity with Soviet literature' (1973: 93). State control of culture and ideological control over the schools, forms and techniques of art culminate perhaps in the 1946 Central Committee proclamation on literature: 'The function of Soviet literature is to aid the State in properly educating young people... That is why everything that tends to foster... "Art for Art's sake" is foreign to Soviet literature and is harmful to the interests of the people and the Soviet State' (cited in Arvon, 1973: 91).

The Gramscian turn

From the embarrassing excesses of Zdhanovism, we can turn to the fresh air brought to the marxist debates on culture by Antonio Gramsci. From an attempt (largely successful) at closure, we turn to a desire (eventually successful) for openness. Against all variants of economism and reductionism Gramsci comes to symbolize an open, fluid, less 'necessitarian' brand of marxism. Of course, his dispersed, difficult, practically coded prison notebooks do not amount to a 'Gramscian' system of thought. In that, I would disagree with the assertion of Renate Holub (in what is nevertheless a remarkable book on Gramsci 'beyond' marxism and postmodernism) that Gramsci's 'research programme' was 'to write a definitive Marxist cultural theory' (1992: 40). The Gramsci industry has produced a variety of Gramscis, not all of which are plausible versions. Gramsci has also been 'used' quite literally to justify particular political or cultural positions. Yet in all the Gramscis and Gramscianisms there is an understanding that classical marxism neglected culture and had a mechanical conception of how people lived their lives and contested the oppressive conditions under which they lived. The plasticity of Gramsci's marxism, perhaps inevitably, become a stepping stone to post-marxism, as we shall shortly see.

Antonio Gramsci broke decisively with the mechanistic marxist tendency to take literally the base/superstructure analogy of how societies work. For Gramsci: 'The claim, presented as an essential postulate of historical materialism, that every fluctuation of politics and ideology can be presented and expounded as an immediate expression of the structure, must be contested in theory as primitive infantilism, and combated in practice' (1971: 407). It was in a critique of Bukharin's *Popular Manual* of historical materialism that Gramsci most explicitly rejected the claims to Marx's authority of the subsequent 'scientific' renderings of his thought. Gramsci derided the attempt to reduce Marx to the search for 'so-called laws' typical of the new 'Marxist–Leninist–Stalinist' positivism. Necessity and determination were not terms with which Gramsci was happy. In an explicit rejection of economism in particular, Gramsci wrote of Bukharin's work that: 'One of the most blatant traces of old-fashioned metaphysics in the *Popular Manual* is the attempt to reduce everything to a single ultimate or final cause' (ibid.: 437). This reference to determination 'in the last instance' by the economic base (or structure) of society Gramsci places, appropriately, in the long line of attempts to 'search for God'.

In relation to the concept of ideology, Gramsci developed one strand of Marx's contradictory accounts, namely that which has become known as the 'positive' as against the 'critical' view of ideology (see Larrain, 1983). For Gramsci, ideology is neither an 'illusion' nor a simple 'reflection' of an economic process. Instead, it is, above all, a contested terrain, a key arena for political struggle. Gramsci usefully distinguishes between two types of ideology: 'philosophy', which refers to organized sets of conceptions about the world; and 'common sense', by which he refers to the lived culture of particular social classes or groups. As ideology is no longer just an illusory representation of what is happening in the economic 'base', Gramsci is free to prioritize the political struggle over ideas and culture. As Michèle Barrett puts it: 'Gramsci sees what is now generally called "ideological struggle" as politically effective and significant in its own right' (1991: 28). His understanding of 'common sense' or popular culture is typically nuanced, accepting that, while these contain 'ideological elements' (in the negative sense), they also contain much 'good sense'. What emerges from this contested terrain depends on agency above all, and cannot be predetermined.

What is undoubtedly the central and most influential of Gramsci's concepts in following this through is that of 'hegemony'. Gramsci understands that no ruling class rules through coercion alone. Briefly, for Gramsci, *egemonia* refers to the social and cultural organization of consent in society: 'if the ruling class has lost its consensus, it is no longer "leading", but only "dominant", exercising coercive force alone, this means precisely that the great masses have become detached from their traditional ideologies' (Gramsci, 1971: 275–6). The hegemony of a given social group over society as a whole is achieved through a wide range of institutions within civil society such as schools, the church, the media and even trade unions. Not only does this conception of contemporary capitalist society redress the balance from Lenin's focus on the coercive element of state power, but it lays the basis for a cultural programme of social transformation. If in Lenin's Russia a 'war of manoeuvre' may have been appropriate, in Gramsci's Italy a 'war of position' was called for. Where one advocated the seizure of state power in a politics akin to trench warfare, the latter moved towards a subtle analysis of how 'hearts and minds' are won in contemporary capitalist societies and emphasizes the need for broad popular consensus around a transformation project.

Where Gramsci's ideas have probably been most creatively taken up has been in relation to the 'national–popular'. Though developed in various ways (see Forgas, 1984) this couplet generally refers to the formation of a 'historic bloc' in society which unites national and popular aspirations. It forms the basis for a cultural policy for social transformation and also for a more directly political strategy of a 'post-class' popular-democratic struggle. It is thus the site on which bourgeois hegemony operates and on which popular hegemony might be constructed. For Gramsci, for example, Catholicism needed to be understood in all its complexity and not simply wished away by a secular, socialist hegemonic project. He also understood, 'the role which Fascism played in Italy in "hegemonizing" the backward character of the national popular culture … and refashioning it into a reactionary national formation, with a genuine popular basis and support' (Hall, 1996b: 439). This subtle, open-ended engagement with the national–popular, and in particular its discursive construction, was followed through by Stuart Hall, among others, in his original analyses of 'Thatcherism', which grasped some of its popular appeal and refused the easy option of 'false consciousness' or 'reflection' of economic transformations.

In terms of the production of that prolific field of study now known as 'cultural studies' Gramsci was a watershed. As Stuart Hall recalls, in his account of the emergence of cultural studies in the 1970s, while Gramsci belonged to the problematic of marxism, 'his importance for … cultural studies is precisely the degree to which he radically *displaced* some of the inheritances of marxism in cultural studies' (Hall, 1996a: 267). We have seen how far removed Gramsci was from earlier marxist cultural theorists in breaking with the mechanical base/superstructure distinctions and in understanding the autonomy of the political and ideological/cultural domains. The new cultural paradigm which emerged focused particularly on the 'way of life' of particular social groups, their 'common sense' and their sense of agency. In Althusser, ideologies are seen to 'interpellate' (hail or address) a 'subject' but, as Richard Johnson reminds us, that 'subject' is never naked: 'Outside some structuralist texts, the "lonely hour" of the unitary, primary, primordial and cultureless interpellation "never comes". Ideologies always work upon a *ground*: that ground is *culture*' (1979: 234). Cultural studies may later, in the 1980s, have become institutionalized and depoliticized (see Davies, 1995), but if it did no more than remind us of this it would have served a useful function for a marxist understanding of culture and society.

Gramsci was also a key figure in that other flourishing area of study known as postcolonial studies (see Ashcroft, Griffith and Tiffin [eds], 1995). Its origins can be traced back to Edward Said's *Orientalism* (1985) which examined how the West had constructed the Orient as an object of knowledge and domination. *Orientalism* shows how Western cultures 'make representations of foreign cultures, the better to master or in some way control them' (ibid.: 120). Central to *Orientalism* is the Gramscian concept of 'hegemony' and the role of intellectuals in constructing and reproducing it. Orientalism is shown by Said to be a hegemonic Western discourse, a 'cultural and political fact'. While aware that 'most attempts to rub culture's nose in the mud of politics have been crudely iconoclastic' (ibid.: 210) Said has, in *Orientalism* but particularly in his subsequent *Culture and Imperialism* (1993), begun to fill an enormous gap in bringing these two domains together. *Orientalism* has been criticized for producing an over-monolithic, totalizing or over-hegemonic view of this discourse and for neglecting or downplaying agency or resistance. Nevertheless, it more or less single-handedly brought postcolonialism to the fore as a dynamic new area of critical cultural studies.

Another related 'Gramscian' area of study is that of 'subaltern studies', which emerged in India but also had a significant influence in Latin America. For the Subaltern Studies Group, Gramsci's concept of subaltern is taken 'as a name for the general attribute of subordination in South Asian society whether this is expressed in terms of class, race, age, gender and office or in any other way' (Guha [ed.], 1982: vii). Colonial history always ignored the politics of the people, and subaltern activity in particular. The subaltern studies approach stresses cultural autonomy, authenticity and consciousness, and thus is very much in the Gramscian tradition. For Ranajit Guha, in particular, the subaltern study project has shown that popular culture and resistance in India meant that the

British colonial project was never truly hegemonic (ibid.). Gayatri Spivak critiques and extends the subaltern studies project, focusing not only on the knowledge–power couplet, but bringing gender squarely into this critical area of study. Her influential *Can the Subaltern Speak?* (1993) focuses on the figure of the subaltern South Asian woman, whose contradictory location is both constructed and controlled by colonialism and traditional patriarchy. The increasing influence of Foucault in Said and Spivak is, of course, taking our account beyond the 'Gramscian turn'.

Internationally, Gramsci's thought was probably most influential politically (as against in the academy) in Latin America. The much earlier reception of Gramsci in Spanish is part of the reason, but also a marked 'fit' between the type of problematic Gramsci was dealing with and the reality of Latin America. Work by Jose Aricó (1988) and Juan Carlos Portantiero (1983) are some examples of the sophisticated political use to which Gramsci was put in Latin American progressive circles. A whole range of social, political and historical enquiries were guided by the Gramscian concepts of passive revolution, historic bloc, hegemony and civil society. The perverse, practically 'postmodern', nature of the modernization process in Latin America proved fertile ground for the application and development of Gramsci's concepts. In the cultural domain, Gramsci's influence has been equally significant, for example in the recent influential work by Nestor García Canclini on 'hybrid cultures' (1995). As political practice now moves beyond the state-centric model, so the Gramscian influence is likely to be even more strongly felt. The growing importance of the cultural domain in terms of creating the conditions for development and for democratic citizenship is giving rise to new diverse debates, often under the explicit or implicit sign of Gramsci.

To round off this cursory account of the Gramscian turn in marxist cultural studies it might be useful to recall the controversy between so-called 'culturalists' and 'structuralists'. In terms of Marx's legacy, the 'culturalists' (such as E. P. Thompson) would lay stress on people 'making their own history', whereas the structuralists would stress the element of 'not in conditions of their own making'. Thompson's history of the 'making' of the English working class stressed the active process of class formation and the element of conscious agency: 'The working class did not rise like the sun at the appointed time. It was present at its own making' (1970: 9). Yet, structuralists would note a lack of basic objective co-ordinates in this story of the cultural development of a class, such as the size and composition of the working class. While it is possible to short-circuit this discussion by pointing to the obvious 'dialectical' interaction between structure and agency (or voluntarism and determinism, in another language), the fact remains that Thompson (and Raymond Williams) helped define a crucial absence in traditional marxist theory. Thompson's concern with culture, values and ideas, along with Williams's focus on culture as a 'way of life' represent a significant enrichment of the marxist tradition. The structuralists, meanwhile, were becoming 'poststructuralists', the theme of our next section.

Postmodernism and culture

If Gramsci brought culture squarely back into the marxist vocabulary, postmodernism seemed to put it on a pedestal. In this era of post-everything 'the word "culture"…seems to be appearing everywhere, its meaning stretched to the point that attempts to specify the non-cultural run into severe difficulties', as Adam and Allan put it, in their recent attempt at theorizing culture, after postmodernism (1995: xiii). Whereas marxism, but also much of social science, had neglected culture, now the postmodernists seemed to be proclaiming the death of society and the rule of culture. As culture was/is an expansive and ever-inclusive concept, this tendency towards conceptual inflation was, perhaps, inevitable. So, not only has culture gained a more important role in critical social analysis but there are those of extreme tendencies (for example, Baudrillard) who argue that 'everything' is culture. Also apparent is the tendency for the postmodern turn in cultural studies to be studiously apolitical, especially compared to the likes of Raymond Williams or Stuart Hall. It would, however, be quite inadequate to leave the verdict on postmodern cultural studies at 'culturalist' and 'apolitical'. A knee-jerk marxist reaction 'against postmodernism' (for example, Callinicos) both impoverishes marxism and allows the reactionary tendencies in postmodernism to run unchecked.

It is probably impossible to summarize the main tenets of postmodern cultural theory in a short space, certainly impossible to capture its flavour, but some main ideas are clear enough. Probably above all else, postmodernism implies a mistrust of 'metanarratives' or master narratives, such as wealth creation or workers' revolution. All paradigms of progress based on science are also rejected as incredulous. Rejecting foundational truths and global knowledge, postmodernism turns instead to 'local' or grounded knowledge, forms of knowledge which stress openness, discontinuity and reflexivity. The postmodernist also rejects the studiously disinterested language of representation, seen as typical of modernism. The world is not simply out there – 'objective reality' – waiting to be represented. Boyne and Rattansi write of 'a series of crises of representations, in which older modes of defining, appropriating and recomposing the objects of artistic, philosophical, literary and social scientific languages are no longer credible' (1990: 12). The boundary between the object and language seems to have been dissolved and we are now more prone to take a 'perspectival' view of things. The universality of Reason – the cornerstone of the Enlightenment of which Marx was of course part – seems to have run into a brick wall and dissolved into relativism.

In relation to culture, postmodernism rejects the idea of art as unique, based on the creative genius of the artist. For Baudrillard, in particular, there is nothing real or original, we have only simulations, we can only copy. Thus the boundary between 'high' and popular art, which marxist cultural critics usually shared, is dissolved. The boundaries between reality and images fade away. Images and simulations take on a life of their own. It is not all free play and heterogeneity because postmodernism also deconstructs, interrogates and disrupts traditional cultural forms, such as their highly gendered nature. Cultural metadiscourses are seen as masks for the partiality and prejudice of the powerful. However, this subversive element is at least matched by what Mike Featherstone refers to as postmodernism's 'aestheticization of the mode of perception and the aestheticization of everyday life' (1991: 124). Images of war, sexual violence and famine shamelessly sell products to the consumer society. Politics and war (the Gulf War, for example) are reduced to images. The aesthetic becomes a new master paradigm, all is culture, everything is discourse, all sense of reality, oppression and justice disappears. Postmodern cultural theory can thus destabilize its predecessors but can also be as one-sided as any theory of ideology ever was.

Existing as a bridge between marxism and 'postmarxism' via postmodernism, is the figure of Antonio Gramsci, very much a limit case before marxism was seen to collapse, at least in its traditional form. Ernesto Laclau (then Laclau and Chantal Mouffe) began in the mid-1970s the break with class reductionism via an original and dynamic engagement with the work of Gramsci. The Laclau and Mouffe text on radical democratic politics is even entitled *Hegemony and Socialist Strategy* (1985). Gramsci, as we saw above, had developed a non-reductionist conception of ideology and his conception of hegemony broke decisively with economism. However, he would simply have taken for granted that ideologies 'belonged' to classes, an assumption that post-marxism would come to challenge in developing its conception of non-class political ideologies. While ideology and culture, for Gramsci, could not be reduced to, or explained by, the economic base, they were always part of the political, basically class, struggle. As Michèle Barrett notes: 'Gramsci is a pivotal figure for Laclau and Mouffe because he represents the furthest point that can be reached within Marxism and the intrinsic limitations of the theoretical problematic' (1991: 63). This leads Laclau and Mouffe to recognize 'the impossibility of society' (as a unitary object of cognition) and a turn from class essentialism to the pluralist demands of the 'new' social movements of gender, anti-racism, peace, ecology, and so on.

We have already seen the influence of Foucault alongside Gramsci in producing a ferment in marxist cultural studies. Foucault turns from science versus ideology to knowledge and power. Foucault cuts across the science/non-science division with his 'archaeology' of knowledge and his particular conception of discourse. For Foucault a discourse is what constrains or enables what we write and speak within historical limits. Against all forms of idealism, Foucault is acutely aware of the non-discursive domain, however. What he does is supersede the traditional marxist distinction between base and superstructure. It is not that 'all is discourse', but that we cannot separate in a mechanical, unilinear and hierarchial manner, words from things. For Foucault, marxism is a 'totalizing discourse' and its claim to scientificity an instrument of domination. Foucault, as others, rejects the grand narrative, the grand theory and the great truth and directs our attention to local, fragmented and subaltern knowledges. Culture – in the sense of how people live, think and speak – is central to Foucault. Cultural resistance emerges in specific struggles, because 'one should not assume a massive and primal condition of domination, a binary structure with "dominators" on one side and "dominated" on the other ...' (1980: 142).

If Foucault could be useful even to a structuralist marxist such as Nicos Poulantzas in his last writings on power (Poulantzas, 1978), the impact of Derrida was seemingly more corrosive, less assimilable. Derrida once (in)famously declared that 'Il n'ya pas d'hors texte' literally 'there is nothing outside the text'. In fact he was saying no more than Laclau and Mouffe were to say, namely that 'society' is not a valid object of discourse. The idea of society as a self-contained and integrated totality – base and superstructure – was, of course, central to marxism. Derrida shows how thought-systems based on foundations or first principles are eventually metaphysical, and how 'binary oppositions' can always be deconstructed. For Derrida there is no direct, transparent and unmediated knowledge of the world. As Madan Sarup puts it,

'Derrida wants to emphasize the culturally produced (as against natural) character of thought and perception' (1993: 56). Meaning cannot be absolute, it is always positional, as against traditional beliefs in the fixity of meaning. An issue to be developed in Chapter 8, it is worth mentioning at this stage that Derrida's poststructuralist advocacy of deconstruction is opposed to some postmodernists' refusal of ethical choices, irrationalism or nihilistic political outlook.

Having cast a cursory glance at certain moves in the postmodern turn, we can, perhaps, return to what postmodernism 'is'. Nowhere better to start than Frederic Jameson's influential 1984 essay (Jameson, 1991) on postmodernism as 'the cultural logic of late capitalism'. For Jameson, the cultural transformations of late capitalism express a deeper logic of the system. Where market capitalism produced realism and monopoly capitalism led to modernism, late or consumer capitalism has spawned postmodernism as its cultural expression. As commodity production expands throughout society, and accelerates constantly, so aesthetic innovation and experimentation take on 'an increasingly essential structural function and position' (ibid.: 5). This new dominant or hege-monic cultural logic is characterized by its 'depthlessness' and what Jameson calls 'multi-phrenic intensities', which refers to the break-down of individual identity though cultural bombardment by frag-mented images and signs. Aware that he is using 'a different language', Jameson argues that culture can no longer be characterized by its 'semi-autonomy', rather it is 'to be imagined in terms of an explosion: a prodigious expansion of culture throughout the social realm, to the point at which everything in our social life … can be said to have become "cultural" on some original and yet untheorized sense' (ibid.: 48).

It is interesting to note that Jameson has since been accused of being an irresponsible postmodernist *and* an apologist for marxism. This is not surprising, in that he explicitly seeks to follow Marx's diagnosis of capitalism in *both* its negative consequences and positive potential. Far easier to question is his (admittedly broad brush) periodization of capitalism, and his (rather appealing) 'Hegelianism'. However, it is true to say that Jameson sees history in terms of a relentless logic of develop-ment, and there is rather too seamless a fit between culture and society in his narrative. Also, while it is true that postmodernism (or contem-porary society) has become fragmented, this cannot be contrasted to a golden age, unified or integrated past. To say that today's advanced industrial societies are culturally saturated implies some sort of non-saturated other past or different society. Jameson is seeking to develop a new cultural politics adequate to the era in which we are living, but simply to 'unmask' postmodernism as the cultural logic of late capitalism may ultimately prove too reductionist, too necessitarian, and may constrain the options that need to be considered in an epoch of unprecedented fragmentation and flux.

What I would wish to foreground, in conclusion is the postcolonial moment of postmodernism which radically decentres the West and registers its declining cultural role in the postcolonial world. Politics are back in command and the relativist slip into nihilism has little place in this radical postmodernist hybrid. There has been a spatial relativization of the Western Enlightenment tradition, a 'provincialization' of Europe, as the Subaltern Studies Group puts it. Cultural complexity, hybridity and syncretism are now seen as important components in the increasingly important cultural sphere. Where postmodernism sought to deconstruct the master narratives of European culture, the postcolonial project is to dismantle the binary opposition of centre–periphery typical of imperialist discourse. Yet against a certain universalizing (even Euro-American-centredness) tendency of postmodernism, postcolonialism gives voice to the colonized and seeks to subvert the discursive and material effects of imperialism. It has the added bonus of correcting the economism of marxist theories of imperialism, by recognizing the multiple axes of cultural formation, including those of race, gender, sexuality, religion and family discourses.

The postcolonial 'movement' is potentially, at least, a source of cultural resistance and reconstruction. There are, however, serious objections to it as a totalizing framework. Why centre colonialism, when it is largely superseded in most areas of the 'Third World'? Is Latin America postcolonial? Is North America postcolonial? For Aijaz Ahmad, postcolonialism takes upon itself to privilege colonialism in structuring other people's histories (1992). Instead of decentring imperialist history, the very singularity of the term 'postcolonialism' seems to reassert European historical time and bring colonialism in through the back door. Certainly there is a risk of homogenizing the 'non-European' cultural experience by using the simple label 'postcolonial' too literally. However, as with postmodernism, there is a need to discriminate between variants of postcolonial theory and to understand their contradictory make-up. Ultimately, following Ali Rattansi: 'If there is some commonality in the postmodernist and the postcolonial critique of Western modernity and the Enlightenment's power/knowledge complex, nevertheless postcolonialism must also act as a form of *counter-discourse* to postmodernism, decolonizing the *postmodern* imagination as much as that of modernity' (1997: 494).

7
Difficult Dialogue: Marxism and Nation

For many writers, accounting for nationalism has been marxism's great historical failure. This chapter seeks to examine why that might have been the case. It starts, predictably, with the engagements of Marx and Engels with the pressing national questions of their day. This is followed by a cursory account of the communist movement's interaction with nationalism. These were, after all, competing political movements and the heated debates between Lenin and Rosa Luxemburg on the 'national question' were no mere pedantic or esoteric terminological squabbles. Antonio Gramsci, as we saw in relation to marxist treatments of culture, was also an innovator in terms of nationalism. But our emphasis here lies in the partial, important yet neglected, break in marxist orthodoxy on the national question effected by the Austrian marxist Otto Bauer at the turn of the last century. Finally, we turn to certain crucial postmodern questionings of the whole marxist tradition's limitations regarding the national. Firstly, we examine the deep Eurocentrism in the marxist, as well as liberal, views of the national question. Secondly, we sketch in the necessary engendering of the national question, so long subsumed under an implicit, if not explicit, androcentrism.

Great historical failure?

It was Tom Nairn who famously argued that 'The theory of nationalism represents Marxism's great historical failure. It may have others as well, and some have been more debated ... Yet none ... is as important, as fundamental, as the problem of nationalism, either in theory or in political practice' (1981: 329). This dictum has become something of a truism accepted by non-marxist and marxist writers alike. It is sometimes

118

argued, or implied, that nationalism is so primordial that a political ideology, such as marxism, would find it somehow ungraspable. It is also argued that marxism failed to understand nationalism because of its inherent reductionism (superstructures determined by the economic base) and its class essentialism, because of which only class ideologies were seen. Both these lines of attack are based on certain undeniable features of classical marxism. However, when considering the interaction of Marx and Engels with the 'national question' it is probably best to start by situating them within the politics of the day. They were men of their times, they were not disembodied, they were politicians not sociologists.

In mid-nineteenth-century Europe 'To support nationalist aspirations for unity, autonomy, or independence was to support popular liberties against empire and absolutism' (Benner, 1995: 9). For a Mazzini or a Herder, nationalist icons of the day, the flourishing of nation states was synonymous with democracy. The negative connotations of nationalism after 1914 or 1989 was not even a glimmer on the horizon. Indeed, what was unusual in Marx and Engels was their politically discriminating attitude towards the various national issues of the day. Marx and Engels displayed a normative approach towards the nationalisms of their day, with the guiding light for them being democracy and later, also, internationalism. In a sense they were not interested in analysing nationalism as a unified consistent entity because they did not believe it was such. As Erica Benner writes, they could not have grasped the differences between the new forms of national politics and the democratic politics they advocated had they treated nationalism 'as a phenomenon *sui generis*, rather than analysing national movements as a variety of distinct political programmes based on conflicting social interests' (ibid.: 10). It is this discriminating, deconstructionist approach to nationalism which we now need to outline.

Though Marx and Engels were keen supporters of German unification, they were not German nationalists. For them, national unification was a preliminary task of the German democratic revolution. Marx and Engels were equally sympathetic to the ongoing process of national unification in Italy: 'No people, apart from the Poles, has been so shamefully oppressed by the superior power of its neighbours, no people has so often and so courageously tried to throw off the yoke oppressing it' (Marx and Engels, 1977b: 10). Here we get a hint that support for nationalist demands was not unconditional for the founders of marxism. Rather, it was tied to the big power politics of the day and in particular the dominating role of the Austro-Hungarian and Russian empires.

For Marx and Engels, neither a common language and traditions, nor geographic and historical homogeneity, were sufficient in themselves to define a nation. Rather, a certain level of economic and social development was required, and priority was given, on the whole, to larger units. So, for example, on the question of Germany ceding the Schleswig and Holstein territories to Denmark in 1848, Marx and Engels believed that the German role was revolutionary and progressive and advocated a resolute conduct of the Danish war from the beginning.

In the great historic nations peoples had gained the right to strong, viable national states through their struggles for unity and independence. These nations would be the standard-bearers of progress and civilization for Marx and Engels. This was, indeed, a form of national social Darwinism. Yet who entered the charmed circle would depend on political circumstances. Thus, in 1851 Engels could write to Marx that 'The Poles are *une nation foutue*' (Marx and Engels, 1982: 363) and in 1864 they could refer to the Poles as 'a subjugated people which, with its incessant and heroic struggle against its oppressors, has proven its historic right to national autonomy and self-determination' (Marx, 1974: 380–1). Thus the reunification of Poland was to become a central working-class aim of the First International which Marx and Engels did so much to promote. The right of nations to self-determination was far from absolute for Marx and Engels and depended, rather, on the international political conjuncture and the developments of the class struggle, or lack of it, in each national situation. They were, of course, practical politicians and they were guided on national issues largely by action considerations rather than theory.

Compared to the great 'historic nations' such as Germany, Engels in particular developed the Hegelian notion of 'non-historic' peoples. For Engels, 'these relics of a nation mercilessly trampled under foot in the course of history, as Hegel says, these residual fragments of peoples always become fanatical standard bearers of counter-revolution and remain so until their complete extirpation' (Marx and Engels, 1977: 234). The Southern Slavs – the Czechs, Slovaks, Serbs and Croats – were peoples without a history, were not viable and would never achieve independence. Of course, it was not because they were reactionary 'by nature' that this or that national or ethnic grouping might have remained aloof from the 1848 revolutionary wave or might have entered into counter-revolutionary alliances. Thus, the Basques may have entered an alliance with Don Carlos, but only to defend their democratic *fueros* (autonomy rights) against Spanish absolutism. Furthermore, the concept of 'national viability' is inherently metaphysical and hardly accords with democratic criteria. No national group can be condemned to the counter-revolutionary dustbin of history, nor can any democratic politics call for their annihilation 'by the most determined use of terror' (ibid.: 378) as Engels infamously did on more than one occasion.

The unfortunate categories of historic and non-historic nations were also to frame the writings of Marx and Engels in the world beyond Europe. After the war by the United States on Mexico in 1845–7 which resulted in the annexation of large areas of Mexico, Engels argued that it was in the interests of 'civilization' against the 'lazy' and 'desperate' Mexicans. The conquest of Algeria by France 'is an important and fortunate fact for the progress of civilization' especially given that the 'Bedouins were a nation of robbers' (Avineri [ed.], 1969: 47). Later Engels was to display a much more positive attitude towards resistance in Algeria against French colonial rule. In relation to India Marx and Engels's attitudes were also quite nuanced over the positive and negative aspects of colonialism, at once developing capitalism but also destroying a civilization. The point is probably more general: namely that they tended to view the world outside Europe as mere reflection, its own internal dynamic quite beyond their ken. Thus in relation to Latin America, Marx in his writing on Simón Bolívar, the hero of the independence struggles, seems to share Hegel's judgement of the continent as arbitrary, absurd and irrational in its nature. Thus he could not 'see' a class struggle in Latin America and could only see in Bolívar a pale Third World version of Napoleon III in France.

Where Marx and Engels seem to break with the unfortunate binary opposition between historic and non-historic nations is in regards to Ireland. The 'Irish turn' is clearly signalled by Marx in a letter to Engels in 1867: 'Previously I thought Ireland's separation from England impossible. Now I think it inevitable' (Marx and Engels, 1971: 143). What Marx now prescribed for Ireland was independence, protective tariffs and an agrarian reform. In a glimmer of what would one day be called 'dependency theory', Engels wrote that 'Every time Ireland was about to develop industrially, she was crushed and reconverted into a purely agricultural land' (ibid.: 132). Ireland's domination by British force of arms had converted the country into an agricultural and labour reserve for the Industrial Revolution. Marx and Engels now stood squarely behind the Irish democratic movement for national independence. Their stance was summed up in the single yet eloquent phrase: 'Any nation that oppresses another forges its own chains' (ibid.: 163). It seemed that they were recognizing the fundamental political, even class, differences between a nationalism of the oppressed and the aggressive, expansionist nationalism of the oppressor.

Ireland seems to represent a genuine turning point in Marx and Engels's understanding of the complex relationship between national and class struggles. During a dispute over affiliation of an independent Irish section to the First International, Engels declared unambiguously that 'In a case like that of the Irish, true Internationalism must necessarily be based upon a distinctly national organisation ... The Irish sections' ... most pressing duty, as Irishmen, was to establish their own national independence' (Marx and Engels, 1971: 303). This ringing declaration of support for the democratic right of national independence for Ireland was still, ultimately, couched in terms of its effect on the British and European revolutions rather than its own right. Overall, I would agree with Georges Haupt's verdict that: 'Though the Irish problem [*sic*] leads to a definition of the principled position on the relation between dominant and oppressed nations and allows the national movement to be assigned new functions, the refusal to generalize, to integrate the national dynamic without reservations within the theory of revolution remains manifest' (Haupt, 1974: 19). It seemed thus that Ireland marked the furthest Marx and Engels could go on the national question and the limits of classical marxism's understanding of nationalism, in its democratic and revolutionary variants.

So, what was the legacy of Marx and Engels on the national question? It was probably not the 'great historical failure' it has been portrayed as, although it was certainly contradictory. Though living in the age of nationalism, Marx and Engels preached internationalism and probably exaggerated or over-estimated its homogenizing effect on the world. Furthermore, as Paul James notes: 'ideologies like nationalism were in Marx's writings often reduced to imaginary or fictitious representations of the really real' (1996: 69). As with religion, famously for Marx the 'opium of the people', nationalism was most often seen as a veil over people's eyes, a false consciousness masking the true class struggle. Nationalism belonged to the realm of subjectivity, whereas the class level was somehow more objective and material. Marx was, however, well capable of analysing national traditions, culture and institutions with a flexible methodology which did not reduce national particularities to their economic base. If there was a negative normative yardstick in the shape of 'progress' with which to measure nations, there was also in Marx and Engels a consistent commitment to democracy as the litmus test for an understanding of the political significance of particular nationalist movements.

Communists and nationalism

It is sometimes forgotten that communists and nationalists were political rivals, 'fishing in the same pond', as it were. We should thus reject the idea that one was 'scientific' and rational whereas the other was 'primordial' and irrational. In this regard, we can usefully consider the humorous, but nonetheless pertinent, analysis by Ernest Gellner of 'The Wrong Address Theory' of nationalism he believes is favoured by marxism:

> Just as extreme Shi'ite Muslims held that Archangel Gabriel made a mistake, delivering the Message to Mohamed when it was intended for Ali, so Marxists basically like to think that the spirit of history or human consciousness made a terrible boob. The awakening message was intended for *classes*, but by some terrible postal error was delivered to *nations*. It is now necessary for revolutionary activists to persuade the wrongful recipient to hand over the message, and the zeal it engenders, to the rightful and intended recipient. (Gellner, 1983: 129).

Of course this analysis is not strictly speaking accurate but it does capture some of the deep-rooted incomprehension and hostility which most marxists displayed towards national phenomena. As with the 'woman question' (Chapter 5), communists were often to be found trying to find ways in which their marxist theories could provide a strategy for action towards a recalcitrant social reality they did not always comprehend.

Lenin, as the marxist leader of the multi-ethnic Soviet Union, was called upon to develop the marxist theory of nationalism. His contribution, the so-called 'right of nations to self-determination', has been codified in the Marxist–Leninist system. The right of nations to self-determination had become part of the Bolshevik armoury in 1903 as a response to the more 'nationalist' position of the Jewish workers' organization, the Bund. The 1905 Russian Revolution was to bring the national question more fully into the centre of Bolshevik politics. Lenin took his position against both the demands for Jewish (and Ukrainian) national cultural autonomy and what he saw as the abstract leftist denial of national oppression by Rosa Luxemburg and those among the Bolsheviks who followed her position. Basically, Lenin advocated the right of self-determination (including secession) by smaller nations where they were oppressed by a dominant larger nation. As with Marx though, he preferred larger economic units as being more conducive to economic development. To a large extent Lenin's support for nationalist movements was tactical, designed to undermine the tsarist regime in a Russia he recognized to be 'a prison of peoples'. Once in power the Bolsheviks were loath to put the 'right' to self-determination of these peoples into practice.

There is much that could be said about the Leninist 'principle' of the right of nations to self-determination. I could start (and finish) with Tom Nairn's caustic remarks that what marxist 'orthodoxy required was a plausible way of both supporting and not supporting national movements at the same time. It needed an agile and imposing non-position which would keep its options permanently open. That was what Lenin supplied' (1997: 39). Lenin certainly recognized in his political practice the strategic importance of the national question. He even began to transcend the class reductionism of classical marxism in recognizing the specificity of national oppression. In a remarkable passage, he referred to how 'By transforming capitalism into socialism the proletariat creates the *possibility* of abolishing national oppression; the possibility becomes *reality* 'only' – 'only': – with the establishment of full democracy in all spheres…including complete freedom to secede' (1970: 130). Full democratization of the state and society on the way to socialism would include the democratic rights of national communities. In practice, Russia remained a 'prison of peoples', albeit tempered by considerable degrees of national, especially cultural, autonomy.

Rosa Luxemburg, as in all her political positions and practice, sought to refuse any opportunism on the national question. For her, the 'right' of nations to self-determination made as much sense as the 'right' of workers to eat off gold plates. This right seemed to her either an empty, non-committal phrase which meant nothing, or else it was false and misleading if it implied that socialists had an unconditional duty to support all nationalist aspirations. While welcoming the Russian revolution of 1917, she believed that the Bolshevik policy on national self-determination would lead to the disintegration of Russia and was storing up trouble for the Soviet state. In her critique of the Bolsheviks, Rosa Luxemburg posed the highly pertinent question of who decided a nation's will to secede: 'But who is that "nation" and who has the authority and the "right" to speak for the "nation" and express its will?' (Davis [ed.], 1976: 141). In this Luxemburg was being consistent with her critique of the notion of representation implicit in the Leninist concept of the vanguard party. She was also sensitive to the perspectives of non-European peoples (in her work on imperialism) and also recognised that: 'The working class is interested in the *cultural* and *democratic* content of nationalism, which is to say that workers are interested in such political systems as assure a free development of culture and democracy in national life' (ibid: 175).

As Soviet marxism began to consolidate its grip on the Russian state so its attention turned to spreading the revolution. Orthodox marxism pointed West to the proletariat in the advanced capitalist countries such as Germany. However, Lenin severely underestimated 'the Western proletariat's deep attachment to national and democratic values. The nation and democracy were, historically, products of capitalism, but they were also conquests won by the working masses' (Claudin, 1975: 60). Frustrated in the West, the young Bolshevik revolution turned its sights to the East, with far-reaching consequences. Nationalism came to the fore at the 1920 First Congress of the Peoples of the East held at Baku. The leaders of the Communist (or Third) International wooed the revolutionary nationalist leaders with a discourse which could scarcely be called marxist. Zinoviev proclaimed: 'Brothers, we summon you to a holy war against British imperialism!' while the delegates brandished their sabres and revolvers in the air with cries of 'Jihad' and 'Long live the renaissance in the East' (Carrière d'Encausse and Schram [eds], 1969: 173). It was indeed a renaissance, as communism was reborn in the East in local colours, and an anti-imperialist movement, with communists in the vanguard, became a crucial factor in world history.

Most marxists and then communists would have hitherto held the most circumspect views on the prospects of non-European peoples contributing to the world revolution. Events in India or Ireland, for example, were usually only read in terms of their effect in Britain. The national question was still primarily a European question: for example, how to handle the various ethnic groupings in the Austro-Hungarian Empire. By 1922, however, the Fourth Congress of the Communist International had adopted a position which prefigured the idea of the anti-imperialist united front: 'Taking full cognizance of the fact that those who represent the national will to State independence may... be... of the most varied kind, the Communist International supports *every* national revolutionary movement against imperialism' (Degras [ed.], 1971: 385 [emphasis added]). With the temporary blip of the ultra-left turn between 1928 and 1934, the international communist movement began its adaptation towards and accommodation with Third World nationalist movements. Lenin himself had made the epistemological break to seek a way out of the imperialist blockade of the Soviet Union. Few now remembered his words: 'Marxism cannot be reconciled with nationalism, be it even of the "most just", "purest", most refined and civilised brand' (Lenin, 1963: 34).

It was not just the 'civilized' brand of nationalism which was being wooed by the communists. For example, following a series of executions of communist leaders in Turkey by Mustafa Kemal, who was receiving Soviet military and financial aid, Karl Radek (who earlier held to Rosa Luxemburg's position on the national question) could declare coolly: 'We do not regret for a moment what we said to the Turkish communists: your first duty... will be to support the national liberation movement' (Carrière d'Encausse and Schram [eds], 1969: 173). Thus began a long series of 'betrayals' of Third World communists in the interests of Soviet state policy. Marxism–Leninism was becoming a promoter of 'non-capitalist' national development in the Third World. The lines between marxism and nationalism were becoming very blurred indeed and in many cases a marriage, whether of conviction or convenience, was consummated. This is not intended as a moral critique (although this would probably be legitimate) but simply to point out how the binary opposite of the one-time marxist distance from, if not hostility towards, nationalism had now emerged. This was to persist until the collapse of state socialism or communism in 1989.

As Soviet communism began its final decline towards collapse in 1989, so the national questions in the multi-ethnic state began to come to the fore again. A persistent image is of 'primordial' ethnic or national identities emerging when the authoritarian communist lid was lifted. An example, practically at random, would be Michael Ignatieff in his *Blood and Belonging,* where he argues that liberal civilization now seems to 'run deeply against the human grain' (1994: 189). He portrays a frightening picture of the collapse of communism – with state structures collapsing, no imperial settlement to manage events, and hundreds of ethnic groups being left at the mercy of each other. As democratic discourse and the politics of conciliation had been notable by their absence under communist rule, so violence and force inevitably came to the fore. For Ignatieff: 'Nationalist rhetoric swept through these regions like wildfire because it provided warlords and gunmen with a vocabulary of opportunistic self-justification' (ibid.: 6). According to these images, nationalism is about blood and about belonging and it is so strong, primitive and instinctive that it will out if allowed to do so by a watchful 'liberal civilization'.

The current demonization of nationalism is understandable, but 'liberal civilization' (the United States of America?) is probably no more of an antidote than 'proletarian internationalism' was. If nationalism is seen as a politics and a discursive formation rather than some primeval slime, then post-1989 events are somewhat less cataclysmic or surprising. Imperial collapse was bound to make nationalism an attractive vehicle for articulating a whole series of social and economic grievances. The nationalist form of conflicts does not mean that all is about 'blood and belonging' today. As Erica Benner puts it in a persuasive deployment of Marx and Engels to understand post-1989 nationalisms: 'If extremist nationalism is a powerful force in some formerly communist countries, the rise of blood-lusting nationalist dictatorships is hardly a foregone conclusion in most of them' (1995: 232). Nationalist movements do not operate as some simple, unmediated reflection of a transparent national psyche, always already waiting to explode malevolently. Their politics depends on particular social and economic circumstances which, if unfavourable, as Marx and Engels observed in their day, will give to nationalism a strongly negative connotation.

In conclusion, the engagement of communists with nationalism has not been in theoretical terms too fruitful. In Lenin, ultimately nationalism was conceived as a transient problem in the inexorable march of history towards socialism. The turn towards the non-European colonial world gave rise to a sturdy hybrid of nationalist communism in which, to a large extent, marxism was domesticated by nationalism, and Leninism became an ideology for development. Within European marxism, nationalism continued to be underestimated and misunderstood. Thus, Eric Hobsbawm could write in 1989, in a broad retrospective on nationalism since 1780 that: 'Post-1945 world politics have been basically the politics of revolution and counter-revolution, with national issues intervening only to underline or disturb the main theme' (Hobsbawm, 1990: 176). Hobsbawm has always followed Lenin in not wishing to 'paint nationalism red' but it is difficult to understand such a blinkered view of world politics. If there has been a 'great historical failure', it would probably not be at the theoretical level but at this practical level where an ideology which is supposed to be a guide to action can blind one to the overwhelming importance on the world stage of nationalism and ethnicity in all its variants.

Bauer's break

In most socialist engagements with nationalism, Otto Bauer's work would have been mentioned, if at all, only in relation to a few cutting remarks directed at it by Lenin and Stalin. Yet Kolakowski's encyclopaedic history of marxism refers to Bauer's forgotten 1907 classic 'The Nationalities

Question and Social Democracy' as 'the best treatise on nationality problems to be found in Marxist literature and one of the most significant products of Marxist theory in general' (Kolakowski, 1982: 255). For reasons which will become clear, Bauer's approach was difficult for orthodox marxists to digest, but he did accomplish an important, if partial, break with the reductionism so evident in the classics, a break which has only recently been recognized (cf. Nimni, 1991).

The context of Otto Bauer's writing on nationalism was set by Austrian social democracy, which had to operate within a multinational state. Bauer formed part of the political current known as Austro-Marxism, which describes a number of theorists active in the Austrian socialist movement at the turn of the century (see Bottomore and Goode [eds], 1978). They belonged to a tendency within the social democratic movement, 'The Marxist Centre', led by Kautsky, and after the First World War they sought a third alternative between bankrupt social democracy and the new communist current.

National tensions in the Habsburg Empire posed an obvious threat to the unity of the working-class movement. Until nearly the turn of the century the German-speaking social democrats of Austria had professed what Bauer called a 'naïve cosmopolitanism', which simply rejected nationalism as diversionary and preached a humanist message of fraternization (Bauer, 1979: 298). The Czech workers' movement, on the other hand, was under considerable nationalist influence, not surprisingly given the predominant role of the Germans in the Austrian part of the Hapsburg Empire. As one critic points out, 'what this meant politically was, above all, that the Social Democratic Party lacked any common analysis of national conflicts within the multinational state, and could offer no united guidelines beyond an abstract profession of internationalism' (Loew, 1989: 19).

Support for nationalism was limited because Austrian social democrats wanted to preserve the Empire, rather than see it break up into its national components. The centrifugal tendencies of the national movements were opposed in the name of a reformist political project within the whole state. For this the Austrian social democrats were sometimes referred to as the 'KUK' Social Democrats (Kaiserlich und Königlich: 'imperial and royal'), a reference to the official designation of the Austrian crown (Loew, 1979: 20). Growing national tensions within the Empire had forced the Austrian social democrats to face the national question. This was against the better judgement of their leader, Victor Adler, who considered the question too explosive. Largely inspired by Karl Kautsky, the Brünn programme of 1899 sought to resolve national tensions by allowing each national component of social democracy to present their own cultural demands, while the economic struggle would be waged at the level of the supranational state. Kautsky proposed the democratic transformation of the Austrian state along the lines of the federal structure of six national parties, which the socialist movement had adopted at its 1897 Congress. The Brünn resolution advocated the restructuring of Austria along language divisions, against a minority who called for extra-territorial cultural autonomy. The debate at the Brünn Congress displayed clearly the varying conceptions of nationalism within the social-democrat ranks. Seliger introduced the debate by saying it was ironic that those who were accused of being nationally neutral should be resolving the national problem. He stressed that 'above all, the question of the nationalities should not be seen as a question of power, but as a cultural question' (Bernstein *et al.*, 1978: 187). Delegate Daszynski disputed this view, arguing that 'there is no national question without an economic base' (ibid.: 195). The Ruthenian socialists pledged their support, but reminded the Congress that part of their people lived outside Austria in the Russian-dominated Ukraine: 'We are convinced that the international power of the proletariat will only be developed when each nation can decide its history. We know that social and political liberation also presuppose national liberation' (ibid.: 198).

In attempting to resolve the problem posed by the intersection of national and social struggles most delegates to the congress emphasized that national disputes had to be resolved as a precondition for the advance of the labour movement. A minority argued on the contrary that 'our activity is taken up too much by the national question' and that they had recruited workers often precisely because they did *not* raise the national question (ibid.: 208). The problem was best addressed by the Polish delegation: Polish socialists would act within Austrian workers' organizations but they would also 'act incessantly within the whole Polish people to eliminate the grave national injustice exercised against the Polish people' (ibid.: 216). The struggle of the proletariat could not ignore brutal national oppression and the partition of their country. Mere cultural autonomy could not suffice. Even party leader Victor Adler, who had preferred to ignore the national question, got round the dilemma by saying that internationalists could also be good national patriots. Thus the early abstract stand for internationalism gave way to a limited support for nationalism.

Bauer himself saw the main strength of his work as its description of the derivation of nationalism from the process of economic development, changes in the social structure and the articulation of classes in society (1979: 19). However, much of his work, and the debates to which it gave rise, centred around the definition of 'nation' which he advanced. In a nutshell this was that 'The nation is the totality of human beings bound together through a common destiny into a community of character' (ibid.: 142). The nation was seen as a 'community of fate' whose character resulted from the long history of the conditions under which people laboured to survive, and divided the products of this labour (the social division of labour). Before deriding this conception as a form of idealism, we should note that Bauer repeatedly criticized 'national spiritualism [which] saw the nation as a mysterious spirit of the people' (ibid.: 130). He also explicitly rejected psychological theories of the nation. His working definition of the nation was rather a *methodological* postulate which posed 'the task of understanding the phenomenon of the nation, explaining on the basis of the uniqueness of its history all that constitutes the peculiarity, the individuality of each nation, and which differentiates it from other nations, that is, showing the nationality of each individual as the historical with respect to him, and the historical within him' (ibid.: 14). Only by pursuing this task of uncovering the national components can we dissolve the false appearance of the substantiality of the nation, to which nationalist conceptions of history always succumb, he concludes.

For Bauer, above all, the nation is a product of history. This is true in two respects: firstly, 'in terms of its material content it is a historical phenomenon, since the living national character which operates in every one of its members is the residue of a historical development' and secondly, 'from the point of view of its formal structure it is a historical phenomenon, because diverse broad circles are bound together in a nation by different means and in different ways at the various stages of historical development' (Bauer, 1979: 144). In short, the way in which the 'community of character' is engendered is historically conditioned. It follows that this 'community of character' is not a timeless abstraction, but is modified over time. Bauer refers to national character as something specific to a particular decade and not something which can be traced back to the origins of history. Nor is it seen as an explanation in itself, but as something which needs to be explained. Internationalism cannot simply ignore national characteristics, but must show how they are the result of historical processes.

Bauer also advanced a novel perspective on the future of nations under socialism. For Marx and Engels, 'national differences and antagonisms between peoples are daily more and more vanishing... The supremacy of the proletariat will cause them to vanish still faster' (Marx and Engels, 1976c: 503). For Bauer, however, socialism would lead to '*a growing differentiation of nations* ... a sharper relief of their peculiarities, a sharper distinction of their characteristics' (Bauer, 1979: 116). For Bauer, socialism would lead to the genuine autonomy of nations, the masses would be integrated into the national cultural community, and therefore the 'spiritual' differentiation of nations would flourish freely. The cultural history of the nation, hitherto the history of the ruling classes, would henceforth be appropriated by the masses, who could give free rein to their national characteristics. This meant that 'the task of the International can and should be, not the levelling of national particularities, but the engendering of international unity in national multiplicity' (ibid.: 21). The workers' international should not dictate methods of struggle without considering national diversity and the uniqueness of cultural traditions. Whereas Kautsky meekly lamented that the Second International was an instrument for peacetime, Bauer more realistically recognized that even in peacetime it was not an effective instrument for internationalism when the vested interests of the big states were at stake. Bauer certainly sought the international unity of the working class, but he argued that 'we can only defeat bourgeois nationalism... when we discover the national substance of the international class struggle... We must defeat nationalism on its own ground' (Bauer, 1978a: 184).

Though today Bauer's theory of nationalism suffers from almost total oblivion (an exception is Nimni, 1991), in its day it was a subject of intense polemics. Karl Kautsky was the recognized 'expert' on the national question in the Second International, and it was his task to reassert orthodoxy. Kautsky argued firstly that 'Bauer has not taken sufficiently into account the importance of language both for the nation and the state' (1978: 149). For Kautsky language was the foremost constant in the historic development of the nation. Bauer responded, quite persuasively, that he fully recognized the nation as a 'community of culture' which lay behind the generation, transformation and limits of language (Bauer, 1978a: 176). Kautsky went on to argue, more generally, that the main weakness of Bauer's work was 'its enormous exaggeration of the national factor' (Kautsky, 1978: 166). For Kautsky, it was simply a question of Bauer, not understanding that the proletariat was predominantly international in orientation rather than national. Kautsky saw the proletariat aspiring towards an international rather than national culture, especially as international trade was leading to a worldwide language. To these abstractions, Bauer counterposed a more realistic appraisal of the meshing of class and national struggles. As we have seen above, Bauer sought to confront nationalism on its own ground: 'the art of war teaches us not to avoid the adversary but to take the war to his own country' (Bauer, 1978a: 184). This seems a more fruitful strategy than the development of Esperanto as the key to workers' international solidarity.

Perhaps the most relevant part of Bauer's work today is his consideration of the relation between class struggle and nationalism. In a striking phrase he wrote that 'nationalist hatred is a transformed class hatred' (Bauer, 1979: 259). Bauer was referring specifically to the petty bourgeoisie of the oppressed nation affected by shifts in population and other convulsions engendered by capitalist development. But the point is a more general one, and Bauer shows clearly how class and national struggles were intertwined. For example, in the case of the Czech worker: 'the state which enslaved him [*sic*] was German; German too were the courts which protected property owners and threw the dispossessed into jail; each death sentence was written in German; and orders in the army sent against each strike of the hungry and defenceless workers were given in German' (ibid.: 296). The workers of the 'non-historic' nations adopted in the first instance a 'naïve nationalism' to match the 'naïve cosmopolitanism' of the big nation proletariat. Only gradually does a genuinely international policy develop which overcomes both 'deviations' and recognizes the particularity of the proletariat of all nations. Although Bauer preached the need for *working-class* autonomy in the struggle for the socialist form of production as the best means for seizing power, he argued that 'within capitalist society, national autonomy is, however, the indispensable revindication of a working class which is obliged to carry out its class struggle in a state of (different) nationalities' (ibid.: 314). This was not a 'state-preserving' response, he argued, but was a necessary aim for a proletariat which sought to make the whole people into a nation.

In conclusion, we could argue that Bauer's work represents a major break with economism: politics and ideology are no longer viewed as mere 'reflections' of rigid economic processes. The very context in which Austrian social democracy operated made it particularly sensitive to cultural diversity and to the complex *social* processes of economic development. The economic determinism and basic evolutionism of Second International marxism was implicitly rejected in Bauer's treatise on the national question. In terms of its substantial contribution, Bauer advanced a concept of the nation as historical process, in pages of rich and subtle historical analysis. The nation was no longer seen as a natural phenomenon, but a relative and historical one. This allowed Bauer to break decisively with the Marx–Engels position on 'non-historic' nations, a category still employed by most contemporary marxists. As with Gramsci's much more influential work on the national–popular, we find with Bauer a welcome move beyond most marxists' continuous understanding of nation and nationalism as 'problems' and not just an integral element of the human condition.

Postmodern questions

Nationalism, like marxism, is inextricably bound up with modernity, which sets its parameters and determines its limits. In the era of globalization we may refer to a postmodern nationalism, where the old grand narratives are replaced by cultural management. Traditions become thinned out and are self-consciously 'invented'. Paul James writes of how 'the new nationalism has a febrile fragility' (1996: 36). There is the immediacy of 'nationness' created by the mass media around military or sporting occasions, which cannot overcome the distance from the nation's past as we move into the era of globalization. It is this postmodern-marxist understanding of the nation and nationalism which helps move us into new areas of enquiry. People have multiple identities which interpellate them in various, sometimes contradictory, ways. Marxism and nationalism as modern phenomena are also irrevocably Eurocentric. What implications does that have for a theory of nationalism adequate to the postcolonial era? Nationalism is also cut across by the question of gender. Here is a discourse where gender images and gender roles are absolutely central, yet most marxist theories of nationalism do not intersect with a gendered approach. Here I briefly address the issue of Eurocentrism and androcentrism (or gender blindness) in marxist theories of nationalism.

Elie Kedourie is at least forthright in his conservative manifesto on nationalism, when he asserts that 'Nationalism is a doctrine invented in Europe at the beginning of the nineteenth century' (1960: 28). For Kedourie, every element of the doctrine or discourse can be shown to have a European origin. Nationalism in the non-European world is simply a pale imitation and cannot have an autonomous existence. There are various ways to deconstruct this set of statements. Let us begin by examining to what extent, indeed, nationalism is marked by its European origins. In a sense, we need to go no further than the maps of the globe which draw lines across continents and paint each section a different colour. We see Europe in the middle, and its colonies to the 'South' stand as eloquent testimony to the era of imperialism – the carve-up of Africa, for example. What appears fixed on these maps is, of course, a social construction. Marxism tended to share the related Eurocentric conception of the world and of nationalism in particular. So, even while the colonized peoples were freeing themselves from the colonial yoke, it was assumed that they were doing so with the conceptual tools of the Enlightenment, whether in its liberal or marxist variants.

Tom Nairn's notion of nationalism as Janus-faced (at once looking forward and backwards) is often quoted as an influential, if idiosyncratic marxist theory. After tracing the origins of nationalism in Europe, Nairn tells us: 'We all know how it spread from its West-European source, in concentric circles of upheaval and reaction: though Central and Eastern Europe, Latin America, and then across the other continents' (1981: 340). The struggle between imperialism and anti-colonial resistance is translated by Nairn into 'the battle between scathing cosmopolitan modernists and emotional defenders of the Folk' (ibid.: 340). Now, Nairn begins with an understanding of the 'historic' nation in Europe as entirely unproblematic. These nations are seen as historical subjects with all the attributes of agency, they 'aspire' to things, they 'mobilize', they even have irrational 'ids'. In the non-European world, nationalism arrives by diffusion, by osmosis as it were, with little understanding of the real world of imperialism. Nairn's theory, for all its undeniable engagement and sporadic insights, collapses totally when looking very close to home at Irish nationalism, where he makes a singularly bizzare construction of the Protestant settlers as the real oppressed national group.

Ben Anderson's notion of nation as an 'imagined community' (1983) has achieved considerable diffusion and is a big step forward in terms of its sustained attention to the discursive domain and refusal of reductionism. Anderson goes beyond orthodox marxist views of nationalism as ideology and false consciousness, addressing its 'sacred' role in Weberian terms. Language, literature and the press are seen as crucial in imagining the entity we call 'nation'. Yet it was the same Enlightenment which created European modernity and nationalism, but also the depredations of colonialism. So, then, as Partha Chatterjee asks Anderson rhetorically: 'If nationalisms in the rest of the world have to choose their imagined community from certain "modular" forms already made available to them by Europe and the Americas, what do they have left to imagine?' (1996: 216). It seems that we are back with Hegel, for whom European nations were the only true subjects of history, with the rest of the world mere puppets or pale reflections of European themes. A European focus can only see the rest of the world in these terms and would fail to see, for example, how most Third World nationalisms (including Islamism) are based on their radical difference from Europe and not a mimicry of the master's themes.

That nationalism exists as an international discourse does not mean that it flourished in the non-European world in a simply derivative way, with all the negative connotations that implies. The hybridity of the postcolonial world means also that its nationalisms operated profound displacements, disruptions and subversions of the modernist discourses of nationalism (and marxism for that matter). Nor can we ever forget the extent to which things have been 'erased' or 'glossed over' in the official histories of postcolonialism and nationalism, which 'bear the marks of the people-nation struggling in an inchoate, undirected and wholly unequal battle against forces which have sought to dominate it' (Chatterjee, 1986: 170). The critique of nationalist discourses should not blind us to the popular struggles it has fostered and animated. A Eurocentric marxism could only be part of the West in the postcolonial world. The struggles of the subaltern may take many different forms – nationalist, ethnic, regional and religious among others – and a marxism which seeks to have global influence needs to understand these and not just struggle to 'demystify' them and reassert a 'true' class struggle.

If nationalism was marked by its Eurocentrism, it was also always profoundly androcentric. For a discourse which often constructed the nation as a woman and national wars as the natural pursuit of the male, the analysts of nationalism have seemed singularly uninterested in the question of gender. Only recently has there been a flourishing of interest in the engendering of nationalism, war and citizenship. The introduction to an interesting collection on *Nationalisms and Sexualities* points us to 'the crucial recognition that – like gender – nationality is a relational term whose identity derives from its inherence in a system of differences' (Parker [ed.], 1992: 5). Nations and genders are shaped by what they are not, as much as by what they 'are'. National and gender identities are constituted through difference and are thus clearly relational terms. The concept of nation is also inherently gendered, such as the stereotypical images of women as symbols of the nation. National narratives and cultural identities are also always gendered. It is not only with fascism, but in most nationalisms that the defence of the nation is a task assigned to men. While stressing the solidarity of men in this task, nationalisms are fervently heterosexist and confine 'women and children' to a passive role as victim.

Women are now being written back in to the history of nationalist struggles. Kuman Jayawardena's account of feminism and nationalism in the Third World (1986) carries out a double operation in showing that feminism was no simple import to the postcolonial world and, at the same time, bringing women to the centre of the struggles for independence and national liberation in these countries. A Western feminism, which believed with Virginia Woolf that 'as a woman I find no country', would find some of these histories uncomfortable reading. Many women in many Third World countries have participated actively in nationalist struggles, and felt the common identity of nationality, without forsaking their struggles as women within these movements. That this did not conform to some models of sisterhood proclaimed by Euro-feminism did not particularly concern them. Women also had a contradictory relation towards capitalist modernization which at once created the conditions for a move towards greater equality, and also generated a counter-move of reassertion or reconstruction of traditional social mores as a way to counteract imperialist cultural penetration.

There is a cluster of roles where women play a key role in the social reproduction of nationalism. In a pioneering analysis Floya Anthias and Nira Yuval-Davis point towards the specific and crucial role of women in national or ethnic processes, including:

1. as biological reproducers of ethnic or national collectivities;
2. as reproducers of the boundaries of these collectivities;
3. as crucial in the ideological and cultural reproduction of these collectivities;
4. as signifiers of ethnic/national differences. (Anthias and Yuval-Davis, 1989: 7)

While cognisant of the functionalist implications of the term 'social reproduction', the first three terms point to a set of interrelated processes where women play a crucial role in regards to nationalism. To me it is the last element which is most potent in explaining the gendered dimension of all national discourses. It is through female figures that most nations represent themselves. Women are often icons of the nation, embodiment of its assumed qualities as imagined community, while simultaneously confined to the margins of the actual political community and disempowered as citizens.

A new way of exploring the complex interrelationship between gender, nation and politics would be through a development of the idea of liminality. The liminal points to difference, a betwixt and between, the knowable and the incomprehensible. From a liminal perspective, identities and allegiances are uncertain at best. We can imagine ethnic, territorial and social liminars. In her analysis of this terrain, Anne Norton refers to 'the liminal and definitive role played by women in the structures of the state' (1988: 79). For our purposes here it would be most interesting to extend this analysis to the construction of nations and nationalism. Women are liminars in the making of nationalism in that they are peripheral to the nation (denied citizenship, for example) yet they also symbolically personify the nation. Women's exclusion from state politics is matched by their role as primary symbol of nationality. This ambiguity or ambivalence on the intersection between gender and nation – at once centre and periphery – is crucial to our understanding. Following Anne Norton, we could argue that 'the political significance of liminality lies in [its] capacity to transform weakness into strength' (ibid.: 76). Current debates and campaigns around the concept of engendered citizenship point in this direction.

This final section has exposed the limits of a 'materialist' theory of nationalism which reduces it to mere epiphenomenon of a material (economic) base, just ideology or false consciousness. We are now more likely to understand nationalism as what Michel Foucault called a 'discursive formation', namely 'whenever one can describe, between a number of statements, such as system of dispersion, whenever, between objects, types of statements, concepts, or thematic choices, one can define a regularity (an order, correlations, positions and functionings, transformations)' (Foucault, 1970: 38). From this perspective it is easier to see the limitations of these theories which seek to detect a 'good' (perhaps civic) nationalism to counterpose to the 'bad' (perhaps racist) nationalism often to the fore. For, as Craig Calhoun argues, 'Both positive and negative manifestations of national identity and loyalty are shaped by the common discourse of nationalism' (1997: 3). Many social conflicts take a national form and many grievances are advanced in the rhetoric of nationalism. Understanding nationalism as a discursive formation in all its complexity and contradictory manifestations takes us beyond marxist reductionism on this question. It is not that nationalism is somehow beyond theory (for example, primordial), but it requires a multi-focus approach which would today start from the new globalism, and would include, centrally, a gender focus and an awareness of the postcolonial optic among other things.

8

After the Deluge: Post(modern) Marxism?

The collapse of (most of) the communist regimes after 1989 was bound to unleash a terminal deepening of the crisis of marxism. After this deluge, what could possibly be left of marxism? The first section of this final chapter examines the various reactions to 1989 and the possible relevance of marxism to the new globalized, postmodern world we now live in. Many observers now argue, for example, that globalization is but the fulfilment of predictions in the *Communist Manifesto*. The second section goes back somewhat, to examine the theoretical challenge posed by postmodernism to marxist orthodoxies. Some marxists sought to deal with the postmodern challenge in the same way Marx dealt with religion, as ideological manifestations of real issues. This deadlock, and other related impasses, is tackled in the final section which, essentially, advocates or postulates a postmodern marxism and socialism more suited to the era in which we live. Whether this is a post-marxism, a postmodern marxism or something else entirely is probably an open question. What seems to be opening up now is a new horizon of possibilities to renew the radical impulse motivating Marx and the early 'marxists'.

Practical challenges

Following the challenge to the social order represented by the 'events' of 1968, and the crisis of capitalist stability after 1973, the various political systems and regimes of accumulation began a process of transformation. This led in the capitalist West to what we now call globalization and/or the information society. The state-socialist or communist East was not able to make this transition and collapsed ignominiously almost everywhere in 1989. Twenty years of intense socioeconomic mutation and a seemingly inevitable conservative revolution (Thatcherism, Reaganism, global neoliberalism) had produced a new world order where capitalism ruled unchallenged. The implications for marxists, even those who had always been critical of 'actually existing' socialism as the regimes of the East were euphemistically called, were to be profound. Thus Eric Hobsbawm: 'We are seeing not the crisis of a type of movement, regime and economy, but its end. Those of us who believed that the October Revolution was the gate to the future of world history have been shown to be wrong' (1991: 117). The marxist challenge to capitalism, at least in the form actually implemented by Lenin and each of his successors, had failed without a shadow of a doubt. There was, indeed, no alternative.

What '1989' represented, just like '1968' before it, was much more than the collapse of the communist regimes. As David Held writes, the debates on '1989 and all that' were about 'the character and form of modernity itself: the constitutive processes and structures of the contemporary world' (1992: 14). The book by Francis Fukuyama proclaiming 'the end of history' (1992), contestable though it was, did actually capture something of the mood of the times. There was an epochal mutation going on, even if the extreme conservative optimists and radical pessimists were to be proven wrong very shortly. History had not, of course, come to an end, but capitalism and liberalism did seem to be the only games in town. Soviet socialism seemed as much a bad dream as fascism had been in preventing humanity's progress towards the 'good life'. The West had won the cold war and its triumphalism, for example in the Gulf War, was a terrible and terrifying sight to behold. But it would not be many years before it dawned on supporters and opponents of the new world order alike that this victory might, indeed, be a poisoned chalice and that new contradictions would emerge to challenge capitalist complacency.

There were many reactions on the marxist left to the events of 1989. For those organized in political groups to the left of Soviet marxism, the crisis represented opportunity. The false Soviet god had been torn down, now the one true faith could re-establish its project. Unfortunately, in the real world, people did not tend to distinguish between Soviet-style marxism and the 236 varieties to its supposed left. Another reaction was to develop an acute case of political amnesia where the whole history of marxism was simply forgotten. From embracing the New Times and a critical more liberal marxism, it seemed that '1989' gave licence for a love affair with capitalism itself and the wonders of the free market. The binary opposition between these two positions hardly needs remarking on. For myself, I would go along with Fred Halliday's argument/belief that 'After its long and painful historical detour, the Communist tradition can now return to its point of origin, the critique of, and challenge to capitalist political economy' (1991: 99). We were now back where Marx had been when he looked out at the nascent capitalist world around him. Could Marx, if not the 'communist tradition', have something to say on the eve of the millenium?

It is now necessary to sketch in what the post-1989 brave new world actually looked like, in order to try to establish whether Marx or marxism could make any sense of it. Over and beyond the debates within the globalization literature, and the undoubted conceptual inflation of the concept, there is agreement that the world has 'shrunk' through what Harvey calls time-space compression (1990: 240). Nation-states are today linked through a multiplicity of connections and flows which represents a qualitative break with the 'old' capitalism. The economic, political, cultural and social aspects of globalization point towards a multi-causal logic in its genesis but Marx and the *Communist Manifesto* do seem relevant to its understanding. Marx certainly understood how bourgeois society tended towards internationalization and how globalization was, even in his day, 'giving a cosmopolitan character to production and consumption in every country' (Marx and Engels, 1973: 71). In an even more precise way, in the *Grundrisse* notebooks, Marx foresaw how: 'The tendency to create the *world market* is directly given in the concept of capital itself. Every limit appears as a barrier to be overcome' (Marx, 1973: 408).

If globalization was the context for capitalism's restructuring over the last 20 years or so, its mechanisms would have been even more familiar to Marx. The watchwords of this capitalist revolution were deregulation and the dismantling of the Keynesian social contract between capital and labour. Capitalist restructuring and global expansion would be based on speed and efficiency, flexibility and adaptability. For Manuel Castells, 'in a nutshell', the new capitalist order is based on a three-pronged strategy: 'deepening the capitalist logic of profit-seeking in capital-labor relationships; enhancing the productivity of labor and capital; [and] globalizing production, circulation and markets' (1996: 19). There is nothing in this diagnosis that would have surprised Marx. Indeed, Marx was full of praise and admiration for the dynamism of the bourgeois society whose inequality he detested so much. The picture painted by Castells in his ambitious three-volume work on the nature of contemporary society (1996, 1997, 1998), right through to the pre-eminence of the knowledge and information dimensions,

fits quite well with the prognosis Marx made of the long-term historical development tendencies of capitalism.

In 1997, the *New Yorker* published an unusual article by mainstream
economist John Cassidy, arguing that 'the Next Big Thinker' to hit the
scene would be none other than Karl Marx (Cassidy, 1997). Maybe he
had been right all along in his diagnosis of the dynamics of capitalism.
For example, according to the *New Yorker*: '"Globalization" is the buzz-
word of the late 20th century, on the lips of everybody from Jiang
Zemin to Tony Blair, but Marx predicted most of its ramifications 150
years ago' (ibid.: 11). Cassidy even suggests that one of Marx's most
controversial ideas, the 'theory of immiseration', might be making a
comeback. But, according to Cassidy 'perhaps the most enduring
element of Marx's work is his discussion of where power lies in a capitalist society' (ibid.: 13). Even from the plate-glass windows of the
transnational corporation headquarters, the view of the world is far
from tranquil. Capitalism may have spread its tentacles across the
globe and there is no viable alternative on the horizon, but it is still
a system based on power. Increasingly, the actual architects of globalization are drawing attention, as Marx (their new-found seer) would,
to the down-sides of globalization and the social pressures building up
in its wake.

If capitalism as a global order could make sense in terms of Marx's
Manifesto, who or what would be confronting it? The old distinction
between a political left and right going back to the French Revolution
no longer seemed relevant. And yet, by the mid-1990s the eminent
Italian political philosopher Norberto Bobbio could write a spirited
best-selling defence of 'Left and Right' as a political distinction (1996).
While in the last century it was the 'social question' within individual
states which gave rise to the socialism, today, for Bobbio, it is the
'international social question' (inequality between states) which forms
the basis for a movement for social transformation. Certainly, all available data point towards a deepening of the socioeconomic inequalities
between nation-states, contrary to the gospel of the free-marketeers.
There is now a global hierarchy of power, wealth, privilege and control
which is unprecedented in its scope and its implications. Behind the
rhetoric of global interdependence lies a fierce 'new dependency'
which shocks even the theorists of the original Latin American dependency theory in the 1960s, such as Fernando Henrique Cardoso
(see Cardoso, 1993a).

While globalization spins its capitalist webs across the globe it operates exclusion as much as inclusion. For every country and worker

included in the new virtuous circle of globalization there are many more suffering the vicious circle of social exclusion. As Joan Robinson was fond of saying, if there was anything worse than exploitation, it was not being exploited. Castells captures the new order of inclusion/ exclusion with what he calls a cosmic metaphor, namely 'the black holes of informational capitalism' (1998: 162). People and territories become quite simply 'surplus to requirements' in the new global postmodern order. There is no escape from 'these black holes [which] concentrate in their density all the destructive energy that affects humanity from multiple sources' (ibid.). This 'Fourth World' which exists across the world, both within the advanced capitalist countries (such as the USA) and across whole continents (such as Africa) is elo- quent testimony that the capitalism that Marx knew is still with us today. It would therefore seem that, even though traditional commu- nism has failed, the conditions that gave rise to it still exist and its task in seeking a more just and equitable world is only just beginning.

The 'other' great divide which, arguably, forms the basis for a con- temporary movement towards social transformation, is that between women and men. In reflective mode some Western marxists realized 20 years ago that the 'gender question' could lead to a greater revolution than the class struggle then seeming to be winding down, 'if only' women could act 'like a class'. The problem was that these male marx- ists could not discern an alternative 'feminist mode of production' to ensure the forward march of history once patriarchal capitalism was overthrown. Now, Manuel Castells, one-time structuralist marxist who understood the new social movements, can declare that the rapid spread of women's consciousness across the globe over the last 20 years represents 'the most important revolution because it goes to the roots of society and to the heart of who we are. And it is irreversible' (Castells, 1997: 135). In this regard, globalization has had the dual pos- itive effect of absorbing vast layers of women into paid employment and has allowed for the global spread of the motivating ideas of feminism. The cultural politics of feminism have irreversibly altered the original socialist project of liberation whether or not the 'end of patriarchalism' is actually on the cards in the foreseeable future.

Theoretical challenges

What is interesting, if we step back from 1989 by a decade, is that precisely when the high tide of communism occurred in the late 1970s (remember Afghanistan, Grenada and Nicaragua) the 'crisis of marxism' was coming to a head, particularly in the Latin countries. Marxism seemed to be running out of steam (notwithstanding its growing prestige in the Western academy) because it did not renovate itself after 1968 as successfully as capitalism did. The main theoretical challenge to marxism's claim to the radical mantle came from that cluster of ideas, theories and movements grouped loosely under the umbrella(s) of postmodernism. It was Louis Althusser who, in retrospect, acted as a bridge from structuralist marxism to the new post-structuralist theoretical and political variants. This has been recognized not only by those who believe that 'Marxism needs to avail itself of the insights of postmodernism' (Callari and Ruccio, 1996: 27) but orthodox opponents of the postmodern turn such as Ellen Meiskins Wood, who severely attacked Louis Althusser's 'scientific' marxism precisely because it 'became the main theoretical channel through which Western marxism travelled in its passage to post-marxism and beyond' (Wood, 1995: 8). It is to that journey we now turn.

An interesting case to examine is that of the late Jean-François Lyotard, who was one of the few theorists deemed 'postmodern' who actually accepted the term. His mid-1950s writings on Algeria in the maverick marxist journal *Socialisme ou barbarie* throw new light on his postmodernism. His main concern was the way marxist categories failed to grasp the particularities of the Algerian situation, seeing it instead as a simple rerun of the Russian Revolution. This was not, for Lyotard, a 'pure situation' amenable to analysis by the rigid and dogmatic marxism of the day. Algeria became symbolic, for Lyotard, of marxism's lack of touch with reality and confirmed its ideological decay. In light of recent work on postcolonialism, it is highly significant that Lyotard made his break with marxism over the colonial question and the failures of metropolitan marxism regarding the nation–colonial revolution. By the early 1960s, Lyotard began to move beyond a critical marxism towards what is now called postmodernism only after this. As Stuart Sim puts it: 'Postmodernism is embraced only after Lyotard has painstakingly catalogued Marxism's failings in a concrete political situation over a period of several years' (1996: 3). The point is that Lyotard, as Derrida and Foucault for that matter, engaged with marxism (and Marx) for a long time and the new theories and politics did not just drop down from the sky.

To describe the postmodern challenge it is probably appropriate to begin with Lyotard's 1979 text *The Postmodern Condition* (Lyotard, 1984). In it Lyotard describes the postmodern age in terms of technological and social changes which would not be unfamiliar to the marxists of the day. However, he goes beyond this substantive focus to develop an epistemological analysis of modernity's limitations. Lyotard questions the Enlightenment's view of knowledge as scientific, holistic, progressive, universal, rational and objective. Lyotard encapsulates postmodernism as a 'scepticism towards all metanarratives' (ibid.: xxiii) by which he refers to all those stories based on absolute or universal truths such as the creation of wealth (Adam Smith), the evolution of life (Darwin) and, of course inevitably, the emancipation of humanity through that of the working class (Karl Marx). With knowledge thus deconstructed and desacralized, we are taken onto a new terrain where foundational claims are rejected, as is the constant search for 'deeper' truths. No views are privileged, everything is provisional, representation is futile and the future is uncertain. In an era where all is fragmentation and flux, destinies make little sense. Postmodernism became, if nothing else, a widespread mood in the arts and humanities during the course of the 1980s.

No taxonomy and diagnosis of the postmodernisms is ever totally convincing, but it is important not to think that all cats in the night are simply black. Two distinctions I have found useful in delving into this area are those between sceptical and affirmative postmodernists (Rosenau, 1992: 15) and between a conservative and an oppositional postmodernism (Santos, 1995: 92). Baudrillard would be a postmodernist-sceptic who not only had a negative prognosis of the era characterized by disintegration, chaos and meaninglessness, but actually revelled in it. An affirmative-postmodernist position would share the critique of modernity but would be more hopeful about the current era, not shying away, for example, from ethico-political choices. The conservative/oppositional distinction has a similar tenor but, with Sousa Santos, the oppositional takes on a much more radical bent than the basically liberal North American affirmative strand. For him, oppositional postmodernism:

> captures the perspectives for social transformation at the end of the century better than any other. The emancipatory postmodern knowledge that I have been calling for aims at investing, inventing or promoting the progressive alternatives that such a transformation may entail. It is an intellectual utopia that makes a political utopia possible. (Santos, 1996: 92)

We are a long way here from the Baudrillard who once (in)famously declared that the Gulf War was just a media spectacle.

There is another dimension to postmodernism usually neglected in the Western textbooks, namely its relation to postcolonialism. As the editors of a reader in postcolonial studies put it: 'the major project of post-modernism – the deconstruction of the centralised, logocentric master narratives of European culture – is very similar to the post-colonial project of dismantling the Centre/Margin binarism of imperial discourse' (Ashcroft *et al.* [eds], 1995: 117). In some ways while post-modernism has led to an aestheticization of politics, postcolonialism has led to a politicization of aesthetic studies. More pertinently, per-haps, postmodernism has in practice become the privileged domain of a North Atlantic intelligentsia. Even postcolonialism has, to some extent, become an academic niche for Third World intellectuals in the West. Nevertheless, especially when we combine postmodernism with postcolonial politics, we have a very powerful discursive movement seeking to decentre and destabilize the ontological security of the West. Eurocentrism is alive and well within postmodernism, which accounts for its hostile reception among many Third World radicals. However, from a broad historical perspective, postmodernism does seem at least to allow some space for the postcolonial Other to speak.

There is no single or simple politics of postmodernism because there is no one postmodernism: its politics will thus be as diverse, fluid and contradictory as the 'movement' is. However, there are certain themes we can discern among 'affirmative' or 'oppositional' postmodernists. Foucault (not necessarily a postmodernist) had already advocated very strongly a move away from grand, totalizing, contestatory politics to a micro-politics more appropriate to the way capitalism works today. Felix Guattari goes one step further in advocating a micro-politics that will set loose 'a whole host of expressions and experimentations – those of children, of schizophrenics, of homosexuals, or prisoners, or misfits of every kind – that all work to penetrate and enter into the semiology of the dominant order' (1984: 184). At a more prosaic level, the oppositional postmodernist celebrates diversity, encourages politi-cal pluralism and works at a grass-roots level in favour of radical democracy. Postmodern politics stresses autonomy and identity, rejecting the master-plan for 'emancipation'. As Ernesto Laclau (again not necessarily a postmodernist) puts it: 'We are today coming to terms with our finitude and with the political possibilities that it opens. This is the point from which the potentially liberatory dis-courses of our postmodern era have to start. We can perhaps say that today we are at the end of emancipation and at the beginning of free-dom' (1996: 18).

But what of the objection that postmodernists all share Nietzsche's dangerous nihilistic beliefs in 'Beyond Good and Evil', a relativism which can only end badly? Sceptical-postmodernists do not believe in any form of representation (for example, of others' political interests) or of value judgements (such as leftwing–rightwing, good–bad), so democratic politics becomes impossible. Political agnosticism leads them to reject all global projects of transformation, so they end up supporting the *status quo* and begin to see considerable virtues in the respectable right. Given the virtual end of history and the absence of truth, what Baudrillard terms 'ironic detachment' passes as a progressive political stance. While this is the case, we simply cannot ignore, for example, the very fruitful engagement of (some) feminism(s) with postmodernism. Nor can we retreat to a rejection of all non-class sites of oppression as in the good/bad old days. The new social movements have certainly produced a type of postmodern knowledge and political practice which have forced most marxists to rethink what a radical social theory and politics might look like today. In a sense we can take what we want out of that labile cluster of ideas we call postmodernism.

The political dimension of postmodernism I would wish to stress from a postcolonial perspective is its attention to hybridity as intrinsic to the contemporary human condition. There is none better than Salman Rushdie to explicate how:

> *The Satanic Verses* celebrates hybridity, impurity, intermingling, the transformation that comes of new and unexpected combinations of human beings, cultures, ideas, politics, movies, songs. It rejoices in mongrelization and fears the absolutism of the Pure. *Mélange*, hotchpotch, a bit of this and a bit of that is *how newness enters the world*. (Rushdie, 1991: 394)

The anti-evolutionism of postmodernism helps us think the radical heterogeneity and hybridity which characterizes the postcolonial world. The postmodern problematic (because most of the world does not live in a postmodern age) helps us understand the complex, non-linear paths through and beyond modernity. We live in mixed, confused temporalities – peripheral pre-modernities which are part of global postmodernism – and a politics which would be radical without being fundamentalist needs to grasp this. There are of course risks in moving beyond the ontological and political securities of marxism and liberalism, but the spectre of Nietzsche need not deter us.

What was the reaction of marxists to the postmodern turn/mood/ethos of the 1980s? There was an attempt at co-option, in particular though the influential work of Frederic Jameson (1984). For Jameson, postmodernism is best understood as the 'cultural logic of late capitalism'. Somewhat misusing Ernest Mandel's (1975) periodization of late capitalism, Jameson ties in cultural developments of the 1960s with a new stage of capitalism. His cultural analysis is simply breathtaking and he situates artistic forms imaginatively within socioeconomic developments. For Jameson, the link between culture and economics is direct, arguing as he does that 'the whole global, yet American postmodern culture [is] the internal and superstructural expression of a whole new wave of American military and economic domination throughout the world' (Jameson, 1991: 57). While accepting the valuable contribution that Jameson makes to an understanding of the postmodern condition, we could argue, firstly, that there is a certain conceptual crudity in his attempt to incorporate/domesticate postmodernism within traditional marxist schemas; and, secondly, that his own particular brand of Hegelian marxism, with its acceptance of the old base-superstructure dualism, is a poor base from which to think the new in a radical fashion.

More orthodox marxists, such as Alex Callinicos (1989) and Terry Eagleton (1996) mounted a less subtle counter-offensive against postmodernism. In good sociological reductionist mode, Callinicos argues that: 'The discourse of postmodernism is best seen as the product of a socially mobile intelligentsia in a climate dominated by the retreat of the Western labour movement' (1989: 170–1). Callinicos and, in much wittier vein, Eagleton basically see postmodernism as the product of radical intellectuals disillusioned or disappointed after the failure of '1968' to deliver on its revolutionary promise. It is a turn away from the 'god that failed' to aestheticism. Eagleton refers, with merited passion to 'The political illiteracy and historical oblivion fostered by much postmodernism, with its cult of flash, theoretical fashion' (Eagleton, 1996: 23). It is good practice to historicize postmodernism and to expose some of its darker political facets and relativize its sometimes grandiose claims. However, what the orthodox marxist response tends to produce as an alternative – in this contestatory, gladiatorial contest – is simply a restatement of old platitudes. We know that social class 'still matters', we know that culture is not 'everything' and we understand that postmodernism does not have all the answers. The question is whether it at least asks some of the right questions.

Beyond the impasse(s)

There would seem to be an impasse between postmodernism and orthodox marxism, judging from some of the above. There was also some sort of an impasse between those who thought 1989 represented a total catastrophe for marxism and those for whom it represented a wonderful opportunity for 'true' socialism. Finally, there seems to be an impasse in the globalized postmodern times in which we are living, only tangentially captured by the literature on *fin de siècle* blues. Not to 'transcend' but to confront these interlocked impasses, I shall develop the notion of a postmodern-marxism–socialism. Prompting for the first leg of this project comes from none other than Jacques Derrida, once assumed to be an implacable enemy of marxism. It is, indeed, the case that Derrida's critique of logocentrism, and his deconstructionist approach undermines the mechanical materialism of orthodox marxism. However, Derrida went on to re-evaluate his position on Marx himself and by the early 1990s was declaring (against the fashion) that: 'Marxism remains at once indispensable and structurally insufficient: it is still necessary but provided it be transformed and adapted to new conditions and to a new thinking … This transformation and this opening up of Marxism are in conformity with the *spirit of Marxism*' (1994: 58–9).

   Derrida rejects logocentric thought which claims legitimacy in terms of an external, universally truthful proposition because he believes that this can only be circular and self-referential. For a postmodernist perspective these systems of thought are only grounded in a self-constituted logic. Marxism would appear to be such a system of thought. For Derrida, though, 'When the dogma machine and the "Marxist" ideological apparatuses … are in the process of disappearing' (1994: 13) we have no excuse not to reconsider Marx as the first deconstructionist. This approach or philosophy – Derrida will not call it a method – advocates an inworming or internal subversion of the text, to reveal its contradictions and assumptions. It does not do so, however, from the perspective of an external validation, nor does it seek to offer a better text. Thought systems are assumed to rest on binary oppositions (good/bad, true/false, nature/culture, man/woman, and so on), with an assumed privilege of one over the other. One side is primary, the other derivative. So, Derrida's approach, somewhat too briefly, is as follows: 'One of the two terms governs the other … To deconstruct the opposition … is to overturn the hierarchy at a given moment' (Derrida, 1981: 41). Not surprisingly, this approach can be used to destabilize the assumed hierarchies behind race or gender inequality and class exploitation.

Derrida's deconstructionism does not seek simply to neutralize binary oppositions, as would be the case with Hegel's idealist method and, arguably, much of marxism. Deconstruction, rather, involves reversal and displacement. It does not accept the false appearance of resolution, and – on the basis that difference is always present – would be sceptical of a communist society without difference which could only be sustained by force. Derrida rejects what he sees as our metaphysical need for closure, to make ends and means coincide. He questions the accepted notions of truth and believes that no interpretation can be the final one. So, deconstruction, unlike most marxisms, does not set out to unmask 'error' because that assumes we know what 'truth' is. Deconstruction directs us to the margins of a text, it bids us look for the excluded, the conceded, the unnamed. Deconstruction, then, following Gayatri Spivak's introduction to Derrida, seeks 'to locate the promising marginal text, to disclose the undecidable moment, to pry it loose with the positive lever of the signifier, to reverse the resident hierarchy, only to displace it; to dismantle in order to reconstitute what is always already inscribed' (1976: xxvii). So, what response can marxism have to this deconstructionist enterprise?

For Terry Eagleton 'many of the vauntedly novel themes of deconstruction do little more than reproduce some of the most commonplace topics of bourgeois liberalism' (1996: 17). To privilege plurality and heterogeneity, to oppose totalizing knowledge and to advocate indeterminacy may, indeed, appear to be liberal virtues. However, there are a number of social and political theorists now working on the border between marxism and deconstruction. Thus, Michael Ryan has explicitly argued for a 'critical articulation' (note, not marriage) between marxism and deconstruction (1982). Marx and Derrida are both sharp critics of metaphysics. Derrida helps correct the linear evolutionism of a certain marxism and a naïve belief in the finalistic resolution of socialism. Deconstruction provides marxism with a critical vantage point which is not merely oppositional but can lead to a politics of transformation. Derrida, for his part, now embraces 'an affirmative thinking of the messianic and emancipatory promise of marxism' (1994: 71). Against a certain postmodern nihilism, he believes that this emancipatory promise is 'undeconstructible'. A marxism prepared to undertake its self-critique – as Derrida believes Marx always was – would then not be absent from the social and political struggles of the next century.

For marxism, the critical articulation with deconstruction would have several advantages. It seems to make the marxist critical function more acute insofar as it is not based on some false notion of 'truth' (proletarian, or otherwise) and a, frankly, unsustainable notion of a mechanical development towards communism. At a more pragmatic level, it takes marxism into the various poststructuralist fields where much remains to be learnt, and into the politics of the new social movements from which a politics of transformation may arise. Deconstruction will also be changed by this encounter. As Bill Martin puts it in his marxist dialogue with Derrida: 'The point is that deconstruction has to be deepened, made more powerful, by criticizing everything in it that can render deconstruction merely academic' (Martin, 1995: 10). Apart from taking deconstruction away from North American professors of literature, marxism can assist it in becoming more critical of conventional terms such as 'economy', 'democracy', and so on, which are usually untheorized in the deconstructionist discourse. A marxism extracted from the totalizing prison of modernism would, essentially, be a useful antidote to the unspoken, taken-for-granted, liberalism which permeates much of the postmodernist literature.

If a postmodern marxism can be envisaged, what about a postmodern socialism, or is this simply an oxymoron? It would certainly be a hybrid, but that would be in keeping with the global postmodern era in which we live. Peter Beilharz is one who has articulated the need for 'a postmodern socialism which is differentiated, sceptical, pragmatic, and seeks like [Walter] Benjamin always to speak about culture and power together' (Beilharz, 1994: 105). The basic pressure is that modernity has exhausted its progressive potential. Indeed, this potential was never much in evidence in what we used to call the Third World. So, if socialism grew up in the shadow of modernity, it is unlikely to have much purchase on postmodern problems. It would be tilting at windmills to use the tools of yesteryear on today's problems. Barbarism or (postmodern) socialism do remain on the horizon today as much as they did for Rosa Luxemburg. The new transformative politics which will undoubtedly emerge in the decades to come will almost definitely not be called socialist. As a provisional label to think the new democratic alternative to barbarism, postmodern socialism may be a convenient way of exploring the horizon of possibilities now opening up.

The new discursive, hybrid postmodern socialism could probably learn from the original and productive engagement between feminism(s) and postmodernism(s). Feminism began unambiguously as and still is, by and large, a modernist discourse, sharing (or wanting to share) in the values of the Enlightenment. Yet the universalistic discourse of Enlightenment rationalism did not allow (most) women to bask in its warm glow any more than it did the postcolonial peoples. A move began within the various feminist movements during the 1970s away from a rhetoric of equality to a discourse of difference. From here the parallel and cross-fertilization with the new poststructuralist theories became evident. The new politics of location, standpoint epistemologies and identity politics had hit the scene. Foucault was appropriated for feminism (for example, McNay, 1992) and the debate with/against Lacan opened up new dimensions. Derrida, of course, would help obliterate the man/woman hierarchy. Even the category of 'woman', central of course to a feminist politics, was to be revealed as an unstable if not false category. All these things were exciting but also dangerous in terms of the feminist project, especially in its socialist variants.

Luce Irgaray asked (im)pertinently if postmodernism was not, in fact, the 'last ruse' of patriarchy (1985). Just as women (and the postcolonial peoples) were finding their voices, postmodernism conveniently proclaimed the death of the subject. Perhaps some aspects of postmodernism had to be put on hold and some of the old-fashioned (if theoretically dubious) virtues of the Enlightenment rediscovered. Yet the case for a postmodern feminism is (for me) quite persuasive. One need not 'buy in' to some postmodern themes such as relativism and nihilism. Derrida allows us to merge the critique of phallocentrism and logocentrism. The revolutionary character of Derrida's thinking as it relates to feminism is closely argued by Susan Hekman, for whom:

> Derrida's contribution to feminism, then, lies in his displacement of binary logic and his new inscription of difference. The binary logic of western thought is displaced through a supplementary logic that uses the concept 'woman' to overthrow the polarities of the metaphysics of presence. Feminist deconstruction entails a radical restructuring of western thought and practice … This discourse speaks in a multiplicity of sexual voices, it is a discourse which has no centre, neither masculine and feminine, yet does not erase either the masculine or the feminine. (Hekman, 1980: 175)

What implications might this line of enquiry/intervention have for a putative postmodern socialism?

One of the things a postmodern socialism would need to do would be to de-demonize capitalism. Here it is extraordinary to note to what extent many marxists have themselves made capitalism into a seamless, impregnable monster. J. K. Gibson-Graham has developed a strong critique of marxist essentialism, a belief in a true essence, something irreducible which is constitutive of a given social phenomenon (1996: 24). Thus capitalism in the mainstream marxist discourse has been seen as all-powerful, all-persuasive, self-reproducing and dynamic, conferring identity on all of us and giving meaning to all social life. What if capitalism is really a 'paper tiger' or has 'feet of clay'? Or, as Gibson-Graham put it, more theoretically, 'Theorizing capitalism itself as different from itself – as having in other words, no essential or coherent identity – multiplies (infinitely) the possibilities of alterity' (ibid.: 15). This feminist critique of radical political economy, especially associated with a discourse–theoretical approach, would allow us to see, for example, to what extent the phallic images of transnational corporations penetrating the Third World as part of globalization can be deconstructed, deflated and diverted or subverted.

Would our sensible, practical and realist postmodern socialism not need a utopia to motivate it? Well, Derrida has no problem with the messianic message of marxism, so why not something akin to Foucault's *heterotopia* – not the invention of a new place but a displacement of the one we live in, a move from the centre to the margins? As Boaventura de Sousa Santos puts it: 'We must, therefore, reinvent the future by opening up a new horizon of possibilities mapped out by new radical alternatives' (Santos, 1995: 479). If our present is marked by undecidability so will our future be. There can be no blueprints for a new society after Hitler, Stalin and Pol Pot. However, there can be and there are a number of possibilities on the horizon. The South, uneven development, globalization and, for that matter, imperialism remain as major parameters for the prospects of transformation. Others will explore the gendering and the greening of this non-utopian utopia. What Marx had to say about capitalism, and his egalitarian ethic which ran through from his 'young' to his mature phase, will probably be part of the equation. History really did not end in 1989.

Bibliography

Adam, B. and Allan, S. (1995) 'Theorizing Culture: An Introduction', in B. Adam and S. Allan (eds), *Theorizing Culture: An Interdisciplinary Critique after Postmodernism*, London: UCL Press.

Adams, B. (1993) 'Sustainable Development and the Greening of Development Theory', in F. Schuurman (ed.), *Beyond the Impasse: New Directions in Development Theory*, London: Zed Books.

Adams, M. L. (1994) 'There's No Place Like Home: On the Face of Identity in Feminist Politics', in M. Evans (ed.), *The Woman Question*, 2nd Edn, London: Sage.

Ahmad, A. (1992) *In Theory: Classes, Nations, Literatures*, London: Verso.

Althusser, L. (1984) 'A Reply on Art in Reply to André Daspre', in *Essays on Ideology*, London: Verso.

Anderson, B. (1983) *Imagined Communities: Reflections on the Origin and Spread of Nationalism*, London: Verso.

Anderson, P. (1976) *Consideration on Western Marxism*, London: Verso.

Anthias, F. and Yuval-Davis, N. (1989) 'Introduction', in N. Yuval-Davis and F. Anthias (eds), *Woman-Nation-State*, London: Macmillan.

Anweiler, O. (1974) *The Soviets*, New York: Simon & Schuster.

Aricó, J. (1988) *La Cola del Diablo. Itinerario de Gramsci en América Latina*, Buenos Aires: Puntosur.

Aronowitz, F. and Di Fazio, W. (1994) *The Jobless Future*, Minneapolis: University of Minnesota Press.

Aronson, R. (1995) *After Marxism*, New York: Guildford Press.

Arrighi, G., Hopkins, T. and Wallerstein, I. (1989) *Antisystemic Movements*, London: Verso.

Arvon, H. (1973) *Marxist Esthetics*, Ithaca: Cornell University Press.

Ashcroft, B., Griffiths, G. and Tiffin, H. (eds) (1995) *The Post-Colonial Reader*, London: Routledge.

Avineri, S. (ed.) (1969) *Karl Marx on Colonialism and Modernization*, New York: Anchor.

Bahro, R. (1978) *The Alternative in Eastern Europe*, London: Verso.

—— (1984) *From Red to Green*, London: Verso.

Bailey, A. and Llobera, J. (eds) (1981) *The Asiatic Mode of Production: Science and Politics*, London: Routledge & Kegan Paul.

Balibar, E. (1992) 'Foucault and Marx: The question of nominalism', in T. Armstrong (ed.), *Michel Foucault, Philosopher*, New York: Routledge.

—— (1995) *The Philosophy of Marx*, London: Verso.

Baran, P. (1968) *The Political Economy of Growth*, New York: Modern Reader Paperback.

Barrett, M. (1980) *Women's Oppression Today*, London: Verso.

—— (1983) 'Marxist-Feminism and the Work of Karl Marx', in B. Matthews (ed.), *Marx: A Hundred Years On*, London: Lawrence & Wishart.

—— (1988) *Women's Oppression Today*, London: Verso.

—— (1991) *The Politics of Truth, From Marx to Foucault*, Cambridge: Polity.

Bauer, O. (1978a) 'Observaciones sobre la cuestíon de las nacionalidades' (Bemer-kungen zur Nationalitätenfrage, *Die Neue Zeit*, 1908).

—— (1978b) 'El obrero y la nación (Der Arbeiter und die Nation, *Der Kampf*, 1912) in Calwer *et al.*, *La Segunda Internacional y el Problema Nacional y Colonial (segunda parte)*, Cuadernos de Pasado y Presente 74, Mexico; Siglo XXI.

—— (1979) *La Cuestión de la Nacionalidades y la Socialdemocracia* (Die Nationalitäten en frago und die Socialdemokratie, 1907). Mexico; Siglo XXI.

Bauman, Z. (1976) *Socialism: The Active Utopia*, London: Allen & Unwin.

Baxandall, R., Ewen, E. and Gordon, L. (1976) 'The Working Class Has Two Sexes', *Monthly Review*, 28(3).

Beilharz, P. (1992) *Labour's Utopias: Bolshevism, Fabianism, Social Democracy*, London: Routledge.

—— (1994) *Postmodern Socialism: Romanticism, City and State*, Victoria: Melbourne University Press.

Benner, E. (1995) *Really Existing Nationalisms: A Post-Communist View from Marx and Engels*, Oxford: Clarendon.

Benton, T. (1992) 'Ecology, Socialism and the Mastery of Nature: A Reply to Reiner Grundmann', *New Left Review*, 194.

Benton, T. and Redclift, M. (1994) 'Introduction', in M. Redclift and T. Benton (eds), *Social Theory and the Global Environment*, London: Routledge.

Berman, M. (1983) *All That Is Solid Melts Into Air: The Experience of Modernity*, London: Verso.

Bernstein, E., Belfort Bax, E., Kautsky, K. and Renner, K. (1978) *La Segunda Internacional y el Problema Nacional y Colonial (primera parte)*, Cuadernos de Pasado y Presente 73, Mexico; Siglo XXI.

Bernstein, H. (1993) *The Preconditions of Socialism*, Cambridge University Press.

Bideleux, R. (1985) *Communism and Development*, London: Methuen.

Bloch, E. (1970) *A Philosophy of the Future*, New York: Herder & Herder.

Bobbio, N. (1996) *Left and Right: The Significance of a Political Distinction*, Cambridge: Polity.

Boggs, C. (1995) *The Socialist Tradition: From Crisis to Decline*, New York: Routledge.

Bookchin, M. (1980–1) 'Review of A. Gorz's Ecology as Politics', *Telos*, 46.

Bottomore, T. and Goode, P. (eds) (1978) *Austro-Marxism*, Oxford: Clarendon.

Boyne, A. and Rattansi, A. (1990) 'The Theory and Politics of Postmodernism: By Way of an Introduction', in R. Boyne and A. Rattansi (eds), *Postmodernism and Society*, London: Macmillan.

Braverman, N. (1974) *Labor and Monopoly Capital*, New York: Monthly Review Press.

Brewer, A. (1980) *Marxist Theories of Imperialism: A Critical Study*, London: Routledge.

Brundtland, H. (1987) *Our Common Future*, Oxford University Press.

Bryson, V. (1992) *Feminist Political Theory: An Introduction*, London: Macmillan.

Buck, G. and James, S. (1992) 'Introduction: Contextualizing Equality and Difference', in G. Buck and S. James (eds.), *Beyond Equality and Difference: Citizenship, Feminist Politics and Female Subjectivity*, London: Routledge.

Calhoun, C. (1997) *Nationalism*, Buckingham: Open University Press.

Callari, A. and Ruccio, D. (1996) 'Introduction: Postmodern Materialism and the Future of Marxist Theory', in A. Callari and D. Ruccio (eds), *Postmodern Materialism and the Future of Marxist Theory: Essays in the Althusserian Tradition*, Hanover and London: Wesleyan University Press.

Callinicos, A. (1989) *Against Postmodernism: A Marxist Critique*, Cambridge, Polity.

Camilleri, J. and Falk, J. (1992) *The End of Sovereignty? The Politics of a Shrinking and Fragmenting World*, Aldershot: Edward Elgar.

Cardoso, F. H. (1993a) 'New North/South Relations in the Present Context: A New Dependency?', in M. Carnoy *et al.*, *The New Global Economy in the Information Age*, University Park, PA: Penn State University Press.

—— (1993b) 'Desafios de la Socialdemocracia en América Latina', in M. Vellinga (ed.), *Democracia y Política en América Latina*, Mexico: Siglo xxi.

Carlassare, E. (1994) 'Destabilizing the Criticisms of Essentialism in Ecofeminist Discourse', *Capitalism, Nature, Socialism*, 5(3).

Carr, E. (1970) *Socialism in One Country of 1924–1926. Volume One*. Harmondsworth: Penguin.

Carrière d'Encausse, H. and Schram, S. (eds) (1969) *Marxism and Asia*, London: Allen Lanes Penguin.

Casey, C. (1996) *Work, Self and Society after Industrialism*, London: Routledge.

Cassidy, J. (1997) 'The Next Big Thinker', *Independent on Sunday*, 7 December.

Castells, M. (1996) *The Information Age: Economy, Society and Culture, Vol. I: The Rise of the Network Society*, Oxford: Blackwell.

—— (1997) *The Information Age: Economy, Society and Culture, Vol. II: The Power of Identity*, Oxford: Blackwell.

—— (1998) *The Information Age: Economy, Society and Culture, Vol. III: End of Millenium*, Oxford: Blackwell.

Caudwell, C. (1970) *Romance and Realism*, Princeton University Press.

—— (1973) *Illusion and Reality: A Study of the Sources of Poetry*, London: Lawrence & Wishart.

Chatterjee, P. (1986) *Nationalist Thought and the Colonial World – A Derivative Discourse*, London: Zed Books.

—— (1996) 'Whose Imagined Community?', in G. Balakrishnan (ed.), *Mapping the Nation*, London: Verso.

Claudin, F. (1975) *The Communist Movement: From Comintern to Cominform*, Harmondsworth: Penguin.

Cleaver, H. (1979) *Reading Capital Politically*, Brighton: Harvester.

Cohen, G. A. (1978) *Karl Marx's Theory of History*, Oxford: Clarendon.

Cohen, S. (1980) *Bukharin and the Bolshevik Revolution: A Political Biography, 1888–1938*, Oxford University Press.

Collins, P. (1991) *Black Feminist Thought*, London: Routledge.

Commoner, B. (1973) *The Closing Circle: Confronting the Environmental Crisis*, London: Cape.

Coward, R. (1983) *Patriarchal Precedents: Sexual and Social Relations*, London: Routledge Kegan Paul.

Daly, M. (1979) *Gyn/Ecology: The Meta-Ethics of Radical Feminism*, Boston: Beacon.

Daniels, R. (1969) *The Conscience of the Revolution: Communist Opposition in Soviet Russia*, New York: Simon & Schuster.

Davies, I. (1995) *Cultural Studies and Beyond: Fragments of Empire*, London: Routledge.

Davis, H. B. (ed.) (1976) *The National Question: Selected Writings by Rosa Luxemburg*, New York: Monthly Review Press.

Degras, J. (ed.) (1971) *The Communist International 1919–1943: Documents vol 1*, London: Frank Cass.

Delphy, C. (1984) *Close to Home: A materialist analysis of women's oppression*, London: Hutchinson.

Derrida, J. (1981) *Positions*, University of Chicago Press.

—— (1994) *Spectres of Marx: The State of the Debt, the Work of Mourning, and the New International*, London: Routledge.

Di Stefano, C. (1990) 'Dilemmas of Difference: Feminism, Modernity and Postmodernism', in L. Nicholson (ed.), *Feminism/Postmodernism*, New York: Routledge.

Douglas, M. (1966) *Purity and Danger: An analysis of concepts of pollution and taboo*, London: Routledge.

Dyker, D. (1992) *Restructuring the Soviet Economy*, London: Routledge.

Eagleton, T. (1976) *Marxism and Literary Criticism*, London: Methuen.

—— (1996) *The Illusions of Postmodernism*, Oxford: Blackwell.

Eckersley, R. (1992) *Environmentalism and Political Theory: Towards an Ecocentric Approach*, London: UCL Press.

Edelholm, F., Harris, O. and Young, K. (1977) 'Conceptualising Women', *Critique of Anthropology*, 9/10.

Eisenstein, Z. (1979) 'Developing a Theory of Capitalist Patriarchy and Socialist Feminism', in Z. Eisenstein (ed.), *Capitalist Patriarchy and the Case for Socialist Feminism*, New York: Monthly Review Press.

Engels, F. (1990) 'The Origin of the Family, Private Property and the State. In the Light of the Researches by Lewis H. Morgan', in Karl Marx and F. Engels, *Collected Works, vol. 26*, Moscow: Progress Publishers.

Enzensberger, H.-M. (1974) 'A Critique of Political Ecology', *New Left Review*, 74.

Escobar, A. (1984) 'Discourse and Power in Development': Michel Foucault and the Relevance of his Work in the Third World', *Alternatives*, 10.

Esteva, G. (1992) 'Development', in W. Sachs (ed.), *The Development Dictionary: A Guide to Knowledge and Power*, London: Zed Books.

Featherstone, M. (1991) *Consumer Culture and Postmodernism*, London: Sage.

Fitzgerald, E. V. K (1986) 'Notes on the Analysis of the Small Underdeveloped Economy in Transition', in R. Fagen, C. D. Deere and K. L. Coraggio (eds), *Transition and Development: Problems of Third World Socialism*, New York: Monthly Review Press.

Forgas, D. (1984) 'National-popular: Genealogy of a Concept', in *Formations: of Nations and Peoples*, London: Routledge Kegan Paul.

Foucault, M. (1972) *The Archaeology of Knowledge*, London: Tavistock.

—— (1980) 'Truth and Power', in C. Gordon (ed.), *Power/Knowledge: Selected Interviews and Other Writings, 1972–1977*, Brighton: Harvester.

—— (1984) 'What is the Enlightenment?' in P. Rabinow (ed.), *The Foucault Reader*, London: Penguin.

Frankel, B. (1987) *The Post-Industrial Utopians*, Cambridge: Polity.

Fraser, N. and Nicholson, L. (1990) 'Social Criticism Without Philosophy: An Encounter between Feminism and Postmodernism', in L. Nicholson (ed.), *Feminism/Postmodernism*, New York: Routledge.

Fukuyama, F. (1992) *The End of History and the Last Man*, London: Hamish Hamilton.

Furedi, F. (1986) *The Soviet Union Demystified: A Materialist Analysis*, London: Junius.

García Canclini, N. (1995) *Hybrid Cultures*, Minneapolis: Minnesota University Press.

Garé, A. (1995) *Postmodernism and the Environmental Crisis*, London: Routledge.

Gatens, M. (1992) 'Power, Bodies and Difference', in M. Barrett and A. Phillips (eds), *Destabilizing Theory: Contemporary Feminist Debates*, Cambridge: Polity.

Gellner, E. (1983) *Nations and Nationalism*, Oxford: Basil Blackwell.

Gibson-Graham, J. K. (1996) *The End of Capitalism (as we knew it): A Feminist Critique of Political Economy*, Oxford: Blackwell.

Gilbert, A. (1981) *Marx's Politics: Communists and Citizens*, Oxford: Martin Robertson.

Glenny, M. (1990) *The Rebirth of History: Eastern Europe in the Age of Democracy*, London: Penguin.

Glucksmann, A. (1980) *The Master Thinkers*, Brighton: Harvester.

Gorz, A. (1980) *Ecology as Politics*, London: Pluto.

—— (1982) *Farewell to the Working Class: An Essay on Lost Industrial Socialism*, London: Pluto.

Gramsci, A. (1971) *Selections from the Prison Notebooks*, ed. and trans. by Q. Hoare and G. Nowell Smith, London: Lawrence and Wishart.

—— (1977) 'The Revolution Against "Capital"' in A. Gramsci, *Selections from Political Writings (1910–1920)*, London: Lawrence & Wishart.

Gray, J. (1995) 'Among the Ruins of Marxism', in F. Mount (ed.), *Communism*, London: Harvill.

Griffin, S. (1978) *Woman and Nature: The Roaring Inside Her*, New York: Harper & Row.

Grundmann, R. (1991) *Marxism and Ecology*, Oxford: Clarendon.

Guattari, D. (1984) *Molecular Revolution: Psychiatry and Politics*, Harmondsworth: Penguin.

Guha, R. (1988) 'Preface', in R. Guha and G. C. Spivak (eds), *Selected Subaltern Studies*, Oxford University Press.

Guha, R. (ed.) (1982) *Subaltern Studies, vol I*, Delhi: Oxford University Press.

Hall, S. (1996a) 'Gramsci's Relevance for the Study of Race and Ethnicity', in D. Morley and K. H. Chen (eds), *Stuart Hall: Critical Dialogues in Cultural Studies*, London: Routledge.

—— (1996b) 'Cultural Studies and its Theoretical Legacies', in D. Morley and K. H. Chen (eds), *Stuart Hall: Critical Dialogues in Cultural Studies*, London: Routledge.

Halliday, F. (1991) 'The Ends of the Cold War', in R. Blackburn (ed.), *After the Fall: The Failure of Communism and the Future of Socialism*, London: Verso.

Harding, N. (1971) *Lenin's Political Thought volume 1. Theory and Practice in the Democratic Revolution*, Basingstoke: Macmillan.

Harding, S. (1986) 'What is the Real Material Base of Patriarchy and Capitalism?' in L. Sargent (ed.), *The Unhappy Marriage of Marxism and Feminism*, London: Pluto.

Hartmann, H. (1986) 'The Unhappy Marriage of Marxism and Feminism: Towards a More Progressive Union', in L. Sargent (ed.), *The Unhappy Marriage of Marxism and Feminism*, London: Pluto.

Harvey, D. (1990) *The Condition of Post-Modernity*, Oxford: Blackwell.

Haupt, G. (1974) 'Les marxistes face à la question nationale: l' histoire du problème', in G. Haupt, M. Lowy and C. Weill (eds), *Les Marxistes et la Question Nationale, 1848–1914*, Paris: Maspero.

Hayward, M. (1983) *Writers in Russia: 1917–1978*, London: Harvill.

Hekman, S. (1992) *Gender and Knowledge: Elements of a Postmodern Feminism*, Cambridge: Polity.

Held, D. (1992) 'Liberalism, Marxism and Democracy', in S. Hall, D. Held and T. McGrew (eds), *Modernity and its Futures*, Cambridge: Polity.

Hildyard, N. (1993) 'Foxes in Charge of Chickens', in W. Sachs (ed.), *Global Ecology: A New Arena of Political Conflict*, London: Zed Books.

Hirst, P. (1979) *On Law and Ideology*, London: Macmillan.

Hobsbawm, E. (1990) *Nations and Nationalism Since 1780: Programme, myth, reality*, Cambridge University Press.

—— (1991) 'Goodbye to All That', in R. Blackburn (ed.), *After the Fall: The Failure of Communism and the Future of Socialism*, London: Verso.

Holub, R. (1992) *Antonio Gramsci: Beyond Marxism and Postmodernism*, London: Routledge.

Honeycut, K. (1981) 'Clara Zetkin: A Socialist Approach to the Problem of Women's Oppression', in K. Slaughter and R. Kern (eds), *European Women on the Left, Socialism, Feminism, and the Problems Faced by Political Women, 1880 to the Present*, Westport: Greenwood.

hooks, b. (1991) *Ain't I a Woman: Black Women and Feminism*, Boston: South End Press.

—— (1994) *Feminist Theory: From Margin to Center*, Boston: South End Press.

Ignatieff, M. (1994) *Blood and Belonging: Journeys into the New Nationalism*, London: Vintage.

Il Manifesto (1979) *Power and Opposition in Post-revolutionary Societies*, London: Ink Links.

Irigaray, L. (1985) *Speculism of the Other Woman*, Ithaca: Cornell University Press.

Jackson, C. (1994) 'Gender Analysis and Environmentalisms', in M. Redclift and T. Benton (eds), *Social Theory and the Global Environment*, London: Routledge.

James, P. (1996) *Nation Formation: Towards a Theory of Abstract Community*, London: Sage.

Jameson, F. (1991) *Postmodernism or, The Cultural Logic of Late Capitalism*, London: Verso.

Janmohamed, A. (1995) 'Refiguring values, power, knowledge', in B. Magnuo and S. Callenberg (eds), *Whither Marxism? Global Crises in International Perspective*, London: Routledge.

Jay, M. (1988) *Fin-de-Siècle Socialism*, London: Routledge.

Jayawardena, K. (1986) *Feminism and Nationalism in the Third World*, London: Zed Books.

Johnson, R. (1979) 'Three problematics: elements of a working-class culture', in J. Clarke, C. Critcher and R. Johnson (eds), *Working-Class Culture: Studies in history and theory*, London: Hutchinson.

Kautsky, K. (1978) 'Nacionalidad e internacionalidad' (Nationalität und Internationalität, *Ergänzungshefte zur Neuen Zeit*, 1908) in R. Calwer, *et al.*, *La Segunda Internacional y el problema Nacional y Colonial (segunda parte)*, Cuadernos de Pasado y Presente 74, Mexico; Siglo XXI.

Kay, C. (1989) *Latin American Theories of Development and Underdevelopment*, London: Routledge.

Kay, G. (1975) *Development and Underdevelopment: A Marxist Analysis*, London: Macmillan.

Kedourie, E. (1960) *Nationalism*, London: Hutchinson.

Kolakowski, L. (1978) *Main Currents of Marxism, vol. 1: The Founders*, Oxford University Press.

—— (1981) *Main Currents of Marxism, vol. 2.: The Golden Age*, Oxford University Press.

Kornai, J. (1992) *The Socialist System: The Political Economy of Communism*, Oxford: Clarendon.

Laclau, E. (1996) *Emancipation(s)*, London: Verso.

Laclau, E. and Mouffe, C. (1985) *Hegemony and Socialist Strategy: Towards a Radical Democratic Politics*, London: Verso.

Lane, D. (1974) 'Leninism as an Ideology of Soviet Development', in E. de Kadt and G. Williams (eds), *Sociology and Development*, London: Tavistock.

Larrain, J. (1983) *Marxism and Ideology*, London: Macmillan.

Lecourt, D. (1976) *Lysenko: Histoire réelle d'une 'science proletarienne'*, Paris: Maspero.

Leftwich, A. (1992), 'Is There a Socialist Path to Socialism?', *Third World Quarterly*, 13(1) (Special Issue: 'Rethinking Socialism').

Leibman, M. (1986) 'Reformism Yesterday and Social Democracy Today', in R. Milliband, J. Saville, M. Liebman and L. Panitch (eds), *Socialist Register 1985/86*, London: Merlin.

Leichteim, G. (1970) *A Short History of Socialism*, London: Weidenfeld & Nicolson.

Lenin, vol I. (1963a) 'Self-determination', in *Collected Works, vol. 20*, Moscow: Progress Publishers.

—— (1963b) 'Critical Remarks on the National Question', *Collected Works, vol. 20*, Moscow: Progress Publishers.

—— (1966) *The Emancipation of Women*, New York: International Publishers.

—— (1967) *The Development of Capitalism in Russia*, Moscow: Progress Publishers.

—— (1970a) 'Imperialism, The Highest Stage of Capitalism', in V. I. Lenin, *Selected Works in Three Volumes, vol. 1*, Moscow: Progress Publishers.

—— (1970b) 'Six Theses on the Immediate Tasks of the Soviet Government', in V. I. Lenin, *Selected Works in Three Volumes, vol. 2*, Moscow: Progress Publishers.

—— (1970c) *Questions of National Policy and Proletarian Internationalism*, Moscow: Progress Publishers.

Lévy, B.-H. (1977) *La barbarie à visage humain*, Paris: Grasset.

Lewin, M. (1973) *Lenin's Last Struggle*, London: Pluto.

—— (1975) *Political Undercurrents in Soviet Economic Debates*, London: Pluto.

Lifschitz, M. (1973) *The Philosophy of Art of Karl Marx*, London: Pluto.

Lipietz, A. (1992) *Towards a New Economic Order: Postfordism, Ecology and Democracy*, Oxford: Polity.

Loew, R. (1979) 'The Politics of Austro-Marxism', *New Left Review*, 118.

Lorde, A. (1994) 'The Master's Tools Will Never Dismantle the Master's House', in M. Evans (ed.), *The Woman Question*, 2nd edn, London: Sage.

Lukács, G. (1970) *Lenin: A Study on the Unity of his Thought*, London: Verso.

Lukács, G. (1971) *History and Class Consciousness: Studies in Marxist Dialectics*, London: Merlin.

Lyotard, J. F. (1984) *The Postmodern Condition: A Report on Knowledge*, Manchester University Press.

—— (1993) *Libidinal Economy*, London: Athlone.

Maconachie, M. (1987) 'Engels, Sexual Divisions and the Family', in J. Sayers, M. Evans and N. Redclift (eds), *Engels Revisited: New Feminist Essays*, London: Tavistock.

Mandel, E. (1975) *Late Capitalism*, London: New Left Books.

Manzo, K. (1991) 'Modernist Discourse and the Crisis of Development Theory', *Studies in Comparative International Development*, 26(2).

Marshall, B. (1994) *Engendering Modernity: Feminism, Social Theory and Social Change*, Cambridge: Polity.

Martin, B. (1995) *Humanism and its Aftermath: The Shared Fate of Deconstruction and Politics*, New Jersey: Humanities Press.

Marx, K. (1968) *Selected Works in One Volume*, London: Lawrence & Wishart.

—— (1973a) *Grundrisse: Foundations of the Critique of Political Economy (rough draft)*, Harmondsworth: Penguin.

—— (1973b) *Grundrisse. Introduction to the Critique of Political Economy*, London: Penguin.

—— (1974) *The First International and After, Political Writings, vol. 3*, London: Penguin.

—— (1975) *Early Writings*, London: Penguin.

—— (1976) *Capital: A Critique of Political Economy, vol. 1*, Harmondsworth: Penguin.

Marx, K. and Engels, F. (1971) *Ireland and the Irish Question*, Moscow: Progress Publishers.

—— and —— (1976a) 'The German Ideology', in K. Marx and F. Engels, *Collected Works. vol. 5*, London: Lawrence & Wishart.

—— and —— (1976b) *Collected Works, vol. 5*, London: Lawrence & Wishart.

—— and —— (1976c) *Collected Works, vol. 6*, London: Lawrence & Wishart.

—— and —— (1977a) *Collected Works, vol. 8*, London: Lawrence & Wishart.

—— and —— (1977b) *Collected Works, vol. 9*, London: Lawrence & Wishart.

—— and —— (1977c) 'Manifesto of the Communist Party' in K. Marx, *The Revolutions of 1848. Political Writings vol. 1*, Harmondsworth: Penguin.

—— and —— (1978) *Collected Works, vol. 10*, London: Lawrence & Wishart.

—— and —— (1982) *Collected Works, vol. 38*, London: Lawrence & Wishart.

—— and —— (1987) *Collected Works, vol. 25*, London: Lawrence & Wishart.

McNay, L. (1992) *Foucault and Feminism: Power, Gender and the Self*, Cambridge: Polity.

Mengisteab, K. (1992) 'Responses of Afro-Marxist States to the Crisis of Socialism: A Preliminary Assessment', *Third World Quarterly*, 13(1).

Mies, M. and Shiva, V. (1993) *Ecofeminism*, London: Zed Books.

Mitchell, J. (1971) *A Woman's Estate*, Harmondsworth: Penguin.

—— (1974) *Psychoanalysis and Feminism*, Harmondsworth: Penguin.

Mohanty, C. T. (1992) 'Feminist Encounters: Locating the Politics of Experience', in M. Barrett and A. Phillips (eds), *Destabilizing Theory: Contemporary Feminist Debates*, Cambridge: Polity.

—— (1993) 'Under Western Eyes: Feminist Scholarship and Colonial Discourses', in P. Williams and L. Chrisman (eds), *Colonial Discourse and Post-Colonial Theory*, New York: Harvester-Wheatsheaf.

Molyneux, M. (1981) 'Women in Socialist Societies: Problems of Theory and Practice', in K. Young, C. Wolkowitz and R. McCullagh (eds), *Of Marriage and the Market: Women's Subordination in International Perspective*, London: CSE Books.

—— and Steinberg, D. L. (1995) 'Mies and Shiva's Ecofeminism: A New Testament?', *Feminist Review*, 49.

Morgan, R. (1984) *Sisterhood is Global: The International Women's Movement Anthology*, Harmondsworth: Penguin.

Nairn, T. (1981) *The Break-Up of Britain: Crisis and Neo-Nationalism*, London: New Left Books.

—— (1997) *Faces of Nationalism: Janus Revisited*, London: Verso.

Nietzsche, F. (1964) *Complete Works, vol. 2*, New York: Russell & Russell.

Nimni, E. (1991) *Marxism and Nationalism: Theoretical Origins of a Political Crisis*, London: Pluto.

Norris, C. (1991) *Deconstruction: Theory and Practice*, London: Routledge.

Norton, A. (1988) *Reflections on Political Identity*, Baltimore: Johns Hopkins University Press.

Padgett, S. and Patterson, W. (1991) *A History of Social Democracy in Postwar Europe*, London: Macmillan.

Pannekoek, A. (1978) 'Lucha de clases y nación' (*Klassenkampf und Nation*, 1912), in R. Calwer et al., *La Segunda Internacional y el problema Nacional y Colonial (segunda parte)*, Cuadernos de Pasado y Presente 74, Mexico; Siglo XXI.

Parker, A. (ed.) (1992) *Nationalisms and Sexualities*, New York: Routledge.

Parsons, H. (ed.) (1977) *Marx and Engels on Ecology*, Westport: Greenwood.

Pepper, D. (1993) 'Political Philosophy and Environmentalism in Britain', *Capitalism, Nature, Socialism*, 4(3).

Petras, J. (1978) 'Socialist Revolutions and their Class Components', *New Left Review*, 111.

Plumwood, V. (1988) 'Woman, Humanity and Nature', *Radical Philosophy*, Spring.

Polan, A. J. (1984) *Lenin and the End of Politics*, London: Methuen.

Portantiero, J. C. (1983) *Los Usos de Gramsci*, Buenos Aires: Folios Ediciones.

Post, K. and Wright, P. (1989) *Socialism and Underdevelopment*, London: Routledge.

Poulantzas, N. (1975) *Classes in Contemporary Capitalism*, London: New Left Books.

—— (1980) *State, Power, Socialism*, London: Verso.

Prawer, S. S. (1978) *Karl Marx and World Literature*, Oxford University Press.

Preobrazhensky, E. (1979) *Crisis of Soviet Industrialization*, ed. D. Filtzer, New York: Sharpe.

Rattansi, A. (1997) 'Postcolonialism and its discontents', *Economy and Society*, 26(4).

Redclift, M. (1987), *Sustainable Development: Exploring the Contradiction*, London: Methuen.

Rosenau, P. M. (1992) *Post-Modernism and the Social Sciences: Insights, Inroads, and Intrusions*, Princeton University Press.

Rowbotham, S. (1979) 'The Women's Movement and Organizing for Socialism', in S. Rowbotham, L. Legal and H. Wainwright, *Beyond the Fragments: Feminism and the Making of Socialism*, London: Merlin.

Rushdie, S. (1991) *Imaginary Homelands*, London: Granta.

Ryan, M. (1982) *Marxism and Deconstruction: A Critical Articulation*, Baltimore: Johns Hopkins University Press.

Sachs, W. (1993) 'Global Ecology and the Shadow of 'Development', in W. Sachs (ed.), *Global Ecology: A New Arena of Political Conflict*, London: Zed Books.

Said, E. (1985) *Orientalism*, Harmondsworth: Penguin.

—— (1993) *Culture and Imperialism*. London: Chatto & Windus.

Salvadori, M. (1979) *Karl Kautsky and the Socialist Revolution 1880–1938*, London: Verso.

Santos, B. S. (1995) *Toward a New Common Sense: Law, Science and Politics in the Paradigmatic Transition*, New York: Routledge.

Sarup, M. (1993) *An Introductory Guide to Post-Structuralism and Postmodernism*, London: Harvester.

Schmidt, A. (1971) *The Concept of Nature in Marx*, London: New Left Books.

Scott, J. (1990) 'Deconstructing Equality-versus-Difference', in M. Hirsch and E. F. Keller (eds), *Conflicts in Feminism*, New York: Routledge.

Shanin, T. (ed.) (1983) *Late Marx and the Russian Road*, London: Routledge.

Shiva, V. (1988) *Staying Alive: Women, Ecology and Development*, London: Zed Books.

—— (1993) 'The Greening of the Global Reach', in W. Sachs (ed.), *Global Ecology: A New Arena of Political Conflict*, London: Zed Books.

Sim, S. (1996) *Jean François Lyotard*, London: Prentice-Hall/Harvester.

Sirianni, C. (1982) *Workers' Control and Socialist Democracy: The Soviet Experience*, London: Verso.

Sklair, L. (1994) 'Global Sociology and Global Environmental Change', in M. Redclift and T. Benton (eds), *Social Theory and The Global Environment*, London: Routledge.

Slater, D. (1984) 'Social Movements and a Recasting of the Political, in D. Slater (ed.), *New Social Movements and the State in Latin America*, Amsterdam: CEDLA.

Smith, S. A. (1983) *Red Petrograd: Revolution in the Factories 1917–18*, Cambridge University Press.

Solomon, M. (ed.), (1979) *Marxism and Art*, Brighton: Harvester.

Spivak, G. C. (1976) 'Translator's Preface', in J. Derrida, *Of Grammatology*, Baltimore and London: Johns Hopkins University Press.

—— (1993) 'Can the Subaltern Speak?' in P. Williams and L. Chrisman (eds), *Colonial Discourse and Post-Colonial Theory*, Hemel Hempstead: Harvester– Wheatsheaf.

Stalin (1973) *The Essential Stalin: Major Theoretical Writings 1905–52*. London: Croom Helm.

Stedman Jones, G. (1983) *Languages of Class: Studies in English Working Class History*, Cambridge University Press.

Stites, R. (1978) *The Women's Liberation Movement in Russia: Feminism, Nihilism and Bolshevism, 1860–1930*, Princeton University Press.

Strasser, J. (1978) 'El obrero y la nación' (*Der Arbeiter und die Nation*, 1912) in R. Calwer *et al.*, *La Segunda Internacional y el problema Nacional y Colonial (segunda parte)*, Cuadernos de Pasado y Presente 74, Mexico; Siglo XXI.

Struvé, G. (1972) *Russian Literature under Lenin and Stalin, 1917–1953*, London: Routledge Kegan Paul.

Thomas, P. (1991) 'Critical Reception: Marx Then and Now', in T. Carver (ed.), *The Cambridge Companion to Marx*, Cambridge University Press.

Thompson, E. P. (1970) *The Making of the English Working Class*, Harmondsworth: Penguin.

Vaughan James, C. (1973) *Soviet Socialist Realism: Origins and Theory*, London: Macmillan.

Vogel, L. (1983) *Marxism and the Oppression of Women: Toward a Unitary Theory*, New Brunswick: Rutgers University Press.

Warren, B. (1980) *Imperialism: Pioneer of Capitalism*, London: Verso.

Watts, M. (1995) 'A New Deal in Emotions: Theory and practice and the crisis in development', in J. Crush (ed.), *Power of Development*, London: Routledge.

Weedon, C. (1987) *Feminist Practice and Poststructuralist Theory*, Oxford: Blackwell.

Weiner, D. (1988) *Models of Nature: Ecology, Conservation and Cultural Revolution in Soviet Russia*, Bloomington: Indiana University Press.

Whelan, I. (1995) *Modern Feminist Thought: From the Second Wave to 'Post-Feminism'*, Edinburgh University Press.

White, G. (1983) 'Revolutionary Socialist Development in the Third World: An Overview', in G. White, R. Murray and C. White (eds), *Revolutionary Socialist Development in the Third World*, London: Macmillan.

Williams, R. (1977) *Marxism and Literature*, Oxford University Press.

Wood, E. M. (1981) *The Retreat From Class: A New 'True' Socialism*, London: Verso.

—— (1995) *Democracy against Capitalism: Renewing Historical Materialism*, Cambridge University Press.

Young, I. (1986) 'Beyond the Unhappy Marriage: A Critique of The Dual Systems Theory', in L. Sargent (ed.), *The Unhappy Marriage of Marxism and Feminism*, London: Pluto.

Index